D1106878

THE LAUGHING TRADITION

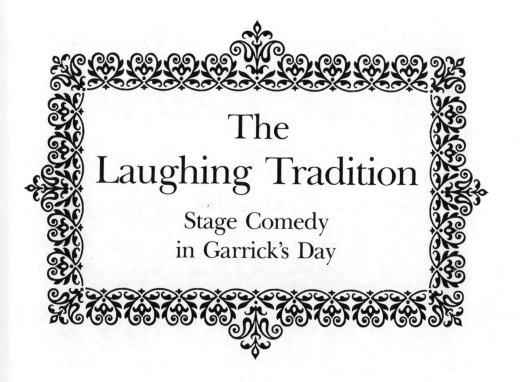

The
Laughing Tradition

Stage Comedy
in Garrick's Day

RICHARD BEVIS

THE UNIVERSITY OF GEORGIA PRESS
ATHENS

Copyright © 1980 by the University of Georgia Press
Athens 30602

All rights reserved

Set in 10 on 13 point Mergenthaler Baskerville type
Printed in the United States of America

Library of Congress Cataloging in Publication Data

Bevis, Richard W
  The laughing tradition.
  Includes bibliographical references and index.
    1. English drama—18th century—History and criti-
cism.   2. English drama (Comedy)—History and criti-
cism.   3. Theater—England—History.   I. Title.
PR708.C6B4 1980   822'.6'09   79–48001
          ISBN 0–8203–0514–6

Contents

Foreword

A decade and a half ago, when *The London Stage 1660–1800* appeared and I began work on the subject of this book, the prevailing dogma held that comedy on the eighteenth-century London stage was mainly sentimental, and the "laughing tradition" virtually moribund, until Goldsmith arrived with his curative potion in "five Draughts." When I found I could not agree, I was reminded of how Johnson dealt with Boswell on a similar occasion: "Nay, Sir, there is no talking with a man who will dispute what every body knows."

But indisputables come and go; what every body knows at one time will not pass so easily at another. There is sufficient evidence in current research to suggest a widespread impatience with the old orthodoxy, sufficient to indicate that a reformation has begun. The voice that seemed to cry in the wilderness is suddenly borne on the crest of a wave. Perhaps we have almost reached a point where *sentiment*, which has been the reigning word of Georgian dramatic criticism for a century, can be dethroned.

Almost—but not quite. The older view still recurs, now usually as a passing generalization, and these reversions to obsolete dogma show the work that remains to be done. In this book I have tried to accomplish at least a part of that task, whose importance, along with the bases of my procedure, is explained in the chapters that follow. After reading them, as Boswell wrote in response to Johnson's remark, "my readers will decide upon this dispute."

After more than fifteen years of research in this field I have incurred more debts to people, books and institutions than I could enumerate in a single page, so I must begin by apologizing to those whom the necessity of selection forces me to omit thanking by name, asking instead that they consider themselves included in this general expression of gratitude to the minds and hearts that have helped along the way. But even if limited to a single sentence I would have to record my obligations to Bertrand Bronson, Professor Emeritus of English, University of California, Berkeley, for his judicious guidance. Professors Gardiner Stout of Berkeley, John Loftis of Stanford and Robert Hume of Cornell offered encouragement at crucial junctures that I will not forget. And among the many typists at various stages I must single out my wife, who made me an offer I could not refuse, for special appreciation.

I am also indebted to the University of California at Berkeley and the American University of Beirut for travel and research grants; to the University of British Columbia for a study leave during which I drafted the book; to the Oxford University Press for help in obtaining photostatic copies of faraway manuscripts and for permission to quote from the poem by W. R. Rodgers; to the Huntington Library for permission to publish excerpts from numerous Larpent manuscripts; and to the Canadian Federation for the Humanities for an aid-to-publication grant, using funds provided by the Social Sciences and Humanities Research Council of Canada.

R. B.

Prologue

Prologue

English dramatic comedy is often held to have fallen on evil days in the eighteenth century. To some extent Georgian critics believed this: they looked back to Shakespeare with reverent nostalgia, and worried over the hold that pantomime, slapstick, and sentimental comedy had acquired on the stage of their day. Yet other voices could praise contemporary comedy as a worthy offspring of its sixteenth- and seventeenth-century forebears, and some Victorians, such as Lamb and Hazlitt, looked back to eighteenth-century comedy with nostalgia, if not reverence. It is modern criticism, beginning with Edmund Gosse in the last quarter of the nineteenth century, that has been almost unanimous in its denigration of the Georgian stage. Twentieth-century historians of the period from Cibber to Goldsmith have usually either alleged a serious dearth of comedy, or suggested the survival of a comic tradition without going into detail, or dismissed it as given over to sentimentalism.[1] "Sentiment," indeed, has been the great critical shibboleth of this drama for nearly a century. Until quite recently, most general studies of eighteenth-century comedy have focused upon "the drama of sensibility," "English sentimental drama," or "genteel" comedy, regarding its humorous episodes as faint echoes of Restoration wit.

This critical tradition has had serious consequences, for the sentimental tag is at least partly responsible for the current low esteem of the age's comedy and its scant appeal to students. So great is the odium we attach to sentimental indulgences in art that a reexamination of sentimentality on the eighteenth-century stage must be at the heart of any improvement in our diplomatic relations with the drama of that period. If, as the traditional interpretation argues, comedy in Garrick's day became generally lachrymose, then it will remain alien to us during the foreseeable

3

future. That is why the claim that sentiment overcame comedy from, say, Steele to Cumberland needs a sober assessment.

First, we will need some working definitions that provide clear distinctions between terms, for it makes a great deal of difference whether one is claiming a disappearance or sentimentalization of *comedy*, the *comic tradition*, the *comic spirit, laughing comedy* or the *laughing tradition*. *Comedy* is the oldest of the terms, with a thick deposit of theory and definition going back to Aristotle. Originally applied only to drama, it has since been broadened to include other genres, and some critical pronouncements about "eighteenth-century comedy" suit the novel better than they do the drama. Aristotle tells us disappointingly little about comedy in the surviving portions of the *Poetics*, though he does mention that the word is assumed to come from the *comoe* or country revels, which were phallic in character. Hence, presumably, stem the rituals of fruition (Roman *saturnalia*) that conclude most comedies: songs, dances and hymeneal feasts. Aristotle also observes that comedy portrays people who are worse than average, a criterion that was used against sentimental writers who wanted to call their exemplary plays comedies.[2] Historically, we can distinguish Aristophanic or Old Comedy, which was particularly satiric, and the New Comedy of Menander, Plautus, and Terence, which was romantic, generally satiric, and saturnalian.

Most of the other terms derive from the classical usage. *The comic spirit* is the vaguest; it can mean the mind or frame of mind in which life is seen comically and thus produces literary comedy, or refer to a quality of the work, the Latin *vis comica* (comic energy), or to the philosophical Over-spirit of George Meredith's *The Idea of Comedy and the Uses of the Comic Spirit* (1877, better known as *An Essay on Comedy*). Meredith's comic spirit, with its "calm curious eye," is elevated, intellectual, salutary, and rare, a "fountain of sound sense" playing on the follies of society. But in practice the term more frequently alludes to the outlook of a writer or the *vis comica* of a work or an age.

Laughing comedy is the phrase Goldsmith coined to distinguish "traditional" from "sentimental" comedy. As he used it, the term seems to mean all regular, full-length (mainpiece) comedy except the sentimental variety but excludes afterpieces, which he held in low esteem. From our perspective, however, that exclusion makes little sense unless one has

4

eyes only for high comedy; in fact it passes over an important component of the comic drama found on the Georgian stage. I have therefore taken the liberty of referring to "the laughing tradition," an extrapolated coinage which preserves Goldsmith's meaning in regard to mainpiece comedy (non-sentimental), but adds to it the non-sentimental short comedies and farces that flourished in the eighteenth century. The matter is discussed further at the beginning of chapter five.

Comic tradition is potentially the most misleading of these terms, because it is easy to confuse with *traditional comedy*, which means *non-sentimental comedy*, Old or New. *Comic tradition* also connotes non- (or pre-) sentimental comic drama if used of the period before 1700; in the eighteenth century, however, the "comic tradition" as practiced unquestionably came to include sentimental forms and influences to some extent, and it would be exclusivist or polemical to rule otherwise. The *comic tradition*, then, properly refers to the full range of forms which have been offered as dramatic comedy, including (when applied to the eighteenth century or later) sentimental comedies. One often finds these terms applied inconsistently by critics of all ages, but I have tried to remain within the bounds of the usages stipulated here.

We must next try to understand exactly what is, and what is not, intended by those who hold that stage comedy was moribund in the eighteenth century. In the first place, that diagnosis clearly cannot be applied to drama as performed in Georgian London; no one could describe as "weak" a comic tradition that included nightly performances of Shakespearean, Jonsonian, and Restoration comedies, together with those of their imitators, plus merry song and dance, in addition to sentimental plays.[3] The successive volumes of *The London Stage 1660–1800* portray it in that period as an unparalleled storehouse of the accumulated riches of Western comedy. Every genre and style that had ever graced or debased a stage anywhere was represented: the numerous progeny of Aristophanes and Molière, Plautus and Terence, the commedia dell 'arte (as the pantomime), farce, and so on. In short, stage performance of comic drama was alive and flourishing.

It is, then, dramatic comedy *as written* in eighteenth-century England that is at issue, the contention being that all or most new comedies were sentimental, or simply that very little comedy was produced, until

5

Goldsmith and Sheridan. These claims are nearer the bone, and a full response is the purpose of this entire book: particularly, on the question of sentiment, addressed in chapter three. But a preliminary point must be made here. The dramatic history of the eighteenth century falls naturally into two segments of approximately one-third and two-thirds, divided by the Licensing Act of 1737, and comedy did not expire in the first third. Even a quick look at the major playwrights of this era, included by Ian Donaldson in the "Golden Age of English Comedy,"[4] will establish that a laughing tradition existed intact at least up to 1737.

At the beginning of the period George Farquhar, and Gay and Fielding towards its end, are well known and require least comment. The work of the latter playwrights is widely accepted as satirical and amusing; sometimes it is antisentimental. Farquhar is usually regarded as a bridge between the cynical and licentious comedy typical of the Restoration, and the moralized, more humane variety composed in the eighteenth century. Though Richmore's reform in *The Twin-Rivals* (v.iv) and Aimwell's recantation to Dorinda in *The Beaux' Stratagem*, v.iv ("Such goodness who could injure!"), have been held by some to partake of the sentimental influence, and certainly indicate a shift in comic tone, the consensus has been that these plays and Farquhar's work as a whole have strong roots in traditional laughing comedy and satire. Farquhar is genial but comic; his mellowness of spirit is a return to abiding comic norms, not a declaration for Cibber and Steele.

Colley Cibber is customarily credited with fathering the sentimental comedy in *Love's Last Shift* (1696). However this may be, over half of his plays are notably non-sentimental. *Woman's Wit*, which failed in 1697, is recognizably a Restoration comedy of intrigue and manners, long, dull, and overly complex in plot, but not sentimental. *Love Makes a Man* (1700), composed in the then-popular genre of Spanish intrigue, has traditional characters of humors and some moralistic reform at the end, a description that also holds for *She Would, and She Would Not* (1702), long a stock piece. Both have been judged non-sentimental by most authorities. In *The Careless Husband* (1704) and *The Lady's Last Stake* (1707) Cibber went back to the formula of *Love's Last Shift*: four acts of fashionable intrigue, capped by a scene of fulsome reconciliation between husband and wife in act 5. Though all three are usually classed as sentimental comedies, they raise the difficult question of just when a racy

6

comedy of manners becomes, on balance, "sentimental." *The Double Gallant* and *The Comical Lovers* (both 1707) cause no such difficulties—they are laughing comedies of intrigue and manners, quite without sentiment—but *The Non-Juror* (1717, from *Tartuffe*) is a problem. Some have found it sentimental, yet it is rather *sui generis*, for no "sentimental" comedy is so preoccupied with religious and political issues vital to the state and currently controversial. *The Non-Juror* is a serious, didactic play, somewhat relieved by the liveliness of Maria, with patches of patriotic sentiment, lovers' distresses and a tearful reunion. *The Refusal* (1721) is a straightforward comedy of manners and premarital intrigue, alternately pleasant and dull, set against the background of the South Sea Bubble.

Cibber's final comedy, *The Provoked Husband* (1728), an alteration and completion of Vanbrugh's *A Journey to London*, again raises the issue of classification, more pressing this time because it was popular enough to be considered the eighteenth-century standard for comic authors to aim at until Goldsmith. Several writers have described *The Provoked Husband* as "sentimental," though it is so in only one scene (v.ii) of one plot. Cibber's recent biographer points up the difficulties attending categorization when he calls it a "sentimental comedy of manners combining feeling and wit,"[5] and the playwright himself was, in the last analysis, equally amphibious. Even in the *Apology* he is equivocal about his motives. After the fact Cibber can announce that he wrote with "virtue always in view,"[6] though on the previous page he has spoken of his "muse" as "only call'd upon, by family duty," and throughout he emphasizes the necessitous character of his work. He not only explains that he wrote *Love's Last Shift* in order to get a good part for himself, but adds that he was "honoured" to have Vanbrugh write *The Relapse*, a sequel which fundamentally contradicts its antecedent, and to act in it (pp. 118–20). These various statements, while not entirely irreconcilable, when taken together with his mixed bag of work at least suggest that he was not a philosophic or principled sentimentalist on the order of Steele or Cumberland. It is worth recalling that Cibber is supposed to have added the low servant humor, the "Tom and Phillis" portions, to *The Conscious Lovers*, in order to leaven its didacticism.

Even Steele, however, contributed to the laughing tradition. *The Funeral* (1701) has divided commentators with its Cibberian mixture of emphases. Steele's editor, Shirley S. Kenny, considers it touched by sentimentalism, while Bonamy Dobrée agrees with the *Comparison Between the Two Stages* (1702) in classing the play as a farce.[7] Each has a point; *The Funeral* mixes amusing and realistic comedy (Sable and his mourners, Lord Hardy and his "company of foot") with the rather sentimental character of Trusty and one sentimental scene (v.iv) of Lord Brumpton's emotional reunion with his children. *The Lying Lover* (1703) is felt by all critics to be almost unrelievedly sentimental, but *The Tender Husband* (1705) "retreated from sentimentalism."[8] It is Steele's best written, most tightly constructed and most traditional comedy. From its fast opening—"Well, Mr. Fainlove, how do you go on in your Amour with my wife?"—to the ending, where Mrs. Clerimont, more realistic than most reforming characters, agrees to "slide out of [her] Foppery by degrees" (v.i.152–53), *The Tender Husband* seldom flags. After its cool reception, however, Steele did not produce a play for seventeen years. *The Conscious Lovers* (1722) is the acknowledged *locus classicus* of Augustan sentimental comedy; Parson Adams paired it with *Cato* as the only plays "fit for a Christian to read," for it contains "some things almost solemn enough for a sermon."[9] Sentimental it certainly is, and heavily moralized, but *The Conscious Lovers* should not be (though it sometimes is) taken as typical, for even among sentimental comedies or Steele's plays it was extreme.

By the year 1900, only four non-Shakespearean comedies written before 1750 were still being performed regularly in Britain and America. One was Massinger's *New Way to Pay Old Debts*, a second Cibber's *She Would and She Would Not,* and the other two (*The Busy Body* and *The Wonder*) were by Susannah Freeman Carroll Centlivre.[10] "The celebrated Mrs. Centlivre" commands respectful notice from students of laughing comedy, though she is described by Bonamy Dobrée as representative of "the popular, clever, meaningless theatre of the time" (p. 226) and charged with possessing " 'a sense of the theatre' and little other sense at all" (p. 236). Dobrée's disgust is excessive. After a nine-year apprenticeship in all types of comedy, the most substantial of which was the brisk but rather sentimental *The Gamester* (1705), Mrs. Centlivre made her mark with *The Busy Body* (1709). This fast-moving intrigue piece with characters in the humors tradition was the most frequently performed comedy at Covent Garden between 1747 and 1776.[11] More distinguished is *The Wonder: A Woman Keeps a Secret* (1714), a mixture of

Spanish intrigue with low servant humor and the play with which both Kitty Clive and David Garrick chose to retire. Mrs. Centlivre's last contribution to laughing comedy was *A Bold Stroke for a Wife* (1718), which gave Simon Pure to the stage and the language. The well-constructed plot has a classic simplicity: the four guardians who "block" the love of Colonel Feignwell and Anne Lovely must be duped into giving their consents. Even Dobrée finds this play "refreshing" and "more amusing" than *The Busy Body* (p. 236), and it is as original as such a thing can be. *A Bold Stroke* was performed well over two hundred times in the eighteenth century and, like *The Busy Body* and *The Wonder*, was still acted in the late nineteenth (Bowyer, pp. 216, 218). Her last comedy, *The Artifice* (1722), is a falling-off; the construction is disappointing, and some writers consider it sentimental.

This brief and superficial sketch is intended only to review the main evidence for a generally accepted argument: that a recognizable tradition of laughing comedy survived at least through Fielding. In the first decade of the century alone over a dozen new laughing comedies by well-known dramatists appeared. Even if we limit ourselves to undisputed plays by major playwrights, leaving out such peripheral figures as William Burnaby, Mrs. Haywood, and Charles Shadwell, at least sixteen traditionally comic mainpieces were composed and produced between 1700 and 1728, when *The Beggar's Opera* initiated a decade of vigorous dramatic satire. Throw in half a dozen comedies and burlesques by lesser dramatists, allow something, if you will, for a couple of doubtful cases and the laughing portions of the sentimental comedies, and you have a laughing tradition which, if not precisely thriving between Farquhar's day and Gay's, was nevertheless unbroken. The renaissance of Old Comedy subsequently promoted by Fielding at the Haymarket was lively enough to alarm the authorities with its sociopolitical criticism in the years preceding the Licensing Act. The sentimentalists had a few notable successes, influenced traditional comedy significantly, and gained some adherents; yet not over six comedies are widely agreed to be "sentimental" in the first third of the century, and even if we include the doubtfuls the results do not justify an inference that traditional comedy had perished.

The case for its disappearance, then, must be drawn from plays written and produced in the latter two-thirds of the century, a period profoundly affected by the Licensing Act of 1737. By this measure the Walpole government sought principally to stifle Fielding's satires, but it had other consequences both immediate and far-reaching. Fielding himself was shunted from the stage to the novel, which henceforth diverted potential literary talent from the drama. Covent Garden and Drury Lane were given an effective monopoly on legitimate drama in London, but were required to submit all their scripts to the Lord Chamberlain's Examiner of Plays for censorship prior to performance.[12] Fortunately for theater historians, the office of Examiner left a valuable legacy of Georgian dramatic manuscripts (hundreds of them unpublished) which today permits a close and thorough study of that period of stage history.[13] But the combination of censorship and restricted outlets discouraged more dramatists than Fielding, and had a generally pernicious effect on drama in Garrick's day.[14].

In the late seventies the first generation of playwrights to cope with conditions under the Licensing Act—the only one to cope at all successfully—was closing shop. By 1780 Goldsmith, Garrick, and Foote were dead, Murphy and Sheridan had produced their last comedies, and George Colman (the Elder) had written his important plays. A general sense of postlapsarian malaise set in among drama critics. "Indeed," wrote John Pinkerton glumly in 1785,

> pantomime is now the best entertainment we find in our theatres. It is quite astonishing to remark how much our stage hath declined within this half dozen years, since the retreat of Garrick. It is overwhelmed with floods of Irish nonsense, and stuff more stupid than stupidity, where not one glimmer of sense or wit appears. Had those Irishmen, female scribblers, etc., offered their trash to a Bartholomew-fair audience a few years ago, they would have been hissed to scorn.[15]

Similarly, but with a longer perspective, Arthur Murphy lamented in 1801 an "eclipse of all genius since Mr. Sheridan's *School for Scandal* in May, 1777," and the "inundation of nonsense, which has for some time been the reigning fashion."[16] May 1777 is perhaps a bit early for "universal Darkness"—*The Critic* appeared in 1779—but modern historians would generally agree with Pinkerton and Murphy that after 1780 the comic tradition becomes almost unrecognizable (until, say, Robertson), and one must certainly grant that it enters a different phase then. A new group of comic dramatists—Mmes Inchbald and Cowley, Mssrs Holcroft, Cumberland, Reynolds, Burgoyne, and Colman the Younger—were taking over and, by and large, devoting themselves to farce, spectacle, "benevolist" comedy, and melodrama to a degree that almost excluded traditional comedy. So tenuous does the genre become that little is lost by rounding off our study at about 1780, and I have therefore undertaken no systematic coverage beyond that time.

My purpose holds, then, to trace the comic, and especially the laughing, tradition on the stages of London during the supposed interregnum after the overthrow of Fielding in 1737. In place of the conventional view of eighteenth-century theater as sentiment-ridden, I shall be proposing a view in which laughing comedy looms large, though farce, spectacle, vaudeville, and a host of other minor and "illegitimate" forms bulk larger, while sentimental comedy is for the most part only an interesting entr'acte. Because the supporting arguments are long, the exhibits unfamiliar and the assertions unusual, I offer the following list of "workpoints" as an abstract of the chapters that follow and a guide to their plan:

PART I

We need to take a fresh look at eighteenth-century dramatic comedy because:

1. The combination of the original audiences' prejudices and their opportunities for direct, violent recourse against any play (often for nondramatic motives) caused the failure or obscurity of some comedies that might please contemporary taste or affect our preconceptions (chapter one).

2. Publishing conditions of the time have presented a biased selection by favoring the publication (other things being equal) of sentimental plays, and by emphasizing the sentimental in the printed versions of some plays. It is therefore misleading to confine attention to published plays, and it is unnecessary: the comic plays written and produced between 1737 and 1780 that were not published (one-third of the total) exist in manuscript in the Larpent Collection of the Huntington Library. Reading these appreciably alters one's image of eighteenth-century comedy (chapter two).

PROLOGUE

PART II

Of the alternatives to traditional comedy,

1. "Sentimental comedy" has been widely misrepresented. It is (a) an oversimplified label for diverse phenomena, (b) occasionally confused with "moralized comedy," (c) closely related to the novel and closet drama, (d) sometimes concerned with "true" versus "false" sentiment, and (e) statistically much less prominent than one is led to expect by textbook generalizations. Though its presence in the eighteenth century is a fact, its assumed dominance is fiction (chapter three).

2. The real threat to traditional comedy was not sentiment, but the mushrooming *illegitimi:* pantomime, burletta, comic opera, spectacle, and a host of other nontraditional forms. After restrictive measures such as the Commonwealth ban and the Licensing Act muffled the traditional voices of the stage, this "minor theater" ultimately overcame both comedy and sentiment to enter the nineteenth century in triumph (chapter four).

PART III

A strong strain of traditional comedy runs through the period from Fielding to Sheridan, but in the mainpiece it is frequently mixed with other elements. Laughing comedy tends to move into the afterpiece, partly because audiences demanded amusement there, partly because comic writers felt more comfortable in the briefer forms. Owing to the influx of talent and its new task of preserving laughter, the afterpiece becomes an independent art-form, obeying its own principles and producing an appropriate pleasure (chapters five and six).

PART IV

Goldsmith and Sheridan were writers thoroughly immersed in the drama of their own period, working in a continuous comic tradition that included now-obscure Georgian writers of considerable merit. In addition to sixteenth- and seventeenth-century models, they drew upon the comedy of their own age in demonstrable ways, balancing and synthesizing its heterogeneous components into eighteenth-century statements about eighteenth-century concerns: wit, manners, humanism, civilization, and the nature of feeling (chapters seven and eight).

With this map of the proposed route, the reader may find his way more easily through the confusing stretches. The prime significance of the proposed reinterpretation is that it brings the world of eighteenth-century comedy, especially its weaknesses, much closer to our experience. Widespread indulgence in sentimentality is alien, or at least repugnant, to us; but the vulgarization of art, its impoverishment and diminution into splinter groups, we can understand. All the panoply of contemporary entertainment on radio and television, in music halls and night clubs, was struggling to be born on the stages of Georgian London. A middle-class commercial audience was making its presence felt. Sentimentalism, which had its own internal dialectic, was a side-show; the bulk of the comic drama, particularly the short plays, did not partake of the melancholy, the pre-Romantic, the effete side of the century, but lived in the thicker-skinned London of Smollett, Johnson, Gibbon, the later Burke. It is the prosaic rather than the poetic image of Georgian England that is mirrored in its comedy.

PART I
Contexts of Comedy

The study of the theater has special pitfalls for the literary critic. Drama is the most social of the arts; for the vital spark to leap, a corps of middlemen must be employed, and an audience assembled and actively involved. When a literary historian treats the play simply as a verbal artifact, ignoring its socioeconomic context, a short-circuit occurs: our enlightenment is only partial, and our comprehension of the whole distorted. What a stroboscopic light does to motion, a purely literary approach does to drama. The purpose of part one is to illuminate the sociological background of eighteenth-century comedy as fully and evenly as possible before we try to read the plays themselves.

The Noise and Tumult

A violent party was formed against the author. His piece had been read, and was much commended by several critics of real judgment; but amidst the noise and tumult of a playhouse, the merit of a comic writer is of no avail. A violent party took possession of the pit, and the play did not survive the first night.　　—Arthur Murphy, *The Life of David Garrick*

> Dire is the conflict, dismal is the din,
> Here shouts all Drury, there all Lincoln's Inn.
> —Alexander Pope, *The Dunciad*

We have good reason to believe that the average eighteenth-century play ran a formidable gauntlet of social and physical obstacles in pursuit of theatrical success, and that this trial was not necessarily designed to reward intrinsic value. Comedies of merit as well as dismal farces could fall along the perilous path. Our first need is to see what these conditions were, and how they made for a rather arbitrary selection of the plays to be preserved for posterity.[1]

To begin with, raucous and uninhibited playhouse audiences could seek immediate redress against any play they found exceptionable. They would hiss, stamp, blow catcalls, throw halfpence and ripe fruit or light furniture, call for the curtain or the manager, and threaten or, if thwarted, stage a riot. Their motives for these actions were generally capricious in the extreme, or at least external to the play. For example, Hildebrand Jacob's *The Nest of Plays* was, according to one account, damned in 1738 because it happened to be the first play approved and produced under the Licensing Act of 1737, and Hugh Kelly's *A Word to the Wise* (1769) fell victim to a political prejudice against the author.[2] Richard Cross, prompter at Drury Lane, records a curious confrontation in 1749 over an insignificant farce, *The Little French Lawyer*. At its first performance it had been "well received until ye last scene, then hissed greatly." Withdrawn for alterations, it was presented again three nights later: "Farce greatly hissed and Mr. Woodward promis'd it shou'd be done no more; notwithstanding this they would not suffer us to end it."[3] Whatever the audience found objectionable in the original version, they were probably displeased at the repetition of a play that had been "hissed off." In fact the only unusual aspect of this incident is that the farce was repeated; in most cases the original rejection would have been sufficient to kill it.

> The fate of a play in the twentieth century is decided by the public bookings made over several days following the first night. In the eighteenth and early nineteenth centuries the verdict was given at the time, in the theatre, and by the audience. At the end of the play an actor was appointed to come before the curtain and, as the phrase went, "give out the play for repetition." "Ladies and gentlemen, under the sanction of your kind approbation," he would begin—and then, as Thomas Dibdin remarks, "The Ayes and Noes generally interrupt the remainder." Whether the play was abandoned or continued largely depended on the caprice of that first audience.[4]

And if "that first audience" did not like his work the anxious playwright need not worry about a second, for under the extremely flexible repertory system a manager could determine one night what to offer the next, and while he might for a time withhold what the spectators desired, he dared not give them what they did not like: the police and insurance systems were too primitive, and the actors had to be considered. Arthur Murphy, publishing his short comedy *What We All Must Come To* in 1764 after it had failed the previous fall, sketched what would have taken place had it been allowed to finish: "But, some people were determined not to hear, and the Author could not be induced by any private motives to send the Performers a second time into so painful a service as that of the stage always is, when a few are unwilling to be entertained" (Advertisement to the first edition). The complaints about "some people" and "a few" were frequent throughout the century; apparently a small but well-organized and noisy minority could often ring down the curtain, though a majority quietly approved. Like Kelly, Murphy had political enemies who probably decided to take advantage of the production of two of his plays on the same evening: "it was said, that Party interfered to condemn these two pieces very undeservedly."[5] George Colman claimed similar difficulties with his afterpiece *The Oxonian in Town* (1767, published 1770): "The fate of this little comedy, on its first appearance, was extremely singular. After having been favorably received the first two nights, a violent attempt was made to prevent its exhibition on the third. The pretence for this determined condemnation was, that it contained not only personal, but even national, reflections. . . . The very names of the persons who supposed themselves aggrieved, were unknown to him" (Advertisement to the first edition).

We might, of course, dismiss any one statement as special pleading by a disgruntled playwright, but every student of Georgian theater has found such a variety of reports to the same general effect that the existence of irresponsible abuses of the audience's power can hardly be doubted. "Damning a play was so common a practice in the Georgian theatre that the phrase ranks as a cliché. . . . Judgment was swayed by many things besides a critical consideration of the merits of the play. A piece might be damned in order to attack the manager, as a rebuff to some popular actor, or as the consequence of the smallest affront imagined by that prickly audience."[6] Edward Moore's stage version of *Gil Blas* is said to have failed because of miscasting, William O'Brien's *The Duel* from a never-revealed prejudice against its author.[7] When Richard Bentley had Harlequin gibbetted onstage during *The Wishes* (1761), the spectators took instant exception, hissing and nearly rioting. The play's royal patronage notwithstanding, it lasted only five nights and was not published. So absolute was the audience in its sphere that Hughes suggests the opera house at Parma as the only modern parallel. Playwrights acknowledged this power throughout the century. As early as 1702 George Farquhar noted that "the rules of English comedy don't lie in the compass of Aristotle or his followers but in the pit, box and galleries." Colley Cibber, commenting in 1740 on the "extreme severity" with which audiences were damning plays, called them "pirates" in a theatrical sea, who come "to a new play, like hounds to a carcase." And in 1805 we hear Thomas Holcroft complaining that "dramatic authors must not reason, but comply with the public feeling."[8]

Of course an audience need not riot to kill a play: a cool or mildly hostile reception would often suffice. One of the better-written and most unusual afterpieces of the century expired after one or two performances, and was not published. This was *The Kept Mistress: or, The Mock Orators*, a lively, anonymous two act farce of 1756.[9] The same fate had overtaken Charles Macklin's *A Will and No Will: or, A Bone for the Lawyers*, another *petite pièce*, ten years earlier. Yet the same story (Regnard's *Le Legataire universel*), reworked by Thomas King in a much inferior version entitled *Wit's Last Stake,* enjoyed thirteen performances at Drury Lane in 1768 and was immediately published, though King absurdly moralizes, sweetens, and denatures his and Macklin's source.[10] Thus the more sentimental of the two afterpieces survived in print to help give the period its present reputation, while the traditionally comic version, markedly superior in style and construction, perished with hardly a trace after one night. *The Politician* (1758, anonymous), which Cross reports was "damned and halfpence thrown," is a similar case. A Theophrastan caricature along the lines of Murphy's *The Upholsterer*, this jaunty sketch shows farce near its purest; it was not published either. Yet *The Politician*, trivial as it is, now seems a more interesting and respectable piece of dramatic craftsmanship than many of its brethren which were not damned.

And so on. Each modern reader can compile his own list of curious failures, of comedies inexplicably rejected by the vagaries of the public. Eventually one comes to distrust audience response as an indicator of merit, and to sympathize with distraught authors and the quieter patrons who were steamrollered. Obviously the rowdier elements never intended to give most new plays a "fair" hearing; their behavior was a combination of high spirits, private quarrels, and an expression of British freedom and individual liberty. The Georgian playgoer held himself virtually unaccountable for his actions in the theater. During a riot opposing the performance of a troupe of French dancers "By Authority" at the Haymarket in 1738, shortly after the Licensing Act was imposed, "the many-headed Monster of the Pit" addressed two Westminster justices—representatives of the King— to this effect: "That the Audience had a legal Right to shew their dislike to any Play or Actor; that the common Laws of the Land were nothing but common Custom, and the ancient Usage of the People; that the Judicature of the Pit had been acknowledged and acquiesced to, Time immemorial: and as the present Set of Actors were to take their Fate from the Public, they were free to receive them as they pleased" (Victor, 1:55–56). This right of the audience to judge arbitrarily and irrevocably went unchallenged until the end of the third quarter of the century.[11]

As a rule, damned plays were not published. A well-established author such as Murphy or Colman, a sentimental dramatist who had had the reading public in mind from the first, or an especially aggrieved playwright, might go to the trouble and expense of printing a failure, but generally speaking dissatisfaction in the theater militated against publication for the obvious economic reason that demand would be slight.[12] Since the printed drama we have inherited was influenced by what occurred amid the noise and tumult of the playhouses, we too come under the "Judicature of the Pit" when we content ourselves with the published plays.

If one grows skeptical about Georgian audiences' dramatic judgment in noting what and why they damned, this distrust can only be heightened by a sober contemplation of what they liked. Thomas Sheridan's *Brave Irishman* (1754), for example, today seems thin and puerile compared even with most farces of its own time, yet it was one of the best-attended afterpieces of the mid-century. *The Maid of the Oaks* (1774), a tawdry pastoral-musical-spectacle by General John Burgoyne, enraged the critics, but pit and gallery loved it for three seasons.

> 'Twas fit, as for the public bound to cater
> Our manager should have his fête champêtre

jangled the prologue ominously. That "public" has been characterized as emotional, moralistic, patriotic, prudentially ethical, preoccupied with the "tuneful and spectacular," and fascinated with the social aspect of the theater (Lynch, p. 206). Ashley Thorndike found that mid-century taste ran heavily to "pantomime, opera, and farce" (p. 387). Samuel Foote's burlesque lecture in *The Orators* (1762) is interrupted by Scamper (B.A. Oxon.) calling out from his box:

> Pshaw! there's enough of this dull prosing; come, give us a little of something that's funny. . . .
> FOOTE: What is it you expect?
> SCAMPER: To be jolly, and laugh, to be sure—[13]

Earlier in the century, William Burnaby has a character in *The Reform'd*

Wife (1700) muse: "If I was to write a play . . . I'd have something to divert every Body. I'd have your Atheism to please the Wits—some affectation to entertain the Beaux, a Rape or two to engage the Ladies; and I'd bring in the Bears, before every Act, to secure an interest in the Upper Gallery."[14] Most estimates of audience taste in fact ranged downward from farce; many playgoers seem to have been addicts of "scenery and machinery."[15] Garrick's *A Peep behind the Curtain* (1767) spoofs this kind of vulgarity throughout. Lady Fuz, visiting Drury Lane one morning, begs the dramatist Glib,

> If they are not ready for the Rehearsal, suppose the Manager entertains us with thunder and lightning,—and let us see his traps, and his whims, and his harlequin pantomimes.
>   SIR TOBY FUZ: And a shower of rain, or an eclipse; and I must beg one peep at the Patagonians.[16]

There was, as Pope had said in 1737, such a headlong flight of taste "from heads to ears . . . to eyes" ("To Augustus") that scene designers such as de Loutherbourg could reasonably begin to claim equal importance with dramatic poets.

Surprisingly, sentiment seems not to have been in vogue with the majority of the audience except at certain periods, and the Thespians had to tread carefully among the shifting fashions. In 1768, at about the same time that others were decrying the popularity of the sentimental comedy, Garrick's nervous prologue to Hugh Kelly's *False Delicacy* was apparently trying to forestall criticism of the play's sentiments:

> Write *moral* plays—the blockhead!—why, good people,
> You'll soon expect this house to wear a steeple!
> For our fine piece, to let you into facts,
> Is quite a Sermon,—only preached in Acts.
>   . . . The man may prate,
> And feed these whimsies in his addle pate,
> That you'll protect his muse, because she's good,
> A virgin, and so chaste!—O Lud! O Lud!

As with William Whitehead's *School for Lovers* six years earlier, Garrick—who knew the audiences if anyone did—substituted a comic prologue satirizing sentiment for the serious "moral" one submitted by the author. In 1773 Goldsmith painted a rather different picture, though we must of course allow for an anxious playwright's defensive rhetoric.

Obviously fearful that the "low," farcical portions of *She Stoops to Conquer* would not be acceptable to his "genteel" audiences, he tried to discredit such criticism by having the "third fellow" at The Three Pigeons mouth its great word: "O damn anything that's *low,* I cannot bear it" (I.ii). Hugh Kelly, in the prologue to his unpublished comedy *The Man of Reason* (1776), observes that the comic dramatist maintains a perilous balance, constantly threatened by the whirligig of taste: audiences are "today all charmed with sentiment wrought high / . . . thrust out of doors poor Sentiment tomorrow." Yet if the dramatist grows uproarious, audiences may "mawl the fool as farcical, or low." Kelly resolves to steer a middle course: "We're grave and gay."[17] George Colman the Elder, writing at the same time, generally concurs, but places the onus on the critics: "The most offensive weapon of Modern Criticism is some *reigning word*, with which every literary rifleman arms himself, and does dreadful execution." At one time, he goes on, this word was "low": the genteel reigned, and all humor was suspect (ca. 1767– 72?). "At length, however, the word low has been restored to favor, and the term SENTIMENT in its turn has fallen into disgrace."[18]

The power that audiences possessed ensured that these vacillating fashions would affect the repertoire significantly, by threatening or rewarding those involved in producing drama.[19] The vagaries of theatrical taste, and the plight in which these placed the managers, actors, and playwrights, are concisely described in Samuel Johnson's "Prologue for the Opening of Drury Lane Theatre, 1747," spoken by Garrick, the new manager:

> Hard is his lot, who here by fortune plac'd,
> Must watch the wild vicissitudes of taste;
> With ev'ry meteor of caprice must play,
> And chase the new blown bubble of the day.
> Ah! let not censure term our fate our choice,
> The stage but echoes back the public voice.
> The drama's laws the drama's patrons give,
> For we, who live to please, must please to live.

The picture these lines afford of the relationship between the eighteenth-century stage and its audience has never been seriously faulted. Arthur Murphy found in them an epigraph for Garrick's own later career. Writing of the 1770 season, he observes, "The rage for musical pieces was growing more and more into fashion, and, as *'They who live to please, must please to live,'* the manager was obliged to comply with the public taste" (*Life of Garrick*, 2:76–77). Managers always are, of course, "obliged to comply with the public taste" to a large extent, and we do learn a good deal about eighteenth-century England when we read the plays it approved.

But they are not the whole story, and when we confine ourselves to them, what we learn is as much sociology as it is dramatic history. Johnson's couplet "Ah! let not censure term our fate our choice, / The stage but echoes back the public voice" sounds like a caveat against confusing popular success with the best that dramatists had to offer. Already in the mid-eighteenth century, literature and the stage were beginning to diverge; evidently the best-written and most actable plays of the period were not in all cases the successful and/or published plays. It is significant that Georgian dramatists had few outlets. In modern Britain or America a play that fails to please one director or audience may well please another; one can reasonably assume that drama of any merit will eventually be produced and published. But the Licensing Act of 1737 restricted the production of legitimate drama in London to the two patent houses, Covent Garden and Drury Lane; it was either succeed there or look to the provinces. And these two theaters together produced an everage of only nine new offerings per year during the midcentury: mainpieces and afterpieces, tragedies and comedies, pantomimes and musicals.[20] That was, in effect, the absorptive capacity of the English-speaking world.

The physical conditions in later Georgian theaters also militated increasingly against the success of verbal subtlety or any natural, unexaggerated effect, tending more and more to favor the broader, louder sytles as the century wore on. The early pantomimes and spectaculars created a vicious circle, drawing large crowds, which needed larger houses, which in turn allowed more spectacles, and so on. Drury Lane was enlarged in 1747 and 1762, and many of the new seats were perforce at a greater distance from the action. (Enlargements were carried out at Covent Garden in 1782 and 1792, the year in which Drury Lane was entirely rebuilt; in the nineties both houses trebled the seating capacities they had had in the forties.[21]) The intimate Elizabethan stage, the cozy proscenium theater of the Restoration and early eighteenth century, became a cavernous vaudeville hall, where actors found they had to resort to yells and grimaces. "Exaggeration then, whether comic or tragic, was necessarily the order of the day. The optics and acoustics of the theater imperatively demanded it."[22] Once constructed these auditoriums had to be filled by any available means to meet costs. "House charges" to the author increased formidably, making playwrights as well as managers less able to risk any production but a sure moneymaker, probably a low farce or a scenic spectacle.[23] "Nothing goes down now but mirth and fun," moaned one critic in the eighties, and little wonder.[24] Audiences deserve a measure of understanding if they damned or bypassed some respectable comedies in favor of pieces especially designed to succeed in the larger houses.

The indifferent correlation between stage success and intrinsic merit in the eighteenth century is a well-established fact of dramatic history. Nor was publication a guarantee of either value or popularity: Thomas Mozeen's *The Heiress* (1759), a strong candidate for the most abysmal comedy of the century, was published in 1762 despite failure onstage. There is a striking mixture of the clever and the atrocious, the craftsman-like and the incompetent, in the successful and published plays of the Garrick era. The other side of the coin is that stage failure and nonpublication, while obviously not assurances of merit, are not invariably associated with worthlessness either, for the reasons I have outlined. Our knowledge of theatrical conditions justifies a new look at the whole corpus of Georgian comedy. Plays which might interest us, which collectively might alter our impression of eighteenth-century drama and encourage us to reinterpret better-known comedies, can be found among the unpublished manuscripts and unpopular plays of the time. In our search for the comic tradition in Garrick's time we shall therefore have to remain independent of Georgian judgments, and be prepared to rummage in some pretty unlikely corners.

Stage vs. Closet

The publishing conventions of the eighteenth century, as well as its theatrical conditions, have distorted our picture of Georgian comic drama by selecting and even altering the comedies that now represent it. Two associated phenomena were involved: the economics of the book-selling trade, insofar as it tended to dictate which plays would be published and which would not, and the dichotomy that developed between acting and reading versions. Both tell us something about the playreading public, and both have a bearing on our inherited images.

At the heart of our misconceptions about Georgian comedy is our attempt to read printed plays and then generalize about drama in the theater. Essentially these were two parallel and closely related forms, but often they were distinct and sometimes antagonistic. A few figures will show why they need to be studied separately. Between 1737 and 1777, forty-two mainpiece comedies were submitted to the Examiner of Plays; thirty-seven of these, or 88 percent, were published. For afterpiece comedies and farces in the same period, the figures are fifty-nine of ninety-six, or 61 percent.[1] It may be objected that five-act comedies are by nature more substantial and of more lasting interest than the ephemeral afterpieces, and therefore it is only logical that their rate of publication was 27 percent higher. Waive for the moment the question whether in the eighteenth century the afterpiece was in fact of only passing interest; set aside even the lure of discovering just that ephemeral theater tradition as distinguished from the permanency of print. If in the protracted struggle between the sentimental and traditional approaches to comedy, the one side is represented by mainpieces and the other by afterpieces, then this statistic still means that one camp published a substantially higher proportion of its plays. If, that is, sentiment was generally more welcome in the mainpiece and laughter in the afterpiece, the imbalance in publication becomes significant.

Certainly modern critics have believed that such a division took place. As George Nettleton observes, "While regular comedy was being increasingly sentimentalized and tragedy moralized, Fielding let satirical farce and burlesque trample on the five-act formula and conventional spirit of formal drama."[2] Ashley Thorndike, noting the boisterous, broad-comedy bent of Fielding's *Coffee-House Politician*, adds that "such extravagances of plot and exuberances of fun, though suitable to farce and burlesque, were no longer welcomed in a five-act comedy."[3] A curious shift, involving both authorial practice and audience response, was underway during Fielding's dramatic career in the 1730s. Though "regular" (five-act, mainpiece) comedy became "increasingly sentimentalized" and cool if not hostile to extravagance and fun, no stigma was attached to such goings-on in the afterpiece ("farce and burlesque"). The effect was to separate and purify the genres, a development entirely in keeping with neoclassical criticism. The serious, the high, and the unhappy were reserved for the mainpiece; the low, the broad and the satirical belonged in the afterpiece. Since farce, burlesque, and pantomime, the existing afterpiece forms, were inadequate to bear the new responsibility, the short comedy was developed on the French model to meet the need. As Thorndike puts it, "The farces and the afterpieces and the 'petite comedies' were in the main on the side of the old tradition. Only rarely did they take on a sentimental tone. . . . They not only preserved much of the method and material of the old comedy, they also widened the range of its satire and ridicule."[4]

Even at the time there was considerable awareness of what was happening to comedy. George Colman, a prominent writer of short comedies, closed his Prologue to *The Oxonian in Town* (1767) with the observation:

> Our Piece is call'd a *Comedy* you know;
> A Two-act Comedy: tho' Rome enacts,
> That every Comedy be just Five Acts.
> Hence, parent Dullness the vain title begs
> For squalling, dancing Monsters on five Legs.
> The Bantling of To-night, if rear'd by you,
> Shall run, like Men and Women, upon two. (1770 ed.)

27

These lines repeat the then-common contention that the short comedies exhibited "nature," people as they really were, while mainpiece comedies were unnatural, false and dull. Colman's attitude here (confirmed by his practice) illuminates Goldsmith's dedicatory letter to Johnson on publishing *She Stoops to Conquer* (1773), where he asserts that "the undertaking a comedy not merely sentimental was very dangerous; and Mr. Colman, who saw this piece in its various stages, always thought it so." Goldsmith must have meant that a non-sentimental mainpiece comedy was dangerous, for numerous unsentimental afterpiece comedies were then popular, and neither Colman nor Goldsmith hesitated to write or produce them.

By the end of the century, the division of sentiment and laughter into before and after was virtually codified. Elizabeth Inchbald, whose career extended from 1784 to 1805, is a case in point. Thorndike calls her farces and petite comedies "brisk and unsentimental," yet her "longer plays are all [so] extremely sentimental [that] she may indeed be regarded as the most thoroughgoing exponent and apologist of sentimental comedy" (pp. 463–64). Mrs. Inchbald's prefaces to the individual plays in her twenty-five volume collection *The British Theatre* (1806–9) are interesting in this connection. There was room in her mind for both lofty humanitarian sentiment and boisterous humor, but each had its appropriate niche. She believed that, in Thorndike's words, "fun and merriment might be given rein in such trivial and fanciful pieces as farces and petite comedies, but should have only a slight and secondary place in the works of the imagination extolling, as the sentimental plays assuredly did, 'scrupulous purity of characters and refinement in sensations.' "[5] By precept and example she tended to confirm the generic dichotomy between serious and risible.

The strength of this convention was such that over 75 percent of the afterpieces in the period 1737–77 remained faithful to traditional comedy in every important respect, while only 6 percent can be considered essentially sentimental. The rest achieve some sort of balance or compromise. Though any calculation involving one's own judgment of sentimentality is hazardous, these figures are at least defensible, but I hesitate to make similar computations for mainpiece comedy, where the alloy is so compounded as to make strict categorization impossible and disagreement likely. Nevertheless, it is probably safe to say that a category of "sentimental and mixed" plays would comprise about two-thirds of the five-act comedies in the period. Even among the major defenders of laughter (whose short plays were, almost without exception, traditionally comic), *The Wedding-Day, The Good-Natured Man, The Jealous Wife, The English Merchant, The Man of Business,* and *The Way to Keep Him* (mainpiece version) would probably be so classified.

Evidently this division, once conceived, became a custom whose observance audiences upheld. Isaac Bickerstaffe wrote in the preface to his five-act Spanish intrigue comedy *'Tis Well It's No Worse* (1770) that Garrick had "thought the exhibition of it a hazardous attempt," but staged it in the belief that it had the merit to succeed if it "did not too far clash with the prejudices of prevailing taste." Yet numerous shorter comedies of incident (including Bickerstaffe's *The Absent Man,* 1768) were received without protest at the London theaters every year. Hugh Kelly, worried lest he might be "mawled" as "farcical, or low,"[6] certainly could have been speaking only of mainpieces to a public accustomed to Foote's farces and *The Brave Irishman;* but his remark indicates how insistent the patrons were about theatrical "decorum." The perception that a conservative audience generally expected a serious or at least genteel mainpiece and a humorous afterpiece emphasizes the importance of including the afterpiece in any search for a laughing tradition.

But even if full-length comedies were generally more sentimental, and proportionately more of them were published, no doubt they were printed because they were substantial, full-length plays rather than because they were sentimental. This objection has some truth, and must be partially admitted. Yet, in the first place, it is beside the main point, which is that the printed theater is separate from, and more sentimental than, the acted theater. No causation need be established for this phenomenon. In the second place, the interconnections between sentimental comedy and the reading public were such that it did have a better chance for publication, other things being equal, than traditional comedy. The kinship of sentimental comedy with closet drama and the novel is the heart of the matter.

To the theorem that serious, sentimental, morally grave comedy was usually found in the mainpiece, and farcical, humorous, and satiric "laughing comedy" principally in the afterpiece, we must now add a related proposition: laughing comedy is preeminently stage comedy. Naturally what is designed for the theater, depending partially on visual effects, ought to excel there, and this is particularly true of the active and often farcical comedies of the eighteenth century. James Townley's *High Life below Stairs* (1759), one of the best acting farces of its day, is in no way impressive to read, nor are many other popular afterpieces. Yet "what is dead and repetitious on the printed page may well have been very much alive in the capable hands of a trained *farceur*. Especially in farce, where everything depends upon an instantaneous and vigorous response from the audience, the skill of the actor is paramount."[7] The point holds for higher comedy in the traditional mold. *The School for Scandal*'s famous screen scene, Tony and Mrs. Hardcastle sloughing around the back garden in *She Stoops to Conquer*, the fifth-act bedroom assembly in *The Clandestine Marriage*, the Toby Belch–Andrew Aguecheek scenes of *Twelfth Night*—all gain immensely in stage representation. One would be hard pressed to find similar cases among the sentimental comedies, which depend much more heavily on words alone. Arthur Sherbo, noting the reactions of drama critics in the period 1750–67, found that their strictures upon laughing comedies were usually against the plays read "in the closet," while their stage popularity was conceded. Sentimental plays, on the other hand, if judged on stage performance, were admitted to fail on many occasions.[8]

While the laughing pieces of all types drew louder applause in the playhouse, sentimental comedies appealed more to readers in their "closets." The Rev. Charles Jenner is quite explicit about the matter in his preface to *The Man of Family* (1771), subtitled "A Sentimental Comedy." The dedication to Garrick admits that the nature of the play "made it unfit to be offered to you, as a manager; it is not, therefore, to the manager or actor that I address myself upon this occasion, but to the man of feeling and the scholar." Jenner's preface, noting Diderot's distinction between comedy of "wit and Character" and that of "nature and sentiment," goes on to propose a third kind, the comedy of "stage-trick and decoration" then in possession of the stage. After sketching its characteristics, he laments that "the cast of the times is so *frivole*, as to have banished both nature and sentiment from the stage in such a manner, that the amusements of that and the closet cannot be brought to coincide." It is precisely to the latter category, "the closet," that Jenner directs his appeal, "conscious that refined sentiments, which perish if they are not sown in a warm and genial soil, and even characteristic humor, to which nothing but observation can give a relish, have very little chance of amusing an audience, who go to the theatre to think or to feel.—He therefore wishes his piece, in which he professes to have aimed at a combination of the first two kinds of comedy ['character' and 'sentiment'], without any attention to the last ['stage-trick and decoration'], to be introduced to the closet alone; and judged according to its merit or demerit, by the cool and unbiassed reader." In conclusion, he commits his piece (based on Diderot's *Le Père de famille*) to the public, hoping that writers for the stage "will not grudge him his more confined share [of applause] in the closet." How widespread this attitude was among writers of sentimental comedy is difficult to say, but we have considerable commentary from the eighteenth century which tends to subsume sentimental comedy under closet drama, and to link both to the novel.[9] Various characters in Georgian comedies refer to the novel or the sentimental comedy interchangeably as the proper place for the sententious, the romantic, and the lachrymose.[10] In the first scene of Hugh Kelly's comedy *A Word to the Wise* (1769, pub. 1770), for example, Miss Montagu observes of the amiable Sir George Hastings, "And if his foibles provoke us to an occasional smile, his worth must always excite our warmest admiration." To which Miss Dormer retorts: "Upon my word, Harriot, a very florid winding up of a period, and very proper for an elevated thought in a sentimental Comedy."[11] Modely, in William Whitehead's *School for Lovers*, tells Belmour that he has "heard Caelia talk occasionally, like a queen in a tragedy, or at least like a sentimental lady in a comedy."[12] Both of these speeches from sentimental comedies have a certain self-conscious nervousness about them, a seeming anxiety to forestall possible criticism by making jokes at their own expense. But we tend to derive the stilted, periodic dialogue to which they refer from the sentimental novel or romance, and in fact these speeches are atypical in looking to their own genre for the source of such diction and demeanor. In 1760 George Colman initiated a series of novel-struck heroines with *Polly Honeycombe*, subtitled "A Dramatic Novel." Inevitably, these young ladies' behavior reflects that of their literary idols, with results either instructive or satirical, depending on the author's bent. When the ardors of Belville have finally jolted Lady Frankland, the "Platonic wife" in Elizabeth Griffith's comedy of that name (1765), out of her "sentiments" and into a rational passion for her husband, she exclaims, "How I detest the writers of romance!" (v.i). Both Polly Honeycombe and her more famous descendant Lydia Languish try to make life copy art by envisioning *Clarissa*-like predicaments as their own infatuations unfold, and their speech betrays the novelistic sources of their follies.

> so *sentimental* is the stile,
> So chaste, yet so bewitching all the while!
> Plot, and elopement, passion, rape, and rapture,
> The total sum of ev'ry dear—dear—Chapter.[13]

Sir Charles Somerville, in Mrs. Griffith's *The Double Mistake* (1765), refers to the disguises, duels, cruel stepmothers, mysterious strangers, nocturnal surprises, and other romantic incidents of her sentimental comedy as "the circumstances of this extraordinary novel" (II.i). And Madame Florival, in Colman's *The Deuce Is in Him* (1763), like many a heroine of sentimental comedy, has run away from a tyrannical father and is languishing for the lover he forbade. Says Emily, "I know her whole history; it is quite a little novel."[14] Frances Sheridan, Richard Brinsley's mother, wrote two full-length sentimental comedies, *The Discovery* (1763) and *The Dupe* (1763, pub. 1764). The former, according to the writer for *Bell's British Theater,* is "rather a novel than a comedy—it has no incident that can surprise, and the dialogue is languid, and the sentences loose—they have none of the terse manner so necessary for the stage."[15] The terms of the differentiation are interesting: a novel may be "languid" and "loose"; a stage comedy must have "incident" and be "terse." In fact, Mrs. Sheridan was a writer of sentimental prose fiction (*Sidney Biddulph*), and *The Dupe,* with its grave, sententious heroine, seems a poorly dramatized novel. Perhaps Goldsmith had Mrs. Sheridan or Mrs. Griffith in mind when he remarked acidly that "those abilities that can hammer out a novel are fully sufficient for the production of a sentimental comedy" ("On the Theatre"). Melodrama, sentimental comedy's younger sister, sheds further light on these affinities with prose fiction, for basically melodrama was the Gothic novel staged (cf. Monk Lewis's *The Castle Spectre* and *The Castle of Otranto*). Sentimental comedy in the seventies began to display the romantic plots, black-and-white characterization, wild settings and oversimplification of evil characteristic of most melodrama (e.g., Richard Cumberland's *The Brothers,* 1769).[16] Several playwrights besides Cumberland, notably Frederic Reynolds and General John Burgoyne, moved comfortably back and forth between the two types.

This kind of evidence suggests not only that cross-fertilization between sentimental comedy and the popular novel was a recognized fact in the eighteenth century, but that sentimental comedy may have been primarily a reading phenomenon whose foothold in the theater was tenuous. Its measure of stage popularity seems to have owed much to the vogue of sentimental fiction; "the reading public of the day was so theater-mad that . . . plays were more popular reading than novels" by far.[17] This public received the sentimental closet dramas as avidly as it devoured Richardson, Sterne, and Mackenzie, and the booksellers willingly supplied the demand, which is probably why disproportionate numbers of sentimental plays were published. In this respect, then, sentimental comedy stands apart from the tradition of theatrical comedy.

Small "laughing" pieces, which depended upon the stage for their effect, were less likely to be published than sentimental plays. Among the noteworthy short comedies that remained unprinted were Miles Peter Andrews's *The Conjuror* (1774), Thomas Hull's *The Absent Man* (1764) and *All in the Right* (1766), Macklin's *A Will and No Will* (1746), the anonymous *Mock Orators* (1756), and James Townley's *False Concord* (1764, a possible source of *The Clandestine Marriage*). Several of these were actor's benefit afterpieces designed to be performed only once. There seems to have been no general demand for printing such plays, yet they were so numerous and vivid as to color eighteenth-century theater significantly. Moreover, a comic afterpiece might succeed impressively and still not be published. Foote's *Piety in Pattens* (1773), a clever satire on sentimentalism, had eighteen performances in its first two seasons, and was credited by some with bringing "moral and sentimental comedy . . . into disrepute."[18] Even so it was not printed, perhaps to keep spectators coming to the theater. Yet Hugh Kelly's *A Word to the Wise,* Hildebrand Jacob's *The Nest of Plays,* and Mrs. Griffith's *Patience the Best Remedy,* all sentimental plays which failed completely on the stage, were published at once. One finds few cases in which the situation is reversed. Here again it looks as if the booksellers preferred to print sentimental plays, because there was a market for them among the reading public which did not exist for the stage-oriented laughing comedies.

Another phenomenon tending to link the sentimental play with the reading public, with the "closet" side of the "stage/closet" split, is the discrepancy between plays as acted and plays as printed. The Larpent Collection of plays submitted to the Examiner from 1737 to 1824 consists of manuscripts which represent, approximately, the acting versions. A useful feature of Dougald MacMillan's catalogue of this collection is his comparison of each Larpent MS with the earliest published text of the play. Comments such as "numerous minor differences," "notable differences," "conclusion quite different," and "Acts IV and V very different" abound, and naturally arouse curiosity as to why and how the original stage version was altered for publication. The playwright ordinarily prepared his own play for the press; "he had the opportunity to restore what the manager had eliminated, or to revise the piece in the light of its reception" (MacMillan, p. viii). Since the published play was put together with the reading public in mind, it might incorporate the author's more undramatic ideas. The Larpent MSS afford a unique opportunity to learn what transpired in the theater, but with over twenty-four hundred items in the collection, an exhaustive comparison of MSS with texts would obviously fill tomes, so I have made only a partial and exploratory investigation, oriented to my subject.

The MacMillan catalogue itself drives a sufficient wedge between "stage" and "closet" texts to support Nicoll's recognition of the "popularity of the reading, as distinct from the acting, play" late in the century (Nicoll, *History,* 3:73). Nicoll is here referring chiefly to the almost unstageable *drames,* and Sherbo mentions the "humorless, sententious, unrelievedly dull sentimental comedy which found its way into print for the consumption of many readers, but which never saw stage presentation" (p. 106). These were extreme manifestations of a dichotomy which, in less pronounced forms, was almost ubiquitous. At least as early as Fielding, the playwright was going out of his way to appeal to his readers; the bogus scholarship of *Tom Thumb,* for example, has no theatrical counterpart. Especially if his play fared poorly onstage, the dramatist might produce a press version differing as extensively from the acting script as a full-scale revision of a novel from its first draft. Elizabeth Griffith's *Patience the Best Remedy* (a sentimental comedy) in its first edition

(1772) has "discrepancies in dialogue, order of scenes, and points of division between acts" from the Larpent MS (MacMillan, p. 57). The first edition of *The Rivals* was neither the original stage version nor the subsequent acting script; not until the third edition did the printed text accord closely with the play as acted. Some passages printed by Sheridan were regularly omitted in stage performance by him and Thomas Harris.[19] This common practice is reflected in some of the contemporary collections of plays "regulated from the promptbooks," such as Davies's, or *Bell's British Theatre:* "The lines distinguished by inverted commas, are omitted in the representation." An occasional first edition (e.g., Hannah Cowley's *The Runaway,* 1776) has the same feature.

Of course not all authors were equally careful in preparing plays for the press. Mrs. Griffith found extensive revision necessary in *Patience the Best Remedy,* as did Hugh Kelly in *The School for Wives* (see below). Arthur Murphy, a comic dramatist of a more traditional bent, is said to have rewritten his plays extensively for the 1786 *Works;* the version of *The Choice* (1765) printed there is only "a paraphrase of MS."[20] David Garrick, on the other hand, a very busy man, was not a careful reviser so far as we know. Yet his *Lethe* (1740, pub. 1749 et seq.) showed, by its seventh edition in 1774, the polishing and the accretions of thirty-odd years of acting and experimenting. So independent was it of any written text, so much a thing of the stage, that it evolved continually, molded by its performers. Probably the same process made the 1760 printing of Moses Mendez's *The Double Disappointment* (1746) an almost entirely different version of the play from the Larpent MS (MacMillan, p. 10). In whichever way the discrepancies came about—authorial revision or natural evolution—they demonstrate the distance from stage to page, and the necessity of consulting the acting version in order to know what passed in the theater. Even then we have only the actors' starting point, the prompt book.

Contemporary critics diplomatically recognized the separation of published and acting versions of a play. The anonymous author of *An Examen of the New Comedy, call'd The Suspicious Husband* (London, 1747) describes that comedy as "so much admired, and so impatiently expected in print. . . . It is agreed by all, that it is not only an *acting* but a *reading* play" (pp. 3–4). Another anonymous theatrical commentator prefers English comedy to French, and French to Italian, "and the reason is

obvious; Italian comedies are not composed for the press."[21] Samuel
Foote's comment that the translated plays in *The Comic Theatre* (3 vols.,
1762) were "intended to be performed on the English stage" would have
been superfluous if it had not been for the vogue of closet drama
(Preface, vol. 1). A writer for the *Critical Review* in 1765 claimed that
comedy, unlike tragedy, could as well be enjoyed in the closet as on the
stage (20:331), while Arthur Murphy called *Tancred and Sigismunda* "a
most delightful composition" in the closet, although "stage-effect was not
Thomson's talent."[22] The implicit acceptance of this separation as natural and permissible had profound consequences for the drama as time
went on.

Some general conclusions can be drawn about the nature of changes
made for the press. One tendency was to shorten by omitting scenes,
cutting characters and pruning dialogue judged less effective "in the
closet." The first acted scenes of Garrick's *Miss in Her Teens* and Murphy's
Know Your Own Mind were not printed in the first editions, for example,
and the 1760 text of Mendez's *The Double Disappointment* reduces the
witty servant's onstage machinations. But coexistent with this force was
the author's propensity to lengthen by restoring those bits, discarded for
dramatic exigency, of which he was particularly fond. Both impulses are
discernible in Sheridan's revisions of *The Rivals*. The original MS (predat-
ing even the Larpent copy) was cut drastically to obtain a workable stage
version. Sheridan then added some rejected parts, and made some cuts,
in preparing the first edition, which emerged about five hundred lines
shorter than the Larpent MS (roughly, the acting version).[23] In most cases
the process resembled that of any theatrical company trying out a show
on the road, pruning what is less successful and retaining or elaborating
what works.

Certain of these changes were evidently made with an eye to the
different medium and audience of the printed play. Stage business, for
instance, was often cut from mainpieces, likewise anything "low."[24] The
entire first scene of Arthur Murphy's *Know Your Own Mind* was considered expendable on both counts. The first edition (1778) also omits some
farcical byplay by Sir John Millamour in act 1, a display of "low" servant
humors in act 2, and a scene in act 5 during which Bygrove courts his
lover's maid under the illusion that she is her mistress, and is heartily
laughed at. All of these omissions are typical, especially the last: ridicule,

a classic function of stage comedy, seems to have been judged less suitable for the closet. The 1778 edition adds to the MS a conversation between Millamour and Bygrove in act 1 denoting a conflict in educational philosophies (cf. the nonverbal approach of the MS scene, where servant hustle-and-bustle allows us to experience the disruption of his household by Sir John's capricious temper); a paragraph of fulsome novelistic sentiments by Miss Neville not in the Larpent copy: "Oh! state of dependence! for mere support, to be subject every hour to caprice and arrogance!—Is it pride that makes me feel with this sensibility?—No, my heart can answer it is not" (II.i.), and Dashwould's satirical portraits of London, which are brief verbal sallies in the acting version.

Readers were presumed to have little interest in scene directions, and ordinarily these were not printed in their entirety.[25] The spectacular in general, however prominent on the stage, was played down in print. Isaac Bickerstaffe's *The Sultan* (1775, pub. 1787) is a good example. Stage directions for this opulent, masque-like spectacle were cut wholesale from the first edition, along with several pieces of stage business. Whereas local color and visual novelties dominate the Larpent MS, the text of 1787 emphasizes a moral lesson (mental beauty shines through divergent customs, uniting the world) only implicit in the theater script. In essence Bickerstaffe composed for the press a new piece; he sought to achieve effects appropriate to the printed medium, rather than fidelity to the stage version. Most authors seem to have felt this need to take a different direction in the published play, further contributing to the separation of printed literature and the stage.

As we might expect from the general character of the reading public, printed plays were occasionally "sentimentalized," and that fact has broad implications. Some critics have fixed upon the ending of Hugh Kelly's *School for Wives* (1773, pub. 1774) as a locus classicus for the moral didacticism and self-conscious theorizing of the sentimental dramatist.[26] Thorndike presents it as "a very neat defence of his aim in comedy," and Bernbaum also makes much of it:

> BELVILLE; I sha'n't, therefore part with one of you 'till we have had a hearty laugh at our adventures.
> MISS WALSINGHAM: They have been very whimsical, indeed; yet, if represented on the stage, I hope they would be found not only entertaining,[27] but instructive.

LADY RACHEL: Instructive! Why, the modern critics say that the only business of Comedy is to make people laugh.[28]

BELVILLE: That is degrading the dignity of letters exceedingly, as well as lessening the utility of the stage. A good comedy is a capital effort of genius and should, therefore, be directed to the noblest purposes.

MISS WALSINGHAM: Very true; and unless we learn something while we chuckle, the carpenter who nails a pantomime together will be entitled to more applause than the best comic poet in the Kingdom.

Granted, it is an impressive statement of the creed of the school of morality, placed as it is in a commanding final position, and presented to us by the principal personages of the drama at a receptive moment. But theater audiences never heard it. The acting copy in the Larpent Collection ends with the first-quoted speech of Miss Walsingham; the last three speeches were added for the press. We are not to imagine that Kelly developed his theory between the play's rehearsal period and its publication. The addition is rather due to his consciousness of a different audience, more receptive to the tenets of sentimental comedy. Kelly knew the patrons of the theater would not have been pleased by this bald propaganda. He may have remembered Garrick's sagacity in affixing a comic prologue to *A Word to the Wise* (1770), instead of the serious one he had submitted.

The whole printed text of *The School for Wives* moves toward the sentimental. Several satirical references to people and institutions are cut. A "low" but traditionally comic exposure of imposters (the false justices) in the MS does not appear in the first edition. Another low scene—the encounter of Leeson and Connoly with the bailiffs—is shortened and altered, action in the stage version being replaced by sentiments in print. Taken together with the introduction of sentimental theory at the end, these changes suggest that Kelly, like Murphy, judged the theatrical audience more inclined to traditional stage comedy, and less to the sententious or sentimental, than his readers.

The extent to which such clear-cut sentimentalizing of press versions occurred in the eighteenth century remains a question. One other instance I have come across is worth mentioning. Murphy's farce *The Upholsterer* exists in three Larpent MSS: the original of 1757, and Murphy's alterations of 1763 and 1791. The play as published in 1758 contains in the last scene (II.iv.)—so often the pitfall of *vis comica* in eighteenth-century comedy—a speech by Harriot upon her reunion with her long-absent brother Rovewell, which is virtually the only senti-mental touch in the play: "Tho' your Departure from *England* was too early for my Recollection, yet my Heart feels a ready Inclination to make Acquaintance with you; and I shall ever bless the Hour that has given to my Father so good a Son, to Mr. *Bellman* so warm a Friend, and to me the unexpected Happiness of a Brother, whom I despair'd of ever seeing." Neither 1757 nor 1763 has this speech, clearly addressed to the tearful, the susceptible, and the effusive. Both early MSS pass directly from Rovewell's terse "I must embrace you" to reassertion of the central comic foible of the play, Quidnunc's passion for news: "Pray now *Jack*, how many Ships of the Line has the Admiral with him?" In most comedies these changes are less striking because more minute. They may be confined to the diction, and have no real drift. For instance, Miss Hardcastle's "man of sentiment" in the comic tête à tête with Marlow (*She Stoops to Conquer*, act 2), is only a "man of speculation" in the Larpent MS. This is less a pitch to the novel-readers, however, than a clarification of what type is being undercut, although the nature of the verbal change coincides with typical press alterations.

Traditionally we have accepted a set of generalizations about printed drama of the eighteenth century as if it applied equally to the acted drama, but the evidence at hand suggests that it does not. The selection of plays published was not wholly representative, nor were the texts always accurate; in both cases, and for the same reason, the distortion made the stage look more "sentimental" than it was. Since printed plays of the Georgian period thus falsified the full theatrical reality to some extent, it is necessary to consult the acting versions—in this case, the Larpent Collection—in order to understand the stage. There we have a legitimate point of departure for examining the whole theatrical com-plex, which we have tended to view through the lens of the reading public. In sum, we must take seriously the implications of the stage/closet split for the study of Georgian drama.

PART II
The Rivals
of
Laughing Comedy

To describe sentimental and illegitimate forms as the rivals of traditional comedy is not entirely accurate, for to some extent they entered and even enriched the bloodline of eighteenth-century comedy. A new and livelier drama was born of the wedding of the English and Italian types, a more humane one from the marriage of laughing and satiric comedy with the softening and warming influences of the sentimental idea. The delightful union of all three in the comedies of Sheridan and Goldsmith is a triumph of peaceful coexistence.

On the other hand, a state of war did exist during much of the eighteenth century between the proponents of each type, and in this sense they were rivals. Looking back over the shifting fortunes of each kind in the repertories, we can discern the battles clearly enough. "Harlequin's invasion" is, after all, an eighteenth-century term; and Georgian observers likewise imaged sentimental and laughing comedy as meeting in a series of skirmishes, as when False Delicacy encountered The Good-Natured Man. If their view is occasionally somewhat bald, it nevertheless represents a version of the truth as perceived at the time, and we should be cautious about simply discarding it in favor of our own perspective. One of the tasks of our hindsight can be to mitigate Georgian excesses and soften any harsh contours we may find.

The Muse of the Woeful Countenance

It would be a curious exercise for a gentleman of leisure to write a history of the word "sentimental," and collect instances of its loose and meaningless application. For the past half-century . . . it has become a vague term of abuse which everyone has been free to hurl at everything, not obviously cynical, that he or she happened to dislike.
—William Archer, *The Old Drama and the New*

A MEDITATION ON SENTIMENT

With the single change of *half-century* to *century*, William Archer's words are as apposite today as when he wrote them. Applications of "the word" have continued to be "loose," if not quite "meaningless," and it remains a "vague term of abuse." If he were alive now, Archer would discover that "sentimental" has become a devil-word in modern criticism; nothing, perhaps, will damn a new novel or film to perdition so thoroughly or so fast as the imputation of sentimentality. A recent writer glosses sentimentality as "feeling about nothing." Our present distrust of sentiment as meretricious, illusory, a cheap and outworn emotional costume, is succinctly expressed in a poem by W. R. Rodgers called "White Christmas":

> Punctually at Christmas the soft plush
> Of sentiment snows down, embosoms all
> The sharp and pointed shapes of venom, . . .
> And into obese folds subtracts from sight
> All truculent acts, bleeding the world white.

43

> ... It is a genial time;
> Angels, like stalactites, descend from heaven;
> Bishops distribute their own weight in words,
> Congratulate the poor on Christlike lack.
> . . . .
> But punctually tomorrow you will see
> All this silent and dissembling world
> Of stilted sentiment suddenly melt
> Into mush and watery welter of words
> Beneath the warm and moving traffic of
> Feet and actual fact. Over the stark plain
> The silted mill-chimneys once again spread
> Their sackcloth and ashes, a flowing mane
> Of repentance for the false day that's fled.

Archer placed the commencement of our vendetta against the "sentimental" in "the early days of George Meredith," the 1860s. Probably the semantic deterioration of *sentimental*, coinciding roughly with the generation of Edmund Gosse and A. W. Ward, played a part in the devaluation of eighteenth-century comedy in the eyes of the critics, and Meredith was a key figure in this development. Antisentimentalism is a feature of several of his poems and novels, of *An Essay on Comedy* (1877) and of his comedy *The Sentimentalists* (1910). He believed that "bestiality and sentimentalism were always trying to curb man" in his aspirations, and some of his contemporaries were moving in this same direction.[1]

It is in the twentieth century, however, that literary sentimentalism has become grossly unfashionable, even repugnant. The First World War, that terrible crack in the Western psyche, gapes between us and a time when serious art could indulge in lush displays of fellow-feeling and benevolence without being thought the worse for them. Edwardian writers were already rebellious against sentiment,[2] but it was the Trench Poets who made the irrevocable break. The English literary sensibility has not been the same since Wilfred Owen found "red lips . . . not so red" as "the stained stones kissed by the English dead" in "Greater Love." It may be that 1789 marked the end of the *ancien régime* in politics and philosophy, but for the arts 1914 seems a greater watershed, cutting us off from the "immortal sea / Which brought us hither." It is more than coincidence that two influential works (Nettleton's and Bernbaum's) that stigmatized eighteenth-century comedy for sentimentalism were published during the war years. And the progress of embitterment can easily be traced from Owen through the post-war work of poets such as T. S. Eliot, Michael Roberts, and W. H. Auden. The novel followed suit, with Somerset Maugham shocking readers by his harsh candor, Hemingway, Aldous Huxley, and others maintaining a grimly cynical tone, and the critics leaping on any suspected lapse into sentimentalism.[3] Nor are these examples either extreme or recent; matters have gone much farther since Auschwitz and My Lai.

But our contempt for sentimentality, however understandable or inevitable, puts us in a disadvantageous position with regard to some literature of earlier centuries. We are as far estranged emotionally from many eighteenth- and nineteenth-century authors, for instance, as they were from most seventeenth-century writers.[4] A considerable act of historical imagination is always necessary to read older literature on its own terms. It is sometimes said that the Georgians failed the Metaphysicals in this regard; perhaps it is we who are now failing the Georgians. If so, an appropriate first act of restitution would be to try to understand those unfamiliar premises and conventions which seem to lie beyond a chasm of altered tastes, and no word or concept needs a new effort at understanding more than *sentimental*. How did Georgians use the word and feel about the idea? Did they react to it as we do? It is more than Archer's mere "curious exercise" to find out.

The *Oxford English Dictionary* establishes that *sentimental* was not always a derogatory epithet. In the eighteenth century the root-word, *sentiment*, could mean "a feeling with regard to something," "a mental feeling," "an emotional thought," or "an epigrammatical thought" (this last meaning being particularly important in drama). These basic definitions may still be found in a modern dictionary, but our attitude towards the mixture of feeling with thought has changed. The usages given for the eighteenth century had neutral or slightly positive connotations; context and modifiers allowed the writer to tip the sense either way. Today, however, according to the *OED*, "sentiment" occurs "chiefly in derisive use, conveying an imputation of either insincerity or mawkishness."

"Sentimental" originated in a definitely favorable sense: "everything clever and agreeable is comprehended in that word," writes Lady Bradshaigh to Samuel Richardson in 1749. When Lady Bradshaigh called

45

someone a "man of sentiment," she meant that his nature "comprehended" both sense and sensibility, in balance. After this vogue, however, a reaction set in against the "cant-word," at least partly because sense and sensibility were increasingly seen as distinct and opposed qualities. "Sentimentalism" and "sentimentalize" both appeared in the second decade of the nineteenth century with negative connotations (*Sense and Sensibility* was published in 1811). Since Jane Austen's time a "sentimental" person is apt to be one in whom sense and sensibility are confounded. By the turn of this century the metamorphosis was virtually complete. "I could hardly say more," warns a correspondent in 1908, "without approaching dangerously near to the sentimental." Thus the etymological approach seems to corroborate the semantic development suggested by Archer and supported by recent literary history.

This turns out not to be the whole story, however. When we examine the specifically dramatic usages of *sentimental* we find that the admirable *OED* has partially misled us. Occurrences of the word in drama often have an unfavorable slant; especially after the middle of the century, most come from enemies of the form. This is a case in which generalizations about eighteenth-century literature or society as a whole do not apply equally to the theater. For example, Arthur Sherbo could find only three plays between 1750 and 1800 that called themselves "sentimental comedies," and one of these was Foote's satire *Piety in Pattens*. The *OED* fails to record that "sentiment" in the sense of "an epigrammatical thought" had an adjectival counterpart. Frequently *sentimental* was a synonym for *sententious*. A character (or play) might be termed *sentimental* if he (or it) specialized in *sentiments* or *sentences:* the kind of moral epigrams suitable for stitching into samplers. Two of the period's more notable literary villains—Blifil and Joseph Surface—were given to producing these, a trait which was taken as a symptom of a bad heart. Joseph is actually called "a man of sentiment," by Sir Peter, and "a sentimental knave," by Lady Sneerwell. This is fairly typical of what happened to the sentimentalist in later eighteenth-century comedy, although of course there were those who approved of sentiments and who wrote or applauded what now seems dialogue of maudlin sentimentality. The point is that when eighteenth-century writers called a play or a character sentimental, they might be employing some, all, or none of our connotations. They could mock certain aspects of the idea while accepting others. *Caveat lector*.

Eighteenth-century drama, then, recognized two different faces of sentiment. So do we, who are more ambiguous about sentiment than the foregoing discussion has implied. This becomes obvious as soon as one turns from literature and the intelligentsia to common life. In any popular entertainment, for example, the "sentimental" is still far from discredited, and it has a hallowed place in social camaraderie and ordinary human relations. Even the literati grant that while sentimentality is a mawkish, vain, and excessive display of feeling, from the same impulse, differently channelled, come benevolence, charity, and sensitivity. Though we reject the religious opiate of the Bishop in "White Christmas," we approve intelligent humanitarianism, and while we despise the tearful sensibilities of eighteenth-century précieux, we assiduously cultivate our own. The two faces of sentiment, false and true, meet along the seam still visible in some of our sense-words, a seam that reveals how precariously our attitudes are balanced. *Sensibility* is a "capacity for sensation" that may be either "acuteness of apprehension" or a "liability to feel hurt"; *sensitive* can shade from "responsive" to "easily pained." Feeling is a continuum, not a polarity. Nor do the false and true faces of sentiment simply correspond to *old* and *new,* for the eighteenth century, as we have seen, also recognized both, and placed its emotional desiderata towards the same end of the continuum as ours. Blifil's half-brother is Tom Jones, and the other "surface" of Joseph is Charles.

RECOGNIZING SENTIMENTAL COMEDY

Existing definitions of sentimental comedy are in such disarray that we must either find a new basis of coherence or else abandon the term, as some critics have already done. In an early book, John Loftis adopted the term "exemplary comedy" to describe *The Conscious Lovers;* some years later he decided that there was "no such genre as "sentimental comedy." "[5] Writing in the prestigious *London Stage*, George Winchester Stone, Jr., frankly doubts that we can categorize comedies as laughing or sentimental now, partly because the plays themselves often mixed these

47

modes, partly because critics are not able to agree on firm criteria for either category (pt. 4, 1:clxi). Two dissertations directed by Ricardo Quintana in the late sixties either disregard or challenge our received definitions of sentimental comedy; one of them concludes that neither Murphy, Colman, nor Cumberland even "recognized *sentimental* comedy as a true genre." Much like ourselves, they understood the term as "excessive and unnatural emotionalism" and opposed it.[6] Unfortunately that understanding was not general enough for us to be able to use the historical approach—what the eighteenth century thought about sentimental comedy—with any amount of accuracy or satisfaction: in addition to individual variation and semantic shifts, tastes and standards of critical interpretation have changed too radically.

The most extended statement of the problems one encounters in using the old categorical and qualitative definitions is Arthur Sherbo's *English Sentimental Drama*. Sherbo first establishes a five-point lowest common denominator of modern definitions of sentimental comedy: (1) presence of a moral element; (2) greater emotional than intellectual appeal; (3) artificial, exaggerated, improbable plots and characters; (4) a belief in the goodness or perfectibility of human nature; and (5) an emphasis on tears, pity, and virtuous sufferings. Testing this consensual definition, however, he finds it unsatisfactory, since it does not apply in full to some sentimental plays, and partly describes some non- sentimental plays. He tries adding more criteria himself—repetition and prolongation of sentimental possibilities, the eschewal of humor and bawdry, emphasis on the sentimental plot—in an attempt to bring the sentimental canon into line with the current meaning of the word, but decides that the only real test is the subjective response of the (twentieth-century) reader or auditor to the whole play: "a sentimental speech, character, or situation does not make a sentimental play; a sentimental play is one which leaves reader or spectator with the desired emotional effect un- mixed with disturbingly antagonistic feelings alien to the sentimental response" (p. 75). Sherbo thus replaces the conventional definition-by-certain-traits—reunion and reform motifs, benevolent characters, sententious diction, smug virtue, and the like—which have the disadvantage of also appearing in comedies whose overall effect is clearly not senti-mental, with definition by net psychological/emotional effect on the audience. For him, a sentimental comedy is one that affects us now as disproportionately emotional, mawkish, inappropriately tender, falsely pathetic, and excessively refined. Some find Sherbo's approach too iconoclastic or subjective, but it has subsequently received theoretical support. Elder Olson points out that a comic plot need not be all comic; a play may be part farce, but still be wholly comic. An obvious corollary would be that a wholly comic play could still be partly sentimental: "it is comic if the overall action is comic."[7]

It may well be objected that at this rate there will soon be no sentimental comedies left, for Sherbo, simply by asking if "sentimental comedies" would strike most modern readers as "sentimental" overall, virtually defined the genre out of existence. He concluded that very few of the plays thus labeled could pass the test of "emotional response." For example, Colley Cibber's *Love's Last Shift*, traditionally the first of the "crying comedies," doubtless offered something new and important, but do we find its performance a sentimental experience? The scene in which Loveless reforms (the only "sentimental" scene after four acts of amoral intrigue and prurience) is followed immediately by one in which Snap, Loveless's servant, and Amanda's maid are hauled out of the cellar *in flagrante delicto*. When Loveless offers him a handsome annuity to marry the girl, Snap replies: "I have so much grace left that I can repent,—when I have no more opportunities of being wicked." This annuity, however, is really Amanda's money; Loveless himself was broke when she took him back, and probably we are meant to notice that Snap's remark is a perfectly apt comment on Loveless's own situation, if you change "opportunities" to "need" (cf. Sherbo, pp. 103–6). Overall the scene appears to undermine a sentimental response.

There are so many instances in which each of the traits sometimes used to define sentimental comedy occurs in non-sentimental comedy that we are forced to consider "the whole play." "Sentimental" (i.e., sententious) dialogue, for instance, became a convention in certain situations in eighteenth-century drama. No matter what the "level of conduct" of the play, or the rank of the hero and heroine, their meeting called for effusions and fantastic dialogue inherited from the lovers in romance by way of the novel. Young romantic leads tended to talk priggishly. One or two character types and situations in otherwise unsentimental plays rang a Pavlovian bell for dramatists, and the "sentences" flowed. Sir William, the lover in Thomas Bridges's coarse, primitive

49

satire *The Dutchman* (1775), receives from his Sophy a note containing her plan of escape from her guardian: "But soft, this change so much exceeds my most sanguine expectations, that I cannot persuade myself I am awake. The pleasure that rushes thro' all my senses is too violent to support. Excess of joy is I find, far more dangerous, than excess of sorrow, and if I don't curb mine, it will shake the seat of reason." Some time later he waits for her in a grove, and as the time set for their tryst arrives and passes, he exclaims, "What a situation am I in one moment raised to the highest pinnacle of joy, and the next plung'd into the deepest dungeon of despair" (Larpent MS 391). These melodramatic raptures, which would do credit to Vincent Crummles's troupe in *Nicholas Nickleby,* appear (not as parody) in a farcical sketch, a satyr-play as crude and obscene as would pass the Examiner's Office. Then there is Truman, the romantic hero of Miles Peter Andrews's unpublished farce *The Conjuror* (1774), who learns that the guardian of his beloved Maria plans to marry her himself. "Monstrous!" he cries to Maria's aunt. "What shall we do to hinder the execution of so fatal a design?" (Larpent MS 372). Even Samuel Foote, a confirmed satirist with a good ear for colloquial speech, occasionally wrote sententious speeches for his lovers (e.g., Lydia and Sir James in *The Bankrupt*). This diction may suggest the influence of genteel comedy, and it was called "sentimental" by Georgian critics, but it does not follow that the play in which it occurs can be called "sentimental" in any modern sense.

The shortcomings of qualitative definition force the conclusion that no single element identifies a sentimental comedy; it is rather a clustering of qualities in a certain way without undue interference by antipathetic qualities. Drama, as Olson points out, is not a what but a how: a recognition scene may be serious or comic depending on the handling (pp. 109, 132). Sherbo's subjective criterion of psychic and emotional response to an artistic whole is, finally, the best instrument we have. Here at least we can use our common sense and sensibility, respond to entire plays instead of to artificially isolated components, and avoid entrapment in our own rules.

Modern dramatic criticism has tended to break down the clumsy monolith of sentimental comedy into more precisely discriminated subtypes: reform, benevolist, genteel, exemplary, and so on.[8] The most important of these distinctions is still that between "sentimental" and "moral" or "moralized" comedy, because there is a difference between plays which were rendered "clean" to please the reformers—made decent and perhaps didactic—and those that directed their chief appeal to the susceptible and emotional. Bateson's treatment is standard:

> The rise of "sentimentalism" coincided with the attacks of Jeremy Collier and his fellow moralists on the immorality and profaneness of the stage. Undoubtedly the sentimental dramatists sympathized with these attacks . . . and it is easy to understand the source of this sympathy. The sentimental dramatists, by once again making comedy a mirror of life, had necessarily brought into it the moral laws which govern life. But the movements, none the less, were distinct. . . . There is no reason to believe that Collier ever approved of the sentimental comedies; it is certain that he disapproved of *Love's Last Shift*. . . . As a moralist Collier was indifferent to the inhumanity of the Restoration dramatists; it was their indecency to which he objected. . . . The fact is that the primary object of "sentimentalism" was to humanize the drama, whereas the primary object of Collier was to make it didactic.[9]

The distinction between the words in eighteenth-century dramatic usage approximates that we would draw today. The epilogue to Samuel Foote's *The Englishman Returned from Paris* (1756) propounds a typical statement of moral aims for the period:

> Fain would he send you chearful home to-night,
> And harmless mirth by honest means excite;
> Scorning with luscious phrase or double sense,
> To raise a laughter at the fair's expence.

There is no question of *comédie larmoyante* here: Foote will be "chearful," will produce "mirth" and "laughter," but he fully intends to be decent about it. This same sense is preserved in the phrase "to moralize" an old play, meaning to clean it up, as Garrick did to Wycherley in *The Country Girl*. The word could also signify "explicitly didactic," as in "the moral tag." An intent to sentimentalize, on the other hand, is evident in the prologue to Edward Moore's *The Foundling* (1748), despite the moral preaching advertised in line two:

> He forms a Model of the virtuous Sort,
> And gives you more of moral than of sport;
> He rather aims to draw the melting Sigh,
> Or steal the pitying Tear from Beauty's Eye;

Or touch the Strings, that humanize our Kind,
Man's sweetest Strain, the musick of the Mind.

Moore wants his exemplary play ("a Model . . .") to evoke sympathetic tears, not the cheerful laughter that goes with "sport." He is writing what Sheridan's Sneer called "genteel comedy . . . the true sentimental, and nothing ridiculous in it from beginning to end" (*The Critic,* i.i). In that same conversation two other types are distinguished. Dangle mentions the moralized alteration: "No double-entendre, no smart innuendo admitted; even Vanbrugh and Congreve obliged to undergo a bungling reformation!" And Sneer refers to another species (confusingly called "moral") represented by *The Reformed House-Breaker:* the didactic, social-problem play then gaining in popularity.[10] It is barely possible, even on the basis of eighteenth-century attempts at definition, to discriminate between the "sentimental" but immoral comedy (*Love's Last Shift*), the moral and sentimental play (*The Conscious Lovers*), and the moralized laughing comedy (*The Clandestine Marriage*).

Earlier eighteenth-century dramatists passed on two models, or definitions, of sentimental comedy, for later writers to contemplate; we can conveniently label them the types of Cibber and Steele. One of these, based on *Love's Last Shift,* has already been mentioned: four acts of raking and sexual fun leading to incredible reforms and a fulsome conclusion rewarding Bacchus with Venus and Mammon. This kind had few followers after the Licensing Act, partly as a result of stiffening moral standards, partly because of advancing conceptions of human psychology and humane behavior. Later Georgian audiences seem to have had almost as much difficulty as we in accepting the sincerity of the maudlin confession and reform of Loveless and his kind.[11] Much stronger was the line sired by Steele's *Conscious Lovers,* which differed from the other principally in maintaining a moralistic tone from the beginning, and stressing sententious dialogue and refined character. Edward Moore's *The Foundling,* for example, has few laughs but no smutty innuendoes, being wholly dedicated to virtue and reform. A whole spate of bland comedies during the sixties did homage to Steele. To these inherited types the Garrick era added some of its own—reform, sententious, benevolist, and others—which loosened and diversified the genre considerably.

MID-CENTURY SENTIMENTAL COMEDY

Roughly two dozen full-length sentimental comedies were written and produced in London during the period 1737–77, about equal to the number of mainpiece laughing comedies (I say "roughly" both from the uncertainty of definition and because of ambiguous creatures such as sentimentalized alterations of non-sentimental plays). Of these comedies about twenty were soon published; they point up the variety of strains currently grouped under the heading "sentimental" and the paucity of the unadulterated type. Elizabeth Griffith and Frances Sheridan wrote a sententious kind of comedy, mildly reminiscent of Steele but more of the romantic novel, which fared better in the closet than onstage. One can hardly imagine a "comedy" farther from the traditional type or in more ways sentimental than Mrs. Griffith's *The Double Mistake* (1765); with its wildly romantic plot, reform motif, middle-class consciousness, sentimental dialogue, trembling sensibilities, and benevolent view of human nature, it is a touchstone of sorts. Played as satire it could be brilliant, but another comedy by the author produced earlier that year makes satirical intent unlikely. *The Platonic Wife,* confessedly drawn from one of Marmontel's *Contes moraux* and also resembling Cibber's *The Refusal,* affords a peek into the drawing-rooms of the aristocracy. It specializes in stilted conversations and refined emotions, with a dash of prurience and a touch of satire (on the title-character) thrown in. *Patience the Best Remedy* (1772) is perhaps her most palatable play: the construction is tighter than in the others, and the dialogue of the first act flows more naturally than is usual in comedies of this type and period. But thereafter it declines into a standard reform comedy, full of sentiments. Charlotte Melville is given to utterances like this: "The consciousness of one's own virtue becomes doubly pleasing, from the concurring testimony of an amiable and worthy friend" (II.ii).

Mrs. Sheridan's *The Dupe* (1763), like *The Platonic Wife,* is close to melodrama in the affectation of its language and the flatness of its characterization. The garrulous Mrs. Friendly must have been unbearably tedious onstage, and the audience was (understandably) bored by the interminable pathos of Emily and Wellford. *The Discovery* (1763) is a stronger performance; though the plot-structure is trite and sentimental, there are some stretches of humor and incisive dialogue

53

and one satiric portrait. But Mrs. Sheridan, who was writing the *Memoirs of Miss Sidney Biddulph* in the manner of Richardson at the time, seems incapable of achieving the brisk pace of successful stage comedy for long: she soon falls back into the prolix style of the novel of sensibility. William Whitehead, the Laureate, also belongs to this longwinded group by virtue of the abysmal *School for Lovers* (1762), which Bernbaum identifies as beginning a five-year surge of sentimental comedies. *The Dramatic Censor* (2 vols., 1770) complained justifiably of a "dreadful soporific languor," producing "a poppean lethargy," in his plays (2:474). These and other writers of novelistic comedy created a taste for "sentiments" and "clap-traps" with which later playwrights had to reckon. Their reliance on sententiousness and farfetched situations made stage comedy the competitor of the novel in an area where the latter had every advantage, laying the foundations both for comic drama's quittance of real life and also for its long subjugation to prose fiction. To the extent that comedy went in the direction they pointed, it moved away from its prime sources of strength.

Richard Cumberland, the most productive dramatist of the period, was also one of its major innovators, whatever one may think of his creations. He has been credited with inventing the melodrama, and was also the pioneer and prime representative of a school of "benevolist comedy," in which warm hearts and high-strung sensibilities tremble on the surface of dialogue and action, ready for tears or rapture. His first comedy, *The Brothers* (1769), is a potpourri of proven pleasers out of earlier comedy and romance: feuding brothers, providential shipwreck, marital reunion after long separation, and so forth. In the epilogue Cumberland throws in his lot with the Muse of Comedy, but the play is sentimental in its handling of the reform, reunion, and recognition motifs, in its diction, characterization, and implicit philosophy, and in its lack of humor. It has indeed, as Archer said, "the framework of melodrama" (p. 233).

In *The West Indian* (1771), Cumberland wrote what many consider *the* sentimental comedy of the later eighteenth century, and certainly one of the most successful plays of the period. Despite its reputation, it has its humorous and satiric moments, prompting one recent critic to query whether the large crowds drawn by *The West Indian* (and *False Delicacy*) "were more attracted by the fun or the moralising."[12] The prologue reveals that Cumberland sought benevolent laughter, not tears, as Steele and Moore had. "Rouse . . . / Your good old humour!" he admonishes the audience; since our age is strict and censorious, we will learn to laugh again. But the laughter must be without malice. At Major O'Flaherty he asks us to "laugh, but despise him not, for on his lip / His errors lie; his heart can never trip." Both Cumberland's style and his relationship with his public were emotional and, literally, "hearty":

> In this humble Sketch we hope you'll find
> Some emanations of a noble mind;
> Some little touches which, though void of art,
> May find their way perhaps into the heart.   (Prologue)

"Emanations" and "hearts" were key words for Cumberland; he was the dramatic equivalent of Shaftesburian philosophy and the humanitarian movement. One after the other he rehabilitated the stage Irishman, the stage Scot, the stage Jew, and, of course, the West Indian colonial. Belcour is a Caribbean Tom Jones—hot-blooded and imprudent, but basically good—who is watched over in London by the merchant Stockwell, one of the benevolent incognito relatives dear to all kinds of eighteenth-century comedy. Actually Belcour's unacknowledged father, he wants to test his son's heart before revealing himself. Given Belcour's name (*bel coeur?*), however, there can be little suspense in the matter. Cumberland in fact has difficulty getting Belcour into enough trouble to extricate him from; the device by which he does so in III.i—having Belcour hold on to the Rusport jewels while Stockwell carries the money back to Miss Rusport—is transparently absurd: why doesn't Stockwell take both? None of us ever really believes Belcour's profession of "a thousand faults," nor are we meant to. It is rather, as Stockwell says, that he is "no match for the cunning and contrivances of this intriguing town": his misadventures reflect on London society. Stockwell's fifth-act description of Belcour—"a heart beaming with benevolence, an animated nature, fallible indeed, but not incorrigible"—is unsurprising, for it constitutes no change of opinion. From v.iv. onwards, the audience's pleasure derives from the realization that affairs which were never far wrong are going to be perfectly, beautifully all right. We roll in "conscious" benevolence, material plenty, and the prospect of unbounded but lawful sensual delights for Louisa and Belcour, whose lust is neatly transmuted into marital ardor. Joseph Donohue aptly remarks that *The West Indian* "reads like a pamphlet on 'The Proceedings of Providence Vindicated, Written by a Society for Mutual Esteem.' "[13] Yet if all "sentimental comedy" were this entertaining, the genre would have presented few problems.

Many of these same values are espoused in *The Fashionable Lover* (1772), a sentimental melodrama dwelling long on conscious virtue in distress. In the Advertisement Cumberland restates his theme *fortissime*: "The Comedy, now submitted to the reader, is designed as an attempt upon his heart, and as such proceeds with little deviation from mine; if it should be thought therefore, that I have meant well, the charge of having executed indifferently I shall patiently submit to." Early in the play Mortimer, the anonymous benevolist, notes that if you "sheath a soft heart in a rough case, 'twill wear the longer," and his speeches on benevolence near the end of act 3 bring Shaftesbury from the tea-table to the footlights. *The Choleric Man,* on the other hand, has long been recognized as unsentimental, and is discussed in the chapter on laughing comedy.

The epilogue to Cumberland's two-act farce *The Note of Hand* (1774) suggests that the dramatist was by then "jaded at two heats," but he recovered to write important plays into the nineties, and had several followers in the rising generation of playwrights: Holcroft, Reynolds, Mrs. Inchbald, and George Colman the Younger. Towards the end of his life he grew disillusioned with the London theater, if his *Memoirs* (2 vols., 1807) may be believed. In them he swears, interestingly, that he has always espoused "legitimate comedy," and laments that he has lived to see "buffoonery, spectacle and puerility" triumph on the stage (1:270). For Cumberland, at least, laughter and sentiment ought to have been allies against the threat of illegitimacy.

The work of Hugh Kelly contains a much higher proportion of elements antagonistic to sentimentalism, particularly satire on sentiment. One needs only to compare Kelly's *False Delicacy,* whose very title criticizes a favorite sentimental trait, with Whitehead's *School for Lovers,* a thoroughly sentimental comedy of the same general type, to see how impure and satirically undercut Kelly's "sentimentalism" is. *A Word to the Wise* (1770), however, his second comedy, whether judged by plot, character, thought, or diction, must be listed with the legacy of Steele.

This tedious play, fully as artificial (i.e., unnatural) as any farce, was his most sentimental,[14] least equivocal, and least successful play, though its failure may have been due to political hostility. *The Man of Reason,* possibly by Kelly, will be discussed below with the Larpent plays.

These five writers produced about half the sentimental comedies in the period; beyond them the stream dilutes and ramifies even further. George Colman's *The Man of Business* (1774), a very awkward play to describe, might be called a moralized financial comedy. A social document of the middle-class mercantilists, it owes much to *The London Merchant* and *The Conscious Lovers*. There is a good deal of satire on fashions and prodigality, but little humor; a mild reform motif fades out near the end in favor of a paean to financial responsibility. Colman's only real sentimental comedy, *The English Merchant* (1767), is an adaptation of Voltaire's *L'Écossaise*. Many English sentimental plays have French sources: in time, as Rousseau became known and the *comédies larmoyantes* were translated, sentiment came to be considered a Gallic specialty, though France had taken the original sentimental impulse from England. Belford, in Colman's *The Deuce Is in Him* (1763), finds Tamper's desire to be "loved for himself alone" a "most precious refinement, truly! This is the most high-flown metaphysics in sentiment I ever heard in my life—picked up in one of your expeditions to the coast of France, I suppose—No plain Englishman ever dreamed of such a whim."[15] But despite its sentimentality, *The English Merchant* has the "ejections" of blocking characters and the ridicule associated with traditional comedy.

Occasionally one finds an example of the pure sentimental type that has a surprising charm. Francis Waldron's *The Maid of Kent* (1773, pub. 1778) combines melodrama, romance, and pastoral into a period piece with a fresh innocence usually lacking in sentimental comedy. Emily and George are lovers whose fathers exchanged them when they were infants. Only the revelation that George, not Emily, is the heir, is necessary to complete their happiness. The play has all the symptoms of a horror: "virtue-oppressed" diction, a villain, a father who talks pruriently of marrying the girl he has raised as his daughter, and a roses-and-moonlight ending in which evil is punished and virtue is rewarded with sex and money. Yet Waldron makes the characters lively and interesting, oppressively virtuous though they are. Even Patty, the maidservant whose eccentricities provide the only chuckles, turns into a faithful peasant housewife in a Gainsborough landscape by act 3. In fact, *The Maid of Kent* has closer affinities with the treatment of rural life in eighteenth-century genre-painting than with any dramatic form; a quiet, bucolic *tristesse* and the theme of "worth over birth" pervade the play. *The Maid of Kent* succeeds, after a fashion, through unabashed indulgence in sentimentality.

Three other full-length sentimental comedies of this period were not published, but exist in MS in the Larpent Collection. Two of them are heavily moralized variations on themes by Colley Cibber. Phillipina Burton's *Fashion Display'd* (1771) and the anonymous *Modern Wife* (1771, an alteration of Gay's *The Distressed Wife*) both repeat the unsentimental plot of *The Lady's Last Stake,* in which an errant wife with a passion for gambling is brought into artificial straits and reformed. *Fashion Display'd* (Larpent MS 308) is sententious, studiedly genteel, and totally lacking in any *vis comica;* the reforms are ludicrous. In act 3 for example, Lady Beaufleur offers her panacea for a roving husband: accept his caprices without question and strive to be attractive. After forty-five seconds of the new style Milord falls into line. At times the play tries to scourge society and its misfits (Gallic fops), but without conviction or telling satire, and the involuted language is that of bad eighteenth-century verse. It is difficult to say whether this piece is a sentimental comedy or just a comedy of manners *manqué.*

The alteration from Gay considerably sentimentalizes his play by stressing the reform motif and bourgeois ethics, and by introducing "conscious virtue" and stultifying diction. A reclamation of Lady Willits (copying Cibber's device) is added to Gay's plot, but the difficulties are trumped up by concerned friends, not a scheming enemy. The lowered tension produced by this change is typical of a great deal of later eighteenth-century comedy: she cannot be hurt. The part played by Lord George Brilliant in *The Lady's Last Stake* is taken by Southell, a friend of the family who is so virtuous that he hates posing as evil, though he knows the cause is good: "How distressing to the conscious mind is even the appearance of villainy." It is a good question, which unfortunately the play does not take seriously. A fake duel between Southell and Sir Thomas Willits is staged, whereupon the horrified Lady Willits renounces gaming and instantly reforms. (Gay had merely packed her off, still unregenerate, to the country, where the agents of change would be time and the removal of temptation.) *The Modern Wife* is tired, unoriginal writing, shot through with sentimental and didactic conventions.

The third of the Larpent plays is *The Man of Reason; or, The Reasonable Lover* (1776), said to be by Hugh Kelly. If this is so it adds nothing to his reputation, and not only because it failed after one performance. The complex plot, dealing with *three* potential marital mismatches and father-son clashes, vacillates between the overly ingenious and the dull. This long and dreary play gestures in several directions—humors comedy (Sir James Clifford, the "reasonable lover"), humanitarian reform (Freemore inveighs against cruelty to animals and debtors' prisons) and melodrama (chiefly the villain Lestock)—but never combines these parts into a coherent whole. *The Man of Reason* bears a family resemblance to *False Delicacy* in that Freemore is represented as a man of sentiment whose sentimentality is quite troublesome, but the expositions are so awkward compared to *False Delicacy* as to militate against Kelly's authorship.

The unpublished sentimental mainpieces of this period preserved in the Larpent Collection underscore, then, the poverty of the sentimental impulse in the sixties and seventies, and the scarcity of undiluted sentimental plays, that also characterized the published drama. Compared to the unpublished laughing comedies, it is a weak and wavering performance; nearly all of the significant sentimental plays seem to have been published, which was certainly not the case with the traditional comedies. The overall picture of "sentimental comedy" written at this time is variegated, the plays usually grouped under that heading proving neither uniform nor uniformly uninteresting.

Turning for a moment to the theater, we can see how sentimental comedies, old and new, measured up in performance. Once again the specter of definition rises, and with it the danger that statistics may be abused. To counter these obstacles—and well aware that the reorientation I have proposed for the term *sentimental* will not be acceptable to some—I have sought objectivity by using several different sources of data, various modes of measurement, and others' definitions of sentimental comedy. Since *The London Stage* is the reigning authority, let us start there, with the tabulations George Winchester Stone, Jr., gives for 1747–76. At Covent Garden and Drury Lane, Stone counts 10,545 mainpiece performances and, by his lights, 1,074 performances of sentimental comedy, or just over 10 percent. But the category *mainpieces* has a double disadvantage as a denominator: it includes tragedies, which are hardly relevant to the question, and omits afterpieces, which are pertinent indeed. Excluding tragedies, we have 5,179 comic mainpieces performed at both theaters, 21 percent (1,074) of which Stone calls sentimental: one in five. But if we add in the 4,571 afterpieces that Stone lists as "farce and comedy," for a total of 9,750 comic performances, and assume that 5 percent of those afterpieces were sentimental (about the ratio I found for original short plays 1737–77), the sentimental proportion of the comic repertoire becomes 13.5 percent.

This is all assuming that we accept Stone's categorization of plays, about which he is notably diffident (pt. 4, 1:clxi–xii). But I do not regard *The Suspicious Husband* as "sentimental" (for reasons I explain fully in chapter five), and this is an important disagreement since it was the most popular comedy of the Garrick era at Drury Lane. If its 178 performances at both theaters are subtracted from Stone's total of 1074, then 896 representations of sentimental comedies remain. With that numerator 17.5 percent of all performances of comic mainpieces and 11.5 percent of all comic performances were of sentimental comedy. I also question the sentimental classification of Cibber's *The Provoked Husband,* even more popular judging by its 189 performances, and would like to see what its deduction would do to the percentages, but these are obviously "soft" calculations in the sense that everything depends on what the investigator calls a "sentimental" comedy. I have therefore tried two means of corroborating the results. One was to work from the tabulations in Appendix C of Pedicord's *Theatrical Public in the Time of Garrick.* Pedicord did not have *The London Stage,* and his figures for Covent Garden especially, drawn from early theatrical reference works such as Genest and the *Biographia dramatica,* are far from complete. Also he provides no categorization of plays into sentimental, laughing, and so forth, so I follow the consensus of George Nettleton, Ashley Thorndike and Allardyce Nicoll (in his *History*) as to classification. Omitting musicals and all plays with less than ten performances between 1747 and 1776, we find 9,378 total comic performances at the patent theaters, of which 809 or 8.5 percent were sentimental, by traditional reckoning. Considering all the weaknesses of these data, this is a remarkable corroboration of Stone's calculations.

My other test was to make direct counts of all comic performances listed in *The London Stage* for the patent houses in five selected seasons over the period, again excluding musicals and following received authority as to classification of sentimentality. Here the picture may be clearest in tabular form:

	Total Comic Performances	Sentimental Comedies
1740–41:	760	68 (9%)
1750–51:	478	45 (9.5%)
1760–61:	527	32 (6%)
1770–71:	672	78 (11.5%)
1775–76:	665	48 (7.5%)

It is significant, I think, that three such different modes of reckoning should agree to this extent, as if the figure of about one in ten comic performances being "sentimental" were so firmly established as to be almost independent of the bases of calculation. This is rather a different light on the century that is supposed to have "wept with sentimentalism." The proportion of sentimental comedy written in this period is considerably higher, amounting, as I said, to perhaps half of the comic mainpieces, but put into the context of all comic types—farce, short comedy, pantomime, and other miscellaneous forms—it is still only one-sixth to one-seventh of the total.

Far from flourishing, the sentimental comedy (as distinguished from sentimentalism as an influence or a passing moment) had a tenuous hold on the early Georgian public. Allardyce Nicoll writes, "When we look at the typical dramatic fare of the period, we may be inclined to wonder whether, after all, it was not sentimentalism which was the fashion insecurely planted on the theatre" (*History*, 3:171). Hugh Kelly's compromises, he thinks, show "that sentimentalism as a force was losing ground" (3:165), and we have already seen how careful Garrick was to prepare his audiences for sentiment and morality in the prologues to *The School for Lovers* and *False Delicacy*. If sentiment was the dominant fashion, why was the epilogue to Mrs. Sheridan's *The Discovery* (1763) so nervous?

> If to such innovations you submit
> And swallow tame morality for wit;

If such dull rules you let a woman teach,
Her next attempt, perhaps, will be to—preach.

Charles Dibdin, the theater historian, offered a chronological explanation: that the sentimental play was not a continuous tradition after Cibber and Steele, but a vogue which reappeared in the sixties and died away in the seventies. Hugh Kelly "happened, fortunately for himself, and unluckily for the public taste, to take advantage of the rage that then prevailed for sentiment. Everything was at that time sentiment," but "whatever absurdities the public may have assumed at times, it has not since then [1773] trenched upon the public."[16] For Dibdin, Goldsmith's *The Good-Natured Man* (1768) came out "exactly at the moment when the public began to be under the influence of the sentimental mania" (5:282). The date 1768 sounds late in view of the comedies of Whitehead, Mrs. Sheridan and Mrs. Griffith, and Isaac Bickerstaffe's comic opera *The Maid of the Mill*, in the early and middle sixties. Dibdin probably meant that the vogue reached "mania" proportions only in 1768. In that year Foote complained that "the genius of insipidity" had induced both patent managers to "set up a kind of circulating library, for the vending of dialogue novels."[17] William Archer accepted the view that the sentimental school dated from the sixties, and suggested that later critics such as A. W. Ward had pushed its origins back to Steele and Cibber (p. 203).

Establishing a *terminus ad quem* is more problematical. Dibdin says 1773, and presumably those critics who credited Foote's *Piety in Patterns* with demolishing sentimental comedy would agree.[18] But the comparison Thomas Davies makes with the alleged efficacy of *The Rehearsal* in exterminating heroic tragedy is pertinent: in both cases the supposedly discredited form went right on playing. To judge by the prologue to *The Rivals*, Sheridan did not think sentimental comedy a dead issue in 1775, and we find ample sentimentalism in late eighteenth- and nineteenth-century plays. Dibdin and the others must have meant that sentimental comedy as a genre was dead, that henceforth sentimentalism appeared as an attitude or a style in melodrama and comedy of manners instead of constituting an independent form. Certainly numerous statements testify to some kind of demise by the late 1770s. In James Cobb's *The Contract* (1779, unpublished), Lady D'Orville tells the sentimental heroine, " 'Tis a pity crying comedies are out of fashion, or that speech of yours, with a Proverb tacked at the end of it, would have made a fine figure in a Love Sermon" (Larpent MS 476). And Claude Jones notes that writers for the *Critical Review* grew gradually more sympathetic towards sentimental drama from 1761 to 1777, but swung back with Sheridan. By 1783 the *European Magazine* was reporting that "sentiment is decried, and the very expectation of it is sure to damn a piece" (4:168). Hannah Cowley moaned in the next decade,

> The combinations of interest, the strokes which are meant to reach the heart, we are equally incapable of tasting. LAUGH! LAUGH! LAUGH! is the demand: Not a word must be uttered that looks like instruction, or a sentence that ought to be remembered. . . . Should the luckless bard stumble on a reflection, or a sentiment, the audience yawn, and wait for the next tumble from a chair, or a tripping up of the heels, to put them into attention.[19]

Clearly, to some contemporaries at least, the sentimental comedy was obsolete, a transient fashion that had had its day. This picture contrasts sharply with that of a final triumph of sentimental comedy by about 1780, drawn by critics such as Bernbaum, and Arthur Sherbo, reexamining this claim in detail, concluded that comedy in the last quarter of the century was equivocal, with sentimental drama present but not dominant.[20] Whichever way we turn the question, the importance of sentimental comedy per se seems to have been overestimated.

Harlequin's Invasion

By 1760 traditional comic drama had a dangerous new challenger, or rather an old one who was only now perceived to be within the gates. Its character is implicit in Hannah Cowley's elegy for sentiment, and explicit in elaborate spectacles such as John Burgoyne's *The Maid of the Oaks* (1774), where sentiment is present, but subordinated to song, scenic effects, dancing, vaudeville, masque characters, and pastoral fête. In this species of drama, not in sentimental comedy, lay the degradation of taste and the capitulation of the managers. In the very decade of Goldsmith's and Sheridan's triumphs these illegitimate forms—variously called froth and folly, song and show, mirth and spectacle—were taking over. They had existed, albeit less elaborately and with less audience encouragement, throughout the period, establishing themselves while sentiment and laughter battled for supremacy within legitimate drama, weakening themselves and each other.

The precedent for using a military metaphor to describe this development is *Harlequin's Invasion,* a pantomime by David Garrick, produced at Drury Lane on the last day of 1759. In this piece Garrick visualizes the confrontation of the traditional and nontraditional theaters as an invasion of Parnassus by Harlequin, who is finally put down by Mercury as an agent of Shakespeare. Early in act 1, upon the appearance of Mercury and his retinue, the following chorus is sung:

> Roar Trumpet, Squeak Fife, blow Horn & beat Drum.
> To Dramatica's Realm, from Apollo I come.
> Whereas it is fear'd a French trick may be play'd ye
> Be it known Mons![1] Harlequin, means to invade ye.[1]
> And hither transporting his Legions, He floats
> On an Ocean of Canvass in Flat bottom Boats:

With Fairies, Hags, Genii, Hobgoblins all shocking
And many a Devil in flame colour'd Stocking
Let the light troops of Comedy March to attack him,
And tragedy whack all her daggars to Hack Him.
Let all hands, and hearts, do their utmost Endeavour;
Sound Trumpet, beat Drum, King Shakespeare forever.

In the play Harlequin sinks and Shakespeare rises. In fact, however, Garrick was whistling in the dark; he knew that the actual fortunes of the protagonists were more problematical. Legitimate drama would continue to be threatened and transformed by the pantomimes. The crude novelties of Victorian theater were in large measure the consequence of Harlequin's invasion.[2]

Harlequin here stands for a much larger phenomenon than the encroachment of pantomime on the repertoire. During the eighteenth century a host of other new, nontraditional comic forms—burlesque, burletta, melodrama, interlude and prelude, comic opera, musical farce, entertainments, pieces, and sketches—either appeared or grew in popular recognition, and because of the limitations which the Licensing Act placed on the number of "legitimate" theaters (patent houses), these *illegitimi* crowded the traditional forms for space on the London stages. Patrons at Drury Lane and Covent Garden wanted to see the novelties too, while managers of non-patent houses were specifically precluded by the Act from producing legitimate drama, so their only recourse was to light entertainment. The enormous burgeoning of this minor theater and its successful competition with classical genres was the most significant development on the eighteenth-century stage. Sentiment fought for a time with laughter inside the framework of comedy, but eventually both were annexed into the melodrama, the musical farce, and the extravaganza. The modern entertainment world began to take shape during the Garrick era. Comic strips, the cinema, the circus, the revue, television specials, the rodeo, the solo comic, the musical, the magician were all present at least embryonically in Georgian London, only as yet confined to the playhouse stage, and their effect on legitimate drama was profound. Then as now Shakespeare was hard pressed to outdraw a variety show.

What happened during the century becomes clear from an analysis of the plays submitted to the Licensing Office and now preserved in the

Larpent Collection: statistically speaking, the shorter and the nontraditional forms mushroomed. Between 1737 and 1777, the Examiner of Plays received 42 mainpiece comedies, 96 short comedies and farces, and 63 "miscellaneous comic" pieces for approval. For the years 1778–89, the figures were respectively 45, 93, and 96; a jump of 10 percent (from 31 percent to 41 percent) for the *illegitimi*, a fall of 8 percent (from 33 percent to 25 percent) for comedies of all lengths. Hence it becomes increasingly necessary for the theater historian to take account of a "comic tradition," as distinct from comedy proper, and to search through unpublished manuscripts. Of the plays in the miscellaneous category 69 percent were printed between 1737 and 1777, but only 44 percent in the period 1778–89. For the whole corpus of comic drama, traditional and otherwise, that percentage dropped from 70 to 52. More comic plays were placing more reliance on visual effect and stage-trick; they were increasingly unsuited for reading.

Many traits of later eighteenth-century comedy can be traced to the public's love of various *illegitimi*. Even traditional comic types were influenced by the popular taste for the spectacular, the novel, and the pantomimic. The major components of this irregular tendency in regular comedy were gratuitous "musicalization," a drift towards the melodramatic, the encroachment of pantomime with its typical devices, and an emphasis on spectacle. Every nontraditional form had a shadowy, half-assimilated counterpart in legitimate drama, and it is this reflection of irregular practices in traditional genres, not the pure illegitimate forms themselves, which primarily concerns us here. Yet one must always bear in mind that these upstart forms, especially the popular comic operas and pantomimes, were necessarily produced at the expense of regular drama in the patent theaters' repertoires.

It is difficult to separate the musicalization of comedy from its drift towards spectacle. Both features were present in the Jacobean masque, and only later became autonomous influences on regular drama.[3] The music of the masques affected the development of all forms of English theater music: opera, burletta, and musical farce; and from the masque's use of spectacle, especially imported Italian scenery, were derived in part the increasingly lavish displays of stage-trick and visual wonders after the Restoration. Not all of the eventual effects were pernicious, obviously, but the musical comedy was not born without labor pains. George

Colman's *New Brooms!* (1776) at once brings home the impact of musicalization and testifies to Garrick's reputation as a force for legitimate drama. The "new brooms" are the incoming managers of Drury Lane, including Richard Brinsley Sheridan; Colman graciously contributed *New Brooms!* as an introduction to the season and the neophyte management. One of the more informative "preludes," it compliments Garrick by revealing the plight in which the stage finds itself at his retirement. Crochet, an author writing for Drury Lane, entertains Catcall, a critic, and Phelim, a hopeful actor who claims some talent. "Talents for acting?" exclaims Crochet, surprised. "Lack-a-day, gentlemen! . . . Acting's all over now." "What," asks Phelim, "is the playhouse burnt down?" "No," replies Crochet,

> but plays are worn out, Sir. Otway's a rag, Jonson obsolete, and Shakespeare worn threadbare. Plays!—plays might do well enough formerly indeed, but quite out of fashion now, Sir. Plays and little Roscius left the stage together, Sir!
> PHELIM: What will the stage do then?
> CROCHET: Do? Musical pieces, to be sure—Operas, Sir—our only dependance now.—We have nothing for it now but wind, wire, rosin and catgut. . . . Have you any voice? Can you sing, Sir?

Phelim obliges with a song.

> Well, Sir, that may do very well, introduced into a Comick Opera. . . . Operas are the only real entertainment. The plain unornamented drama is too flat, Sir. Common dialogue is a dry imitation of nature, as insipid as real conversation; but in an opera, the dialogue is refreshed by an air every instant.—Two gentlemen meet in the Park, for example, admire the place and the weather; and after a speech or two the orchestra take their cue, the musick strikes up, one of the characters takes a genteel turn or two on the stage, during the symphony, and then breaks out—
>
> > When the breezes
> > Fan the trees-es
> > Fragrant gales
> > The breath inhales,
> > Warm the heart that sorrow freezes.[4]

Colman was not exaggerating much. Songs had been introduced gratuitously in Restoration comedy (e.g., Congreve, *Love for Love*, beginning of act 3), but the eighteenth century scaled new heights of excess and artificiality in the use of music. Often it is difficult to tell whether a play is a "musical farce" or a comic opera. The unpublished *Bourbon League* (1762) is listed in MacMillan's *Catalogue of Larpent Plays* as a "farce," though it has thirty-one airs in two acts. One important variant of the song-and-speech school was the burletta, imported into London from Italy in 1748, with native imitations following about 1760. In the burletta a classical or mythological plot, treated farcically, was dressed up with new lyrics set to old tunes. Kane O'Hara's *Midas* (1764) and *The Golden Pippin* (1772, pub. 1773, the story of Paris and the beauty contest on Mount Ida) are typical of the genre.

> The later growth and popularity of the burletta was intimately connected with the policies of the minor theatres. The Licensing Act of 1737 had confined the "legitimate drama" to Drury Lane and Covent Garden, and allowed only limited licenses for music and dancing to the smaller houses. In the burlettas the managers of the minor theatres perceived an opportunity for evading the full intentions of the law. Almost anything could be turned into a burletta, so long as the dialogue was sung not spoken. Macready reports that he saw Elliston in 1809 at the Surrey Theatre, acting *Macbeth* as a pantomime.[5]

The Licensing Act thus has more to answer for than at first appears, for the effect of the burlettas on comedy and farce was immediate. The anonymous *Anniversary* (1758, unpublished), a "Dramatick Satire, being a sequel to *Lethe*," has a burletta format. Garrick's original conceit—London mortals allowed to come to Lethe's waters once a year, on the anniversary of Persephone's rape—is "enriched" with songs after almost every character's appearance. Flash and Fribble (from *Miss in Her Teens*) are Charon's first passengers; then a patriotic song is introduced gratuitously:

> Oh the brave monarch of Prussia!
> The Protestant hero I sing.
> (Larpent MS 164)

A "London fine lady" comes on to lament the demise of masquerades, followed by another song, and so on.

In more serious or traditional comedy, the use of song was also frequently inane. In act 3 of Edward Moore's *The Foundling* (a sentimental comedy), Fidelia begins to tell her maid of the dangers of coquetry, but, finding herself tongue-tied, she bursts into explanatory song. In James Miller's *The Picture* (1745), the romantic Celia pleads with her father to heed her choice of a suitor: "Will you not hear me, Sir?" *Song* (I.iii). Even the major comic dramatists were not immune to the rage for musicalization. Dimity, in Murphy's *What We All Must Come To* (1763, pub. 1764), asks Nancy, "What say you then to Mr. Woodley?" Nancy: "Ah!—I don't know what to say—but I can sing something that will explain my mind! 'When first the dear youth passing by,' " etc. (I.i). Garrick wrote a whole play (*May-Day*) for a young singer who could not sustain a regular dramatic role. And Sheridan, the dedicated opponent of sentimentalism, had no such prejudice against musical comedy: witness his *Duenna* (1775), a comic opera, and, if it be his, *Camp* (1778), a musical "dramatic entertainment." Gratuitous musicalization reached its absurd limits in the occasional introduction of a singer into a comedy for the sake of one song. "Ah, Charlotte, I would, but I cannot, sing it. In the next room, however, waits my friend Miss King, the new singer: perhaps she will honor us. Miss King!" *Enter Miss King. Song. Exit.* And exit with her the integrity of music and drama characteristic of Elizabethan comedy.

"Spectacularism"—the exaltation of visual wonder for its own sake—was intimately associated with other symptoms of malaise in eighteenth-century drama. Burletta and pantomime were almost entirely devoted to the fast-paced wedding of tune and spectacle. "Dramatic entertainments" such as *The Camp* and Burgoyne's *The Maid of the Oaks* catered to audiences' love of novelty, music, and scenic ingenuity. The machinations of O'Daub, a painter in Sheridan's playlet, were indicative of a trend. He has come to "take" the military camp at Coxheath for a Drury Lane set:

> You must know I got such credit at the fête champêtre there that little Roscius recommended me to the manager of Drury Lane Theatre, and so I am now a kind of Deputy Superintendent under Mr. Leatherbug[6] the great painter; that is, as soon as he executes any thing, I design it, my jewel; so I'm going to take a front side view of it.
>   GAUGE: And what—are they going to bring the camp on the stage?
>   O'DAUB: You have it—Cox heath by candlelight my jewel.

Even allowing for satiric exaggeration here, the direction of the barb is accurate, and its general truth has been widely confirmed.[7]

Writers of regular comedy also felt the pressure of a spectacle-loving public. As early as 1700, Congreve found audience taste running to farce and show, while at the end of the century, Hannah Cowley complained that these concerns still preoccupied theater patrons and posed an obstacle to the serious dramatist. George Colman's *Man and Wife* (1769, published 1770), ostensibly a gentle satire on Garrick's Shakespeare Jubilee at Stratford-on-Avon, is a legitimate short comedy, but Colman was careful to include in it a sumptuous "Pageant of Shakespearean characters" between acts 2 and 3, for it had to compete with the jubilee procession itself at Drury Lane. Garrick's *The Jubilee,* a spectacular musical pageant, was performed 152 times in three years.

Although he was forced to some serious compromises, Garrick's influence as a manager was fitfully directed towards moderating the onrush of theatrical spectaculars, on which he qualifies as an authority. *A Peep Behind the Curtain* (1767) was for Garrick what *The Critic* and *The Camp* were for Sheridan: wry testimonies to the vagaries of public taste which beset the manager constantly. *A Peep* presents the rehearsal of a new burletta "with all the proper Scenes, Dresses, Machinery, and Music," attended by members of the theater-going public who delight in "traps," "harlequin pantomimes" and "thunder and lightning." The most sympathetic character is Saunders, the carpenter who designs and builds whole plays without a word of credit: "Damn all these new vagaries, that put us all upon our heads topsy-versy—my men have sat up all night, and I have finished every thing but the Dancing Cows" (I.ii). Equally revealing are Garrick's revisions of Whitehead's prologue to *The School for Lovers* (1762), an extremely sentimental comedy. The prologue "as it was intended to have been spoken" goes gravely through a catalogue of Whitehead's past successes, his refined hopes for this comedy, his modest adherence to the rules. Garrick's revision excises only a few of the more pompous and sentimental lines—"and sometimes smiles provoke, and sometimes tears"—until Whitehead ventures

> Form'd on the classic scale his structures rise,
> He shifts no scenes to dazzle and surprize.

Sentiment, discreetly presented, may pass; but clearly this is too much for English audiences to bear. Garrick takes over in midline, and the rest is his:

He shifts no scenes—But here I stop'd him short—
Not change your scenes? said I,—I'm sorry for 't:
My constant friends above, around, below,
Have English tastes, and love both change and show:
Without such aids, even Shakespear would be flat—
Our crowded Pantomimes are proofs of that.
What eager transport stares from every eye,
When pullies rattle, and our Genii fly!
When tin cascades like falling waters gleam:
Or through the canvas—bursts the real stream:
While thirsty Islington laments in vain
Half her New-River roll'd to Drury-Lane.
Lord, Sir, said I, for gallery, boxes, pit,
I'll back my Harlequin against your wit—
. . . .

Still he persists—and let him—*entre nous*—
I know your tastes, and will indulge 'em too.
Change you shall have; so set your hearts at ease:
Write as *he* will, we'll act it as *you* please.

This Garrick—he spoke the prologue himself—has come a long way from the man who, fifteen years earlier, had spoken Johnson's magisterial prologue upon the same stage, bidding the audience help him "to chase the charms of sound, the pomp of shew." The second *School for Lovers* prologue is a document both of the decline of theatrical taste and the omnipotence of the audience.

But spectacularism increased after Garrick's retirement. Newspapers and magazines of the eighties and nineties are full of the diatribes of outraged critics against circus spectacles and monstrous medleys. Charles Dibdin, the theater historian, looking back over the period from the eminence of 1795, remarked sarcastically that Fielding's *Don Quixote in England* was well written but

> ill calculated for the stage, because mere knight errantry without spectacle never yet had success upon the English theatre. If he had carried *Don Quixote* to any other part of the world[8] and . . . introduced a few elephants, or camels, and made him fight half a dozen tygers, and . . . decorated the stage with castles that lose their battlements in the air, about fifteen feet from the ground, the whole an outrage upon nature, and art, the redoubted knight, as mad as his audiences, might have acted every species of extravagance to the admiration of full houses. (5:43)

"An outrage upon nature." Increasingly as the century waned, critics and satirists sounded this tocsin against trick and show, scenes and machines. Mr. Crochet, our acquaintance from *New Brooms*, has plumbed the taste of the times on this point, too:

> CATCALL: I am glad to hear we are to have an opera of yours, Mr. Crochet, this season.
> CROCHET: You are, Sir; and I have got the finest unnatural thought for it!—
> CATCALL: *Natural*, you mean, Mr. Crochet.
> CROCHET: Natural? I thought you knew better, Mr. Catcall. Nature has nothing to do with an Opera—nor with the stage neither, now that little Roscius has left it—we shall go upon quite another plan now, Sir.— (scene 2)

Surprisingly, Colman allows the problems he has brought up to come to an issue in a final debate between Crochet, Mezzetin (a French producer of spectacles), and Sprightly, a writer of comedy. As usual there is compromise. Mezzetin, an advocate of "scenes, machines, chansons & decorations," insists that "vidout my pantomime de new *directeurs* must be ondone." Even Shakespeare will not go down now without a frosting of dance, music, and pantomime. Garrick, he claims, made more money on the *Shakespeare Jubilee* than on all the bard's comedies and tragedies. Crochet agrees to this extent: "Dramatick pieces, unadorned by dance and scenery, and unenlivened by musick, will never be able to make a stand against opera and pantomime." Sprightly, it is clear, bears the standard of Colman and the new managers, and his position is therefore significant. He maintains that "the main body of the stage-enter-tainments should be wrought out of the loom of Shakespeare and his noble assistants," yet "show and sing-song may be admitted as garnish." His summary: "A clear stage, and fair play for all parties! that's all that is required—These too I can venture to assure you are the sentiments of the new managers—." The willingness of the traditionalists to com-promise, and their opponents' determination to please the public and make money anyway, characterized the debate and predetermined its outcome.

Pantomime per se is outside my scope, but its encroachment on regular comedy is not.[9] This encroachment took many forms, including the influence on comedy and taste and the "pantomimization" of old plays, but the most obvious is the space on stages and the time in programs required for the pantomimes. They occupied a portion of the repertoire that could have been given to legitimate drama; the light and air they needed obviously could not be used by two plays at the same time. The burden fell on the afterpiece. At Covent Garden between 1747 and 1776 the four most frequently performed afterpieces were pantomimes, which led all other genres, while at Drury Lane, in those very years of Garrick's stewardship, pantomimes ran one-two-three among the afterpieces, and were second only to farce in total number of performances (*The London Stage*, pt. 4, 1:clxvii). From one point of view pantomime, introduced by John Rich about 1715, was the theatrical success story of the century. From its origin as a crutch for weak plays during a time of sharp interplayhouse rivalry, pantomime soon captivated audiences and frequently threatened to dominate the repertoire in the twenties and thirties.[10] Throughout the century it continued to perform vigorously, a popular and vital form.

From another standpoint, however, it was a disaster. Traditional comedy, rivaled by sentiment and comic opera in the mainpiece, found the afterpiece cluttered with pantomime and more comic opera. The pressure was considerable, space being so limited, and the effect on managers and writers and finally on comedy was debilitating. Garrick, the self-advertised defender of Shakespeare in 1747, wrote and spoke an "Occasional Prologue" in 1750, during the war with Covent Garden, announcing a shift in policy:

> Unwilling we must change the nobler scene,
> And, in our turn, present you Harlequin.

Accordingly, writes Murphy, "in the Christmas holidays, to alarm the monster-breeding breast of the Covent Garden manager, a new pantomime was exhibited, under the title of *Harlequin Fortunatus*. This piece had all the marvelous incidents requisite in such wild productions, a fire, a jig, a battle, and a ball . . . and of course was much followed" (*Life of Garrick*, 1:231). Charles Macklin spoke on behalf of traditional comedy in *Covent Garden Theatre; or, Pasquin Turned Drawcansir* (1752), while at the same time indicating he knew how the land lay.

73

PASQUIN: He who would gain the esteem of a brave, a wise, and a free people, must lash their vices and laugh at their follies.

. . . .

BOB SMART: Have you got ever a Harlequin in the farce of yours, Mr. Drawcansir?

PASQUIN: No sir.

BOB SMART: Then you'll be damn'd sir.[11]

The afterpiece at certain periods (especially the early 1750s) had either to present pantomimic thrills or apologize for not doing so, judging by the prologue to Susannah Cibber's *The Oracle* (1752). Even mainpiece comedy was affected. Richard Bentley's *The Wishes; or, Harlequin's Mouth Opened* (1761, unpublished), a "comedy in the Italian manner," was an attempt to spin a five-act comedy from pantomime materials. Bentley, who viewed his play as the first real transplant of Italian to English comedy, says in the prologue that he wanted "to introduce a relaxation from the tyranny of rules . . . & beside to open a road for all that kind of wit which has not strength of constitution enough to be itself up against regular comedy, to make its appearance to the world in a station made suitable to its ability" (Larpent MS 199). The play was long and dull, and even with Foote acting it failed, but the attempt is indicative of the influence that pantomime was having on comedy. Canker, a critic in Charles Macklin's *The New Play Criticiz'd* (1747) makes an astute comment about Benjamin Hoadly's popular comedy *The Suspicious Husband*. Really it is "a pantomime," he claims, one of "Rich's entertainments," with Ranger as Harlequin (Larpent MS 64). Although the character of Canker is undercut in the play, his observation is sound. Even apart from similarities of character and situation between the comedy and pantomime, *The Suspicious Husband*'s preference for action and intrigue over character exemplifies one of the most profound effects of Italian on English comedy in the eighteenth century. The acrobatic antics of Harlequin, his penchant for surprising escapes from perplexing situations, and his air of hustle-bustle activity, created in spectators a taste for stage business. Neither mainpiece nor afterpiece, sentimental nor laughing comedy was free of this pressure. The "tumble from a chair" and "tripping up of the heels," all the audiences of 1795 cared for in Hannah Cowley's judgment, came to the English stage for good with pantomime, though they began earlier, with farce and Spanish intrigue.

Perhaps the worst horrors were the old plays turned into pantomimes. *Harlequin Macbeth* was mentioned earlier, and the *European Magazine* reviewer choked on a pantomimic production of *Friar Bacon* in December 1783. *Harlequin Faustus* was produced at Covent Garden in 1766 and 1793. When Dr. Primrose met a strolling player in chapter eighteen of *The Vicar of Wakefield* (1766), the practice was already established: "the public think nothing about dialect, or humour, or character; for that is none of their business, they only go to be amused, and find themselves happy when they can enjoy a pantomime under the sanction of Johnson's or Shakespear's name."[12] Macklin must have felt himself a prophet when, in 1751, the ingenious Woodward staged his *Harlequin Ranger* at Drury Lane.

Cumberland's *The Brothers* (1769) has been called the first melodrama (see chapter three), and indeed the drift toward melodramatic stage conventions of thought and action may have owed as much to sentimental comedy as to the irregular minor drama.[13] *The Maid of Kent*, which is very close to melodrama, shows traces of each parent. Its sententiousness, optimism, and humanitarianism are certainly redolent of Shaftesburian dramatists such as Cumberland, but its absolutely flat characterization, black-and-whiteness of motive and tendency to resolve difficulty through action are equally suggestive of the comedies of difficulty and intrigue, the pantomimes and burlettas, and similar miscellanies built entirely on the surprise of a novel plot. For that matter, melodrama has also been regarded as a descendant of the tragicomedy. Whichever way one derives it, the melodramatic tendency was part of the antitraditional erosion of the classical genres, and abetted even less legitimate forms in wearing down regular drama.

Two factors assisted the onslaught of new forms at this time: the Licensing Act and the audiences. The first—and more superficial—is one of a series of political and religious oppressions that have hampered the drama sporadically. Elizabethan and Stuart playhouses were closed by the authorities from time to time on various pretexts. The Commonwealth ban on legitimate theater (1642–60) brought a rash of "drolls," farces, truncated plays and proto-burlettas that circumvented the law and created a precedent and taste for such things. The 1737 Licensing Act was less pernicious in its censorship, an old story, than in its limitation of the number of theaters that could produce legitimate drama to two, and its licensing system for the others. Arthur Murphy recounts a significant anecdote: "Foote complained, that he was likely to pass an idle summer [1761], as he could not obtain a license to perform, as he had usually done, at the Little Theatre at the Haymarket. A man who had a pack of dancing dogs had been before him at the Lord Chamberlain's Office" (*Life of Garrick,* 1:360). This story illustrates better than any generalization what the Licensing Act meant to the playwright and actor: a restriction on creative outlets, an interference in the dramatic by an authority insensitive to it. In a way, of course, the Examiner—if one grants the terms of his appointment—acted sensibly. The dancing dogs could be expected to cause no further trouble. Foote, on the other hand, was a satiric dramatist, and he could hit where it hurt, even among the great. There would be plays to read (at a small emolument), censures to make, a dangerous responsibility enjoined to suppress libelous caricatures. Why bother, since dancing dogs paid a license fee, too? But eighteenth-century drama badly needed the "English Aristophanes": he was the only notable playwright still working the satirical vein of Fielding, ridiculing follies in an age that cried for satire.

The situation at the minor theaters, then—of which the Haymarket was the chief—was dismal.[14] Regular full-length "legitimate" drama might not be performed there at all; the lesser forms, whose role in debasing taste and influencing regular plays we have discussed, had to be licensed, and might assume any shape. This left the patent houses, Drury Lane and Covent Garden: a very limited outlet. The number of new plays produced each year varied considerably over the period, increasing after about 1760. Owing, however, to the conservative tendencies of the repertory system, and the growing necessity, as theaters were enlarged and overhead increased, of being certain each new piece was a money-maker, that number remained low. A liberal estimate, taken from the period as a whole, would be two or three new afterpieces and two new mainpieces (including tragedy) per theater per season, and pantomime, burletta, comic opera and the like cut into these numbers. The mean for both theaters over the period 1737–77 might be seven new comic pieces a year, including the *illegitimi,* or, excluding them, not over five new comedies and farces.

This line of reasoning takes us only so far, however. Five good comedies a year in London over those forty years would have given us a picture vastly different from what we now see. But dramatic composition always involves a chain. There is the society that produces the artist, the artist himself, the managers, the actors, the theater, and the audience and critics (society again). Like all chains, this one is as strong as its weakest link. That link in the eighteenth century appears to have been the audience. John Dennis's explanation of the decline of comedy in terms of the ignorance and vulgarity of its audiences finds echoes everywhere in the century.[15] From the public, after all, the playwright draws not only material success but inspiration. Weaken this link, destroy a balanced give-and-take between dramatist and audience, and the whole frail structure needs only a push to topple it. A society gets the drama it deserves. There will always be entrepreneurs like John Rich,[16] and entertainments like the pantomime, and ultimately the reaction away from them and back towards serious drama will have to come from within. When a resistance to the vulgar, trivial, and mindless is not built in, the drama is living on borrowed time. Charles Macklin has one spectator in *Covent Garden Theatre*, Sir Roger Ringwood, warn a dramatist: "Be it tragedy or farce I don't care a hare's scut, so there is but fun in it. . . . Give us a fair Burst of Fun . . . but if it is any of your New Moral Stuff, according to rule, I shall Tip it a dead Hollow. . . . Think of that and be dull if you dare" (ed. Kern, pp. 29–30). "The fate of the dramatist," comments Dane Smith, "was often the result of the favorable or unfavorable response of just such people."[17] Sentimentality was not the real problem, not the prime weakness of this audience; it was crudity, crassness, a simple-minded delight in the novel and wonderful. Of course there were discerning auditors—all the London *literati* at one time or another—but the repertoire, governed by the laws of supply and demand, proves that their number was insufficient.

We should not be surprised that this audience demanded show and spectacle, nor that, having demanded, they received it. Theaters have to be paying propositions, whatever the dramatic preferences of manager, actor, or playwright: a manager could not pay a dramatist for a satire or a comedy if the audience would not in turn pay him. Encouragement and incentive to write well were low at the beginning of the period, and declined farther. The novel siphoned off some dramatic talent because there were so few opportunities to produce plays; pantomime, spectacle, and musicals drew off more because they could be made to pay, and could be produced in more houses. In the last analysis the *illegitimi* overwhelmed comedy because there was a greater market for them.

PART III
Comic Genres

The third part approaches laughing comedy and the afterpiece as the previous section did sentimental comedy and nontraditional forms: describing, exemplifying, and explicating a class of dramatic phenomena. This section is not, then, a chronicle or history, but rather a general theoretical treatment, a typology, whose major goal is the establishment of an accurate context and an adequate terminology. Wherever possible illustrative material is drawn from plays that were not the productions of major writers and are therefore not covered in part four.

The argument of this and the next section is the central theme of the book: that a "laughing tradition" in comedy existed throughout the mid-eighteenth century, somewhat precariously in the mainpiece, more securely in the afterpiece. "Laughing tradition," again, signifies the continuum of nonsentimental stage comedy in England from the medieval mystery plays on, comprising Shakespeare and Jonson, Congreve and farce, and all that lies within these compass points. This continuum has often been questioned, and sentimentalism seen as the dominant force in Georgian comic drama. Part two questioned this view by challenging the way the word sentimental *has commonly been applied to eighteenth-century comedy, and by proposing the rise of illegitimate forms as a more significant development than sentimentalism in the theater of the period; parts three and four focus upon the wealth of non-sentimental comedy written and produced between the Licensing Act and the last comedies of Sheridan.*

Laughing Comedy

The term *laughing comedy* was first used in the anonymous essay "On the Theatre" published in the January 1773 *Westminster Magazine* and (since 1798) attributed to Oliver Goldsmith. Its general meaning was clear in the context of contemporary dramatic criticism: *laughing comedy* was the opposite of *weeping comedy,* the *comédie larmoyante* (the essay particularly attacks the French stage), better known in England as sentimental comedy. The latter is defined as a play "in which the virtues of private life are exhibited rather than the vices exposed, and the distresses rather than the faults of mankind make our interest."[1] The writer is strongly opposed to this type of drama, asking rhetorically: "Which deserves the preference? The weeping sentimental comedy, so much in fashion at present, or the laughing and even low comedy, which seems to have been last exhibited by Vanbrugh and Cibber?" The concluding phrase introduces a difficulty, but one of our own making: we have been taught to think of Cibber as a "sentimental" dramatist, yet our image must give way if we are to understand the essay at this point. This cannot be the "Vanbrugh and Cibber" of *Love's Last Shift* and *The Relapse,* for those two comedies were held to aim in different directions, and neither is particularly "low." Nor can it be the Cibber of "Cibber and Steele," the supposed sentimental *junta* of the early eighteenth century. In neither case would the example make the point. But Vanbrugh's and Cibber's names were associated in another dramatic venture, *The Provoked Husband* (1728), completed by Cibber from Vanbrugh's fragmentary *Journey to London,* which might be described as "laughing and even low." It is true that most modern critics regard it as a "sentimental comedy," but that is our problem, not Cibber's or Goldsmith's. Possibly the writer is thinking of the two playwrights separately—both wrote laughing comedies—but

81

since Vanbrugh produced his last comedy in 1705, twenty-three years before Cibber's final effort, they would make an odd couple in that sense, and one would expect Farquhar's and Mrs. Centlivre's names to have come up if such were the case. It is altogether more likely that this essayist, like others before him, is using *The Provoked Husband* as the standard measure for good eighteenth-century comedy; "X is the best comedy since *The Provoked Husband*" was the formulaic eulogy at least from *The Suspicious Husband* (1747) to *The Good-Natured Man* (1768). I think we may assume, then, that the Vanbrugh-Cibber *Provoked Husband,* a comedy of manners with considerable satire and one scene of sentimental reform, is being proposed as an example of "laughing and even low comedy."[2] The phrase "and even low" supports the idea of Goldsmith's authorship. This was a sore point with him after the bailiff scene of *The Good-Natured Man* was hissed off as "low," and he feared that *She Stoops to Conquer,* which was about to open, might be condemned on the same grounds, especially as it made fun of the vogue of the word. No other critic of the time is so likely to have inserted that phrase, and to have passed over the risible but genteel *Suspicious Husband* in favor of the more farcical *Provoked Husband* to illustrate what he meant by laughing comedy.

Goldsmith's main argument against sentimental comedy, setting aside a number of rather vague and subjective criticisms which look like advertisements for *She Stoops to Conquer,* is that it steps out of the mainstream of classical authority and tradition: "All the great masters in the dramatic art have but one opinion. . . . Comedy should excite our laughter by ridiculously exhibiting the follies of the lower part of mankind." Laughing comedy is, then, traditional comedy, written according to the precept and practice of the dramatic masters of the past. It must seek laughter (not tears), ridicule follies (not sympathize with distresses), and move among the lower classes (not just the genteel)—presumably an echo of Aristotle's remark that comedy presents people who are worse than average (*Poetics,* chs. 2, 4, 5).

For this primeval definition to be useful to us, we must recognize its polemical dimension. Goldsmith was trying to prepare a way in the theoretical wilderness for *She Stoops to Conquer,* whose qualities, as perceived by him, color the phrasing: "and even low," "the lower part of mankind." He recognizes no comedy of this type since 1728, revealing

two important limitations. He must be excluding comedy which is genteel as well as laughing, or he would have mentioned *The Suspicious
Husband* and *The Way to Keep Him,* at least; and he is ignoring the
afterpieces, or he would have admitted that Fielding, Garrick, Foote,
Colman, Murphy, and others had written scores of low and laughing
comedies in the preceding four decades. These are important exclusions
from a term whose basic meaning, after all, was intended to be "nonsentimental comedy," and I see no reason to follow Goldsmith slavishly here.
Unless otherwise specified, I use *laughing comedy* for traditional, nonsentimental comedies in five acts, and *laughing tradition* when the short
comedies and farces are included.

In assessing the condition of laughing comedy in the mid-eighteenth
century, it is again necessary to distinguish between the picture given by
performance and that drawn from original compositions. The former
gives no support to those who argue that Georgian comedy "drowned"
in sentiment.[3] Performances of laughing comedies account for 79
percent of the comic mainpieces according to George Winchester Stone,
Jr.'s definition of sentimental comedy, and at least 83 percent according
to mine. In his list of the top fifteen comedies at each patent house, Stone
counts both *The Provoked Husband* and *The Suspicious Husband* as
"sentimental comedy."[4] I disagree with both judgments, and Goldsmith
evidently disagreed with the first. If we removed both from his lists
(admittedly an extreme procedure), a full seven-eighths of the
mainpiece comic performances would be laughing; the only sentimental
comedies left would be *The Conscious Lovers* and *The West Indian.* Even a
conservative reckoning, however, places the proportion of laughing
comedy at roughly four in every five comic mainpieces.

When we focus on comedy written in the eighteenth century we
receive a different impression, though not such as to justify the conclusion that gentility and hypocrisy ruled (Kronenberger, p. 186). It is
rather, as James Feibleman once wrote, that the eighteenth century was
"a time of confusion for comedy."[5] Playwrights were collectively divided,
and in some cases individually uncertain, as to what they or the public
wanted. The only consensus seems to have been that the "right" form for
the present would be found by recreating, modernizing, or combining
the great models of the past, rather than by any novel, imaginative leap.
Most "innovations" were actually recombinations, as when James Miller

took hints from both *Robinson Crusoe* and Thomas Southerne's tragedy *Oroonoko* (1695) to create *Art and Nature* (1738), in which a noble savage criticizes England. There were rare exceptions to this radical unoriginality, but generally initiative was rather feeble and hesitation as to the correct mode was widespread. The comic impulse was almost evenly divided between traditional and sentimental outlets: in the forty years from the Licensing Act to *The School for Scandal* I count twenty-five to thirty new laughing comedies, about the same as, or a few more than, the number of arguably sentimental comedies. Possibly as a result of this division of strength, more probably as a hangover from the shock of the Licensing Act, neither type displayed much vigor until about 1760; only five new laughing comedies appeared in those first twenty-three years, and sentiment was no stronger. Except for Moore's *The Foundling,* all the important sentimental comedies were composed after 1760. Thus the weakness or stagnation of the comic mainpiece affected both styles; and conversely, when strength returned, it regenerated both types simultaneously. The renaissance of sentimental comedy in the sixties was matched stride for stride by traditionalists' efforts: *The Way to Keep Him, The Jealous Wife, All in the Wrong* and *The Clandestine Marriage* were all popular before the arrival of Goldsmith and Sheridan.[6] It is very much a potpourri, whose principal virtue is variety.

If "comedy may be said to direct its emphasis upon incident, manners or character,"[7] then eighteenth-century comedy moved increasingly towards the extremes: either incident (often farce and pantomimic stage business) or character (in practice, usually sentimental comedy). The middle ground of manners was seldom achieved, though often essayed; the Restoration comic dramatists were frequently emulated in the period. One symptom of this atrophy of comedy of manners was that writers were hard put to describe it. Isaac Bickerstaffe, defending *'Tis Well It's No Worse* ("Preface," 1770), could conceive of only two kinds of comedy: that of "Character" or "Heart and Understanding," i.e., sentimental comedy, and that of "Intrigue," such as his own. In the next year the Reverend Charles Jenner, a writer of sentimental closet drama, was able to distinguish three. The first two, comedy of "wit and Character" and comedy of "nature and sentiment," he took from Diderot; neither, in his description, sounds like comedy of manners. To these he added a third, the "Comedy of Stage-trick and Decoration," characterized by "an intricate plot, a continued hurry and confusion of incident, a profusion of business and intrigue, detached scenes of flippant dialogue, and an uninteresting catastrophe, foreseen from the first opening of the business" ("Preface," *The Man of Family,* 1771). Thus the Reverend Jenner is left with character, sentiment, and incident as his major comic strains. Similarly, Hannah Cowley cannot visualize an intermediate territory between farce and sentimental comedy in her interesting diatribe against the public prefaced to the second edition of *The Town before You* (1795). Since all the public wants is farce, spectacle and circus, and since her forte is "the strokes which are meant to reach the heart," she has no choice but to withdraw from the stage. The manners tradition would seem to have been menaced by, among other things, an hiatus in comic theory, a void where a concept ought to have been.

But behind the uncertainty in dramatic theory lay the sociology of the playhouses; here, perhaps, is a first cause. If we accept Newell Sawyer's general definition of manners comedy as a "form reflecting the life, thought, and manners of upper-class society, faithful to its traditions and philosophy" (*Comedy of Manners from Sheridan to Maugham,* p. 3), then the demise or radical alteration of the type was the inevitable result of the infiltration of the theater by the bourgeoisie noticed by John Dennis as early as 1702.[8] Most Restoration comedies of manners, being written by middle- to upper-class dramatists for the gentry and nobility, tended to adopt the outlook of a coterie, but the subsequent dilution of aristocratic patronage by the growing middle class caused a shift of tone. Eighteenth-century conditions necessarily changed a courtly form. As the social class of the audiences became more heterogeneous and work-aday, spectators were less interested in seeing titled rakes and idle toasts onstage: they wanted to see themselves.[9] In the course of the eighteenth century Restoration comedies and adaptations of them gradually became less popular, even as Shakespeare, with his broader social range, was becoming more so. Alterations, modernizations, and moralizations of Restoration plays, such as John Hawkesworth's *Amphitryon* (1756) and Garrick's *The Country Girl,* were not notably successful. *The London Stage* shows that Restoration comedy was slowly losing its place in the repertoire; excluding Farquhar, only Vanbrugh's *The Provoked Wife* (fourth at Drury Lane) and *The Way of the World* (fifteenth at Covent Garden) ranked among the more popular comedies in the period 1747–76 (pt. 4,

1:clxiii– xv). During Garrick's managership Restoration comedies accounted for around 10 percent of the comic performances at both theaters, just about the strength of sentimental comedy.

The most obvious effect on dramatic composition of this development was that the eighteenth-century version of the comedy of manners usually portrayed characters some notches lower on the social scale than their Restoration counterparts, and these characters were subject to the restrictions of bourgeois morality. This was a perfectly logical corollary, but it was not immediately perceived how much difference it made to the form; that it made, in a sense, all the difference. Not only is there no one in eighteenth-century comedy who could converse easily with Dorimant, Horner, or Mirabell: there was no eighteenth-century dramatist who could tolerate such a character as Etherege, Wycherley, or Congreve had. Whether a middle- or even an upper-middle-class comedy of manners is a contradiction in terms is a difficult question, but in any case the pure form proved elusive for Georgian comic dramatists; when they reached for it what they grasped was usually situation comedy. Remembering their audiences, we should not be surprised that by the century's end comedy had largely abandoned the realm of aristocratic manners for either situation or sentiment, nor that attempts to recreate the comedy of manners should end in something rather different, until the new classes had established mores of their own: a century's work.

At a time when comedy was struggling with the esthetic problems caused by social changes, one might expect that dramatic criticism would have used its influence to point out promising new paths, but for the most part this was not the case: generally critics of comedy were traditionalists. John Dennis and Oliver Goldsmith were only the most prominent of the many who insisted on judging comedy—especially the sentimental variety—by the standards and precedents of classical antiquity.[10] William Cook's *Elements of Dramatic Criticism* (1775) disbarred sentiment from comedy on the grounds that sentimental comedy lacked both a theory and classical precedent; it could live only through the sanction of a debauched audience, for it nauseated men of sense. Cook adopted the traditional position that "ridicule" is better at "curing the vices" than "examples of rigid virtue" that "intimidate" (p. 145). What is more striking is that Richard Cumberland, defending his sentimental comedies against Goldsmith's onslaught, chose to take his own stand on classical authority as well: "It will appear therefore that *sentiment* or the *pathetic* was not neglected by the ancients; that *Terence* so far from having made the *nearest approaches* to the pathetic, was accused of being deficient in it, and others for that very reason preferred before him, that with respect to *all* the *other comic writers of antiquity;* it cannot be asserted that *ridicule* was their sole aim."[11] Thus both sides of the debate did homage to the ancients.

We might also have expected that the mellowing of humor which is such a well-documented feature of eighteenth-century taste would have influenced the theory of dramatic comedy, but actually it had little effect. Most of the "benevolizers" were nondramatic critics such as Bishop Richard Hurd and Corbyn Morris, who felt that "the BUSINESS OF COMEDY is to exhibit the whimsical unmischievous Oddities, Frolics, and Foibles of Persons in real life; And also to expose and ridicule their real Follies, Meanness, and Vices."[12] Against this clear statement of the compromise view may be set almost any of the pronouncements of the professional theater writers, such as Foote, Colman, or Murphy, on the subject. Murphy's idea of the "business of Comedy," for example, was that it should excite "Laughter and Contempt, by making striking Exhibitions of inconsistent Circumstances, blended together in such a thwarting assemblage, that a gay Contempt ('making us despise and laugh at an Object at the same time') irresistibly shall take possession of us."[13] Nor was the "new amiability" of comedy reflected in the most prestigious dictionary of the time. To his definition of comedy in 1755—"a dramatick representation of the lighter faults of mankind"—Dr. Johnson added in 1773: "with an intention to make vice and folly ridiculous." The traditionalist strain in comic theory, as in comic practice, endured through the midcentury.

Tradition and confused variety were thus the qualities that characterized laughing comedy in this period; most playwrights looked back in reverence to diverse inspirations, and a number of successful plays simply blended venerable dramatic ingredients. A favorite recipe was to combine patches of Shaftesburian benevolence or bourgeois sentimentality with a humorous look at upper-middle-class manners, as in *The Clandestine Marriage* and *The School for Scandal,* or with the rake play (*The Suspicious Husband*), or the reform play (*The Good-Natured Man*). A French strain is also easily discernible; Regnard, La Bruyère, and especially Molière had followers in traditional comedy. Arthur Murphy, for example, based *All in the Wrong* on *Le Cocu imaginaire*, and combined *L'École des femmes*, *L'École des maris*, and *L'Étourdi* to make *The School for Guardians* (1767). Hugh Kelly and Charles Macklin also adapted Molière, whose popularity is further attested by over a dozen plays in the Larpent Collection with "School for" titles.

A somewhat less extensive influence was Elizabethan comedy. Shakespearean romance seems to have been one of Goldsmith's models in writing *She Stoops to Conquer*, and the comic portions of 1 and 2 *Henry IV* were continued by William Kenrick in *Falstaff's Wedding* (1766). There were in addition numerous alterations of Shakespeare's works. Humor characters appeared in many plays, but there were no attempts (with the possible exception of Cumberland's *The Choleric Man*) to write a full-length Jonsonian comedy of humors, satirists of Jonson's persuasion usually confining themselves to the afterpiece. Other Tudor and Stuart comedy was represented by alterations, such as Garrick's *Albumazar* (1773) from Thomas Tomkis, and Mrs. Lennox's *Old City Manners* (1775) from Jonson, Chapman, and Marston's *Eastward Hoe!* For the most part, dramatists were content to let the numerous Elizabethan stock plays in the repertoire supply the demand for romantic comedy, rarely attempting an original one.

Specific classical models evoked only mild interest. Both *The Choleric Man* and *The Jealous Wife* draw on Terence's *The Brothers,* and Plautus' *Amphytrion* (by way of Molière and Dryden) was rewritten by John Hawkesworth in 1756. Of course English and European comedy generally was based on the Roman variety, but there was more overt borrowing from the Latin plays in sentimental comedy and the afterpiece than in laughing comedy.

Reworkings of earlier eighteenth-century drama, including the short comedies, were fairly numerous. *The Rivals* has debts to *Polly Honeycombe* and *The Deuce Is in Him* by Colman, as well as to Garrick's *Miss in Her Teens*. Kenrick's *The Duellist* owes something to *The Conscious Lovers*. *The School for Scandal* repeats devices from *The West Indian* and Foote's *The Author,* and so on.

Yet this approach does not take us far. While influence-hunting among these plays is easy, it has little importance beyond indicating the main alignments of this highly derivative body of material, for dramatic comedy, as Northrop Frye writes, "has been remarkably tenacious of its structural principles and character types."[14] What counts is the end-product, the essence of the distillation; it is therefore more revealing to scrutinize a single laughing comedy that is typical, or symptomatic, of the genre in the eighteenth century. For this purpose Benjamin Hoadly's *The Suspicious Husband* will serve admirably, being virtually a microcosm of Georgian comedy. Only in its authorship and its popularity was it atypical. The largest and most prolific group of playwrights in the Garrick era was composed of professional theater people (Lynch, p. 168), whereas Hoadly was a physician. And *The Suspicious Husband* was an immense success: popular at once, it played often at both patent houses, outperforming every other comedy, ancient or modern, for thirty years at Drury Lane. Two extrinsic factors may help explain its phenomenal appeal. When it appeared in 1747, it ended a long drought: "This was the first good comedy from the time of *The Provoked Husband* in 1727; a long and dreary interval."[15] The anonymous pamphleteer who eulogized the play shortly after its appearance observed that "we now have hopes of seeing comedy revive again, which had been so long given over, & even thought dead among us."[16] And a brilliant cast of actors and actresses, led by David Garrick as Ranger, was certainly a partial cause of its longevity. But the reasons for its continued success go deeper, lying in the play's texture, an amalgam of elements and characteristics, sometimes contradictory ones, dear to eighteenth-century audiences.

Act 1 introduces us to the main characters and the background. Bellamy and Frankly are in love with Jacintha and Clarinda, respectively the ward and house-guest of Mr. and Mrs. Strictland. The Bellamy-Jacintha affair is of long duration, but is opposed by Strictland on the grounds of Bellamy's insufficient fortune; the Frankly-Clarinda liaison began only a few days ago during a dance at Bath, and the principals have yet to find each other in London. Strictland, however, is becoming anxious about the reputation and even the virtue of his wife if she remains in the company of the coquette Clarinda. Ranger, Clarinda's cousin, is a gentleman law-student and rake-about-town known to both Frankly and Bellamy. In act 2 Frankly sees Clarinda in St. James's Park and follows her home, obtaining there a few words and the promise of more later. Strictland, greatly distraught over his wife, peremptorily refuses Jacintha permission to marry Bellamy, whereupon she arranges to elope that night.

Act 3 is a "mistakes of a night" story. Frankly and Bellamy arrive independently at Strictland's house, looking for Clarinda and Jacintha. The latter, disguised in boy's clothes, appears and is mistaken by Frankly for a lover of Clarinda. While they talk Clarinda arrives, sees them together, accuses the perplexed Frankly of infidelity, and stalks away. Enter Bellamy, who sees the now-disabused Frankly with Jacintha and charges him with disloyalty. They postpone an éclaircissement to escape, for by this time Strictland has been aroused and warned; he leads a search for Jacintha and succeeds in recapturing her. Meanwhile Ranger enters, drunk, climbs Jacintha's rope ladder and importunes Mrs. Strictland. When her husband returns with Jacintha Mrs. Strictland hides Ranger in the next room, but his hat, left lying on the floor, creates a row. Only Jacintha's quick-witted fabrication saves the frightened woman. Strictland swears he will take Jacintha back to the country in the morning. After everyone has gone to bed Ranger reemerges and starts to assault Jacintha, but when he learns who she is agrees to "restore" her to Bellamy.

Act 4 provides further confusion but less action. Bellamy and Frankly, temporarily reconciled, meet the Strictlands' maid Lucetta the next morning. Her well-meaning account of what she thought she saw last night, and of Clarinda's unresolved suspicions, sets them upon each other anew. Ranger arrives and pacifies them, but his confused story of the night's frolics turns them against him. The three then part to seek further clarifications. Frankly's letter to Clarinda, arriving after she has gone out, is intercepted by Strictland, who believes it to be a billet-doux to his wife. Though Lucetta disproves this, he is still a "suspicious husband." Ranger follows a "fine woman" to her lodgings and courts her, until she unmasks and proves to be Clarinda. When he boasts of last night's escapades she recognizes the midnight visitor and rebukes him. In retaliation, Ranger implies that Frankly has been hurt in a duel, and Clarinda's response betrays her love.

As the fifth act opens, Strictland is actually writing settlement papers which will disgrace his wife, when an epistle arrives from Mr. and Mrs. Bellamy (!) inviting him to a final-assembly-to-explain-everything.

There, Frankly and Clarinda are easily brought to declare their mutual passion and plight their troth. Strictland, given the combined testimony of Frankly, Clarinda, and Ranger about last night, relents and reaccepts his wife. His renunciation of jealousy is as near to reform as the play comes. All adjourn to dance and feast as Ranger, the only bachelor left, pronounces a benediction on marriage.

Several major strains of mid-century comedy can be found in this play. The world of Restoration comedy of manners is invoked by the settings in St. James's Park, the flirting with lawless love by rakes and masked coquettes, and the occasional polish and wit of Ranger's repartee: "There is a degree of Assurance in you modest Gentlemen, which we impudent Fellows can never come up to—."[17] The characters, drawn from the gentry and well-heeled middle class, occupy themselves with gallantry, raking, or fashion. Strictland's unfounded jealousy, we feel, will not ultimately harm his wife; it is simply a misunderstanding to clear up. The pleasure of *The Suspicious Husband* comes from watching these urbane and comfortably established personages, pale shades of Mirabell and Dorimant, Pinchwife and Margery, Dorinda and Millamant, side-stepping humorous obstacles on their way to socially acceptable and soundly financed unions. But this is a Restoration comedy with eighteenth-century alterations. For one thing, it is moralized. Illicit relationships are contemplated but not consummated; Ranger's raking is ultimately harmless, even wholesome (he helps Jacintha). There are no fallen women or cheated husbands. The Dedication assures us that the play is "free from all Offence against the Rules of Good-Manners and Decency." By the closing curtain all love is brought virtuously within the purview of marriage, and Ranger delivers the irrelevant moral tag:

> Sure joys for ever wait each happy Pair,
> When Sense the Man, and Virtue crowns the Fair;
> And kind Compliance proves their mutual Care.

Moralization of this sort was, as we have seen, expected and approved in eighteenth-century comedy; it was the requisite mask on any dramatic countenance.

Equally typical of the age and of this play are the occasional touches of benevolence and sympathy.

91

> FRANKLY: For all this, Bellamy, [Meggott] has a Heart worthy your Friendship. . . .
> BELLAMY: Now you say something. It is the Heart, Frankly, I value in a Man.
> FRANKLY: Right! (I.iii)

Fellow-feeling is just under the surface of Clarinda's and Jacintha's friendly raillery:

> CLARINDA: Thou art the very first Prude, that ever had Honesty enough to avow her Passion for a Man.
> JACINTHA: And thou art the first finish'd Coquet who ever had any Honesty at all. (II.i)

Such outspoken mutual admiration between eligible single women is almost unheard of in Restoration comedy. Humane beneficence reaches its apex in the last scene of act 3, which is also the crux of the characterization of Ranger. He has caught Jacintha alone, late at night in Strictland's house, and attempts to force her. But when she breaks from him in tears, uttering Bellamy's name, he at once realizes who she is. Admitting aside, "Her Tears affect me strangely," he reveals himself her friend and offers to escort her to Bellamy.

> JACINTHA: Good Heaven, how fortunate this is!
> RANGER: I believe I make myself appear more wicked than I really am. For, damn me, if I do not feel more Satisfaction in the Thoughts of restoring you to my Friend, than I could have Pleasure in any Favour your Bounty could have bestowed.
> JACINTHA: Your Generosity transports me. (III.iii)

The passage documents the mellowing of the eighteenth-century rake and the "benevolization" of his passion. In the final scene, too, we encounter tears and talk of the heart, though not to a fulsome degree. While these moments are too few to give the play an overall sentimental cast, they catered to the taste for articulate feeling and "sentences" in a measure that ensured its popularity on that count.

But above all it is stage business that moves the play. Hoadly manipulated his plot adroitly to take advantage of the rage for intrigue, farcical incident and confused hurry created by Rich's pantomimes and the Spanish influence. The third act especially, with its mistaken identity, sexual cross-encounters, and rope ladder proved extremely agreeable. "The Third and Fourth Acts," says the anonymous pamphleteer, "are a continual laugh from beginning to end" (*Examen*, p. 4), and he goes on to praise inordinately the wealth of humorous and novel incident in the plot. His response indicates how squarely the author had hit the mark, and exactly what mark he had hit: "The Distress of [Frankly and Bellamy] in the Third and Fourth Acts [is] more artfully contrived and interesting, and their Adventures with *Jacyntha* and *Ranger* are more romantick (with the greatest Probability) than any Spanish novel I ever read." He mentions two meritorious "new" characters (Ranger and Strictland) and the sketch of a third (Meggott), but lays his heaviest stress on plot. Adapting Demosthenes, he asserts that action is the first and second excellence of drama, "and I shall produce *The Suspicious Husband* and some Plays of Ben Jonson, as the strongest proofs of my Observation. . . . In short, our author has made wit only a second Consideration: He never stops the Action, to say fine Things." This is true: the characters are kept so busy hustling and bustling that they have little time for conversation. It is a shrewd remark by the critic Canker, in Macklin's farce *The New Play Criticiz'd* (1747), that *The Suspicious Husband* is a pantomime and Ranger is Harlequin (Larpent MS 64). The combination of its long-lived success with its reliance on stage business is a telling comment on eighteenth-century comic theater.

The play succeeded, then, largely because it contrived to combine three strains popular during most of the century: the Restoration rake-play, the benevolent comedy, and the intrigue piece. The evidence for authorial craftiness and connivance with the popular taste should not, however, keep us from seeing that *The Suspicious Husband* is also crafty in the other sense. It not only assembles but skillfully balances these modes. Sentiment is present in strict moderation; intrigue furnishes the chief interest but does not entirely dominate; the Restoration world is faintly evoked so as to appeal to social escapism without bringing a blush to the cheek of Morality, and is made to seem yet alive. Expositions are handled smoothly, and "meritorious characters" are presented, though not studied. The action progresses in a graceful curve from the static, descriptive first act up to the complexly dramatic third, down through the gradual unravelling of the fourth and final assembly of the fifth act.

For all its pot-boiler tendencies, *The Suspicious Husband* should not be dismissed too lightly. Other authors as keen to touch the public's susceptibilities as Hoadly failed for want of his acumen.

Certain qualities of *The Suspicious Husband* also appear in plays by two authors whom one would not normally expect to find treated under the head of "laughing comedy": Richard Cumberland and Hugh Kelly. But no other heading will do for Cumberland's *The Choleric Man* (1774), his fourth major play and last in our period. It is based on Terence's *The Brothers*, and the changes Cumberland made in his source are revealing. He considerably complicates Terence's rather simple plot, turning a comedy of character into a situation play; the Englishman's interest seems to be in gradually "ravelling up" the situation which the Roman presents as *fait accompli* when the play opens. Poses, mistaken identities, cross-purposes and maneuverings of servants replace Terence's confrontation of clashing personalities and educational theories. What is perhaps most surprising is that the one sentimental scene in *The Brothers*—a father forgives his son—is simply omitted by Cumberland. That he should thus create a comedy of incident after the successes of his sentimental plays is interesting. Was Cumberland not such a dedicated sentimentalist after all? Or did he feel that *Piety in Pattens* and *She Stoops to Conquer* had spoiled the audiences for sentiment? In any case, *The Choleric Man* is an accurate barometer of the prevailing weather in the theaters of the time. Ingenious, active entertainment was prized above sentiment, or character, or manners.

If *The Suspicious Husband* exhibits the various comic types that audiences enjoyed in rough balance and superficial reconciliation, the career of Hugh Kelly shows how the pressure to include diverse modes might overwhelm a basically competent comic dramatist. Producing his first and best comedy, *False Delicacy*, during a surge of sentimental comedy in 1768, Kelly built it around sentimentalists (Lady Betty and Winworth) and a favorite sentimental device, the misunderstandings of the sensitive. Winworth, who is mystified by the ways of women, takes Lady Betty's coquettish refusal of his marriage proposal seriously, and consequently transfers his affections. It requires five acts to unravel the complications that result. Yet such is Kelly's use of this material that the question of how he expects us to respond is left open. The play contains amusing comic scenes, including satire on sentimental conventions, chiefly by Cecil and the "merry widow," Mrs. Harley. "You and Lady Betty," she tells Miss Marchmont, "are unaccountably fond of those half-soul'd fellows, who are as mechanically regular as so many pieces of clock-work, and never strike above once an hour upon a new obser-vation—who are so sentimental, and so dull—so wise, and so drowsy."[18] And to Lady Betty herself she objects, "What a work there is with you sentimental folks. . . . Thank heav'n, my sentiments are not sufficiently refin'd to make me unhappy" (II.i). If this is a sentimental comedy, it is remarkably diluted. The sentimentalists' own delicacy (undercut by the title) is actually the villain of the play, as it is this, rather than any character, which delays and almost prevents the destined union of Lady Betty and Winworth.

Kelly, however, includes something for everyone: a feature of his career as well as of this play. Mrs. Harley, who is allowed to be so hard on the delicate ones, is also given some ambiguous moments: "Well, the devil take this delicacy; I don't know any thing it does besides making people miserable:—And yet some how, foolish as it is, one can't help liking it" (II.i). The ending is managed so that one is left unsure of the playwright's own attitude towards the delicacy of his sentimentalists.[19]

Mark Schorer has argued that in each succeeding play Kelly became less sentimental ("Kelly," p. 392), but this is difficult to accept. It is true that Dormer in A Word to the Wise (1770) satirizes sentiment, but he is also an amiable benevolist, and in this case the degree of satiric dilution is not significant. The play has the expression as well as the features of senti-mental comedy, and I have treated it in chapter three, along with The Man of Reason; or, The Reasonable Lover (1776), his last (if it is his) and most tediously sentimental play. But The School for Wives (1773) is an eighteenth-century approximation of the comedy of manners, and cer-tainly Kelly's least sentimental play. The title invokes Molière; there are moments of low comedy (including a bailiff scene), satirical attacks on people and institutions (including Mildew's on sentiment), a hypocritical rake and even some indelicate language. Kelly appears to have been trying to move back towards traditional comic norms without losing his position as a spokesman for sentiment. One way that he attempted to do this was to direct the printed version (1774) toward the presumed sentimentalists in the reading public, adding didactic and sentimental matter that was not presented onstage while omitting much of the satire and anything "low" (see chapter two). It worked in the theater, at least: by 1776 *The School for Wives* had pulled ahead of *False Delicacy* in total performances.

Kelly could be viewed as a shrewd fence-sitter with a mixed style, but his career has an aura of half-starts and backings-off. His sentiment seems undercut by satire and his humor vitiated by the pathetic. He is finally neither traditionalist nor sentimentalist, but an unsatisfactory cross-breed. Evidently the variety of comic styles popular in the Garrick era could be either a strength or a pitfall, and Kelly seems to have tried the boldest but least viable of the possible ways of blending them. While traditional writers used sentiment as a weapon or as a butt for humor in what were basically laughing comedies, and sentimentalists inserted humorous portions into otherwise exemplary plays, Kelly attempted a nearly equal mixture of the genteel and the satiric. His failure to achieve this perilous balance lends weight to Sherbo's contention that a funny sentimental play is a contradiction in terms. Kelly's work did not please audiences for long—after its initial success, *False Delicacy* played only eight times in the next eight seasons—and had little influence on either side of the controversy. He occupies the minor though instructive position of the artist who proves what will not work.

Christopher Fry has called comedy a "narrow escape" from despair into faith.[20] It may be objected that this is the sort of remark that describes mainly the author's own plays; certainly it makes demands that few comedies, only the darkest, can meet. Yet Elder Olson asks much the same thing of comedy when he says that it ought to have comic suffering to be relieved (*Theory*, p. 51). Viewed in this light, most eighteenth-century comedy utterly fails even to qualify for the genre. It has no despair to escape from, little suffering to be relieved; it is light and unproblematical; it lacks tension. Whether or not one accepts Fry's and Olson's stipulations as authoritative requirements for comedy, they do provide a foil against which an essential quality of the eighteenth-century variety shows up. Where and why this quality came to exist is a piquing question, but any answer will surely have to take account of the role of sentimental comedy. Steele's type of drama specialized in distress, and as time passed the sentimental comedies annexed this province altogether. The acquisition went virtually uncontested, for authors of laughing comedy were as anxious to put space between their plays and their opponents' as the latter were to have a clear territory of their own. As a result one of the defining traits of Georgian laughing comedy came to be a freedom from anything resembling despair or suffering. It is one of the ironies of criticism that Goldsmith and Sheridan would almost certainly have told Fry and Olson that they were defining sentimental comedy.

The Combrush of the
Comic Muse

> The orthodox theory is that an insidious disease, a sort of phylloxera or blight, known as "sentiment," had crept into and sterilised the luxuriant vineyard of English comedy. This I hold to be quite a misleading account of the matter. The mass of comedies produced between *The Beaux' Stratagem* and *She Stoops to Conquer* were not in the least sentimental. Where is the sentiment in the lively improvisations of Fielding and Foote? They are thin, slight, trivial, farcical, frothy, extravagant, anything else you please—but sentimental they are not.
> —William Archer, *The Old Drama and the New*

If laughing comedy was surviving in full-length comedy, its extended family, the laughing tradition, was flourishing in the afterpiece. Laughter, restricted to some extent in mainpieces by audiences' expectations of seriousness, found a hospitable refuge in the short plays that closed the evening's program. Stimulated by this fresh responsibility and the influx of new talent and material, the afterpiece developed forms and techniques commensurate with its new status. Dramatists and spectators seemed to feel a pleasure suited to the times in the shortened or "petite" comedies and farces, while writers of regular comedy mined them unashamedly. To view the Georgian comic tradition in its full vigor, one must look at the afterpiece, and learn to see there not merely a reductionist expedient, but an independent art-form.

The story of the afterpiece is a classic of unplanned development, whether one is speaking of a kind of miniature drama or a certain theatrical format. The latter may perhaps be traced to the Elizabethan practice of allowing spectators free admission after act 3, and the former to the "drolls" and farces with which penurious actors tried to evade the Puritan Parliament's suppression of legitimate drama under the Commonwealth.[1] At the same time expatriate Stuart courtiers were seeing afterpieces in France, where the custom was established about 1650; in England, patrons first saw a double bill during the season of 1676–77, when Thomas Otway paired *The Cheats of Scapin* (translated from Molière) with his adaptation of Racine's *Bérénice,* but the idea did not catch on at the time. In 1686, however, the actors began to collect a pittance from latecomers, who in turn demanded more substance for their "after-money." Songs, dances, and masques were used at first—as they had been in Elizabeth's day and would continue to be in the Georgian era—but the definitive answer was found only under the spur of competition between rival playhouses: in 1696 Thomas Betterton's breakaway company at Lincoln's Inn Fields offered a farce after their mainpiece to lure customers from Christopher Rich at Drury Lane. Ironically, it was Rich's son John who established the afterpiece firmly after two decades of sporadic use; in 1714 he took over Lincoln's Inn Fields and staged forty-six afterpieces in a short first season. When Drury Lane returned the fire, the greatest success story of eighteenth-century theater was underway. By the 1720s afterpieces were expected; in the second half of the century they were, according to most reports, better attended than the mainpieces.[2] The hallmark of Georgian theater was its exuberant variety, and the afterpiece was an important part of this characteristic. But double and triple bills produced a theatrical evening of four to five hours, and when, in the late nineteenth century, the changing social habits of the drama's patrons required that it be shortened to two or three, the first casualty was the afterpiece.

While it lasted, the afterpiece's position in the program was a voracious maw into which managers and authors fed dramatic material for quick consumption; a relatively high proportion of these ephemera were performed only a few times. Almost seventy percent of the plays sent to the Licenser between 1737 and 1777 were afterpieces, afterpiece comedies (and farces) outnumbering the five-act variety by ninety-six to forty-two. A good three-quarters of the work produced by the seven major comic playwrights of those years was of afterpiece length. Virtually every species of existing drama was pressed into service, including post-1650 novelties peculiar to the afterpiece; assorted literary oddities were also worked into short plays, and the classical genres—comedy and tragedy—gradually lost authority and dominance.

Unquestionably the most successful of the nontraditional forms was the pantomime, which had actually had a long history on the Continental stage going back to the Roman *pantomimus* by way of the Italian commedia dell'arte. But the form that John Rich introduced in 1717 was based immediately on the harlequinades brought over from France about the turn of the century, which were simply mimed stories based on commedia scenarios. Rich's pantomimes were basically operettas, in which relatively serious scenes, often telling stories from classical mythology, alternated with the silent farce of Harlequin and Columbine, featuring ingenious transformations and frequently spoofing the mythical plot. The freewheeling combination of music, acrobatics, belly laughs, and spectacular scenery enjoyed great favor, especially with Rich (as "Lun") playing Harlequin. In the 1720s and 1750s, particularly, pantomime was so popular that it overwhelmed every other species of afterpiece drama, founding what Allardyce Nicoll has aptly termed a "fantastic empire" (*British Drama,* p. 174).

Pantomime sired the burletta, in which a plot based on mythology or the commedia was snug and narrated, thus satisfying the wishes of some spectators to have audible pantomime. The raison d'être of the burlettas was the need of managers at non-patent theaters to evade the restrictions of the Licensing Act; legally any piece with at least five songs in three acts was not a play, hence not covered by the Act. It was obviously in the interests of such managers to have as many burlettas available as possible, and this pressure led to widespread confusion and abuses in the late eighteenth and early nineteenth centuries. The first English burletta (the form was used earlier on the Continent) is generally held to have been Kane O'Hara's *Midas* (1764), and for the next two decades or so burlettas generally fit the definition later offered by George Colman the Younger while he was Examiner of Plays: "A short comic piece . . . consisting of recitative and singing, wholly accompanied . . . by the orchestra." But burlettas could be "converted" as well as created—a three-act version of *Hamlet* with five songs was technically a burletta—and the term soon bloated beyond all recognition or coherence.[3]

Pantomimes and burlettas accounted for many afterpiece performances, as did a host of other *illegitimi* too numerous and motley to discuss here—circus acts, musicals, pastoral sketches, scenic wonders, and the like—but the farces outdid them all.[4] They had been the first afterpieces and remained the most popular, ineradicably forming the character of the "curtain-dropper." Farce means "stuffing"; the earliest independent farces (as the eighteenth century understood the term) or "drolls" were comic bits lifted out of larger plays and "stuffed" into otherwise legal programs during the Commonwealth, thus performing the law-evading functions that the burletta took over in the following century. In retrospect we trace farce back through the commedia and medieval folk drama to Rome and even Greece, but for most Georgians farce per se dated only to the seventeenth century. They did not define it carefully; a farce was a short, amusing play with low characters, in which improbabilities were admissible and neither trenchant satire nor meaningful ritual was required (many would call it "comedy" today). Often "the farce" meant simply "the afterpiece." Technically, one could recognize the short comedy (taken from the French *petite comédie*) by its saturnalia and avoidance of improbability, but in practice the dividing line between the two was badly blurred. Eighteenth-century usages of the terms were often indiscriminate or polemical; Foote dignified many of his satirical sketches with the label "comedies," while a legitimate shortened comedy—such as *The Kept Mistress*—might be labeled "farce" either by someone who did not like it, or who did not know or care enough to distinguish one from the other, or simply because it was a benefit piece, i.e., a piece whose proceeds after performance went to the actor (or author). Again we have to make our own way through the thicket of definition, recognizing that our efforts are modern constructions on rather swampy Georgian ground.

The traditionality of eighteenth-century English farce poses a nice question, and the answer depends almost entirely upon how we define farce and how we understand traditional comedy. First, it is clear that *farcicality* has a place in the English comic tradition: instances of farce or tendencies toward it occur in many medieval and Elizabethan plays as integrated components of the comedy, or as alternative modes of viewing the material of the comedy. Only a step separates the "low" scenes of 1 and 2 *Henry IV* and *Henry V, Twelfth Night,* the *Secundus pastorum,* and *Friar Bacon* from autonomous farce, and this is precisely the step which the Commonwealth droll took. Here the farce's claim to traditionality turns on whether it is perceived as a logical development from earlier comedy or a radical new departure. If we trace its genealogy to the miracle plays, as some do, then of course its place in the English tradition is unassailable.

Second, to a certain extent the regular comic functions of saturnalia and satire came over from the mainpiece to the afterpiece—but only to a certain extent. These functions were truncated and "farcicalized," and we face the problem of degree: how farcical may comedy become, and still be apprehended as belonging to the comic tradition? Any attempt to exclude farce will necessitate that it be satisfactorily distinguished from the short comedy, which obviously did belong to that tradition. The difficulties of doing so are underscored by Stone's classification of afterpieces in part four of *The London Stage*. Evidently following eighteenth-century labels, he lists among the farces Garrick's *Miss in Her Teens* and Murphy's *The Upholsterer*, both of which seem to me clear examples of short comedy. On the other hand he classifies Foote's *The Lyar* and *The Commissary* as "brief comedies" (accepting Foote's own claims), although most of Foote's contemporaries called them farces, and the latter has all the earmarks of dramatic satire with almost none of the functions of comedy. The problem of definition cannot be approached in a priori fashion; it must be solved for individual plays—a process which will eventually define a genre. Yet since one must, finally, either accept farce or set it aside, I have chosen to include it here, mainly for pragmatic reasons. Lacking a clear-cut distinction between farce and short comedy, it is safest to speak of "afterpiece comedy," which includes both, but is distinguishable from the pantomimes and other clearly untraditional forms.

The afterpiece was an important carrier of the laughing tradition in the eighteenth century. It is not really surprising that the *petites pièces* should have resisted the charms of sentimentalism so adamantly; the original drolls and farces were entirely dedicated to laughter of a trivial sort, and there is no solid evidence to suggest that the afterpiece ever lost, or was asked to lose, that fundamental character, at least to the end of the eighteenth century. (The new forms, such as the pantomime and the burletta, were also devised to provoke laughter and were virtually incapable of sentimentalism.) On the theoretical front, there is the argument that "brevity is inimical to sentimentalism" (Sherbo, p. 36), and satiric comments on sentiment indeed abound in the afterpiece. Of the 109 afterpiece comedies licensed in the period, 86 can confidently be described as "traditionally comic." Another 18 must be called "mixed," in the sense that *The Clandestine Marriage* and *The School for Scandal* are mixtures of traditional and sentimental comedy. Only 5 could be considered "sentimental." Thus about 80 percent of the afterpieces were in the laughing tradition and over 90 percent were non-sentimental, as compared to roughly 50 percent of the mainpieces. The plots, characters, devices and resolutions associated with full-length laughing comedy, romantic or satiric, appear also in the overwhelming majority of the afterpieces. Beginning about 1750, afterpiece writers such as Garrick and Foote began to make serious critical defences of their short plays as comedies. The phenomenon of traditional comedy flowing from mainpiece to afterpiece in the eighteenth century was noted by some earlier historians, and now seems to be gaining recognition.

On the other hand it must be admitted that comedy in the afterpiece was altered, mainly by being "farcicalized." The term is used in Leo Hughes's sense: "When . . . the satirical edge has been dulled by repetition and exaggeration, we are already drawing very near the line separating comedy and farce" (*Century*, p. 32). One might add "the saturnalian edge" as well. The ubiquitous farces—broadly humorous, unreflective, episodic, and incidental—specialized in a cursory treatment of the themes of comedy. Sheridan's *St. Patrick's Day*, a reduction of Farquhar's *The Recruiting Officer*, shows the sketchiness that resulted when regular comedy was adapted to the brisk needs of the afterpiece. A more manageable example is James Townley's *The Tutor* (1765, unpublished, Larpent MS 245), which embodies the essence of the Malvolio idea from *Twelfth Night* in a pedantic tutor, one Diameter System. A conniving household decides to "smoke" him by making him trade his gravity for a beau's costume. The rich widow Mrs. Heartfree is dangled before him, and he quickly decides that "marrying an old woman has something philosophical in it—she really has a kind of classical ugliness about her—." Traps are duly set; he is exposed and ejected, blustering. Curtain. This plot is dispatched in one act (half an hour at most) with a minimum of realism, imaginative ornament, or verbal grace. *The Tutor* represents the tendency toward "mere farce": the traditional comic themes, plots and characters were present, but in a formal way, as a rather mechanical continuation of a once living ritual. This transformation of materials was not wrought overnight, however, nor was it ever complete; the inducements to farce were at times resisted successfully by mid-century writers. The old comic strain surviving in the afterpiece was compromised, on the whole, a good deal less than its mainpiece counterpart. And even to the extent that farce did dominate, this is still a different picture from the one we have inherited.

Three modes of afterpiece comedy were mentioned earlier: sentimental, mixed, and traditional or laughing. The sentimental afterpiece, a *lusus naturae* where all the pressures were against sentiment, occurs only five times in these forty years. Hugh Kelly and Edward Thompson both recount love stories whose principals are returning from India to England. Kelly's *Romance of an Hour* (1774) is a slapdash dramatization of a story by Marmontel; it bears out Sherbo's observation that if a treatment of sentimental themes is brief it lacks emotive power. The dialogue is uniformly dismal, and the "humor" disastrous. Its main gesture is towards humanitarianism: an honest Indian servant resolves a foolish quarrel between English gentlemen. Thompson's *St. Helena* (1776) is a musical farce about a wealthy young sailor (!) who loves a beautiful orphan. Conducted at an infantile level and replete with the patriotic humors of the Navy, it could easily have been the takeoff point for *H.M.S. Pinafore*. Thomas Mozeen's *The Heiress* (1759, pub. 1762) also employs patriotic sentiment to dress up an old romance motif: a girl disguises herself as a boy to be near an interesting young man. Captain Hardy is mildly memorable as a lunatic Anglophile with an anti-Gallican humor, but the purpose of the satire is vague, while motives and morality have all the depth of a wading-pool. The nationalistic vein is also strong in Mrs. Gardner's *Matrimonial Advertisement* (1777, unpub.), the most baldly humanitarian of the sentimental afterpieces. Mrs. Gardner is not behindhand about her claims on our attention:

> Then let humanity my cause defend
> & be the widow'd wife & mother's friend.
> (Larpent MS 435)

Her play contains as perfect a statement of Shaftesburian moral optimism as will be found in Georgian drama. A wealthy widow extends charity to a needy authoress (both surrogates of Mrs. Gardner) with a lofty sentiment—"The hand that relieves, conveys a richer cordial to the feeling mind, than the hand that receives, or the heart that is cheer'd"— that conveys a reasonably accurate impression of the style and mood of the whole. Side by side with sentimental benevolence is a crass materialism about marriage common to both laughing and sentimental comedy (not to mention society) in the period, though perhaps only Mrs. Gardner would write such a line as "What say you to a thousand a year and me?"

None of these plays was successful. *The Heiress* was given a single benefit performance; Thompson's and Mrs. Gardner's plays were not published, and Kelly's probably would not have been without his name. Except for Mozeen's farce, all come from late in the period, and demonstrate the baneful influence of wartime jingoism on the stage: both *St. Helena* and *The Matrimonial Advertisement* are infected with virulent resentment against the French.

Conversely, the earliest of the sentimental afterpieces was also the best. Robert Dodsley's *The Blind Beggar of Bethnal Green* (1740, pub. 1741) is a period piece whose opening scenes have a quiet, stylized bucolic charm. It followed up the successes of his *King and the Miller of Mansfield* and *Sir John Cockle at Court,* in which sentiment appears chiefly as patriotism. Though usually listed as a farce, *The Blind Beggar* is a pastoral with many of the characteristics of melodrama: a helpless, beggared old father, a lovely and virtuous daughter, a flatly diabolic sexual villain, a pure and handsome young rescuer, and a final twist that reveals the "beggar" as Sir Simon Montford (long in hiding from a would-be avenger), who can afford a dowry of five thousand pounds. The play is as improbable as most farces, but there is no humor or slapstick, in fact no interest in *vis comica*. Its affinities with the benevolist comedies are clear from the reflection of the potential rapist Lord Ranby, "Well, there is a pleasure after all in virtue, which we loose fellows know not how to taste"—a fair sample of its tone.

The few sentimental afterpieces of these years show no agreement on how to achieve their effects; they gesture at romance, patriotism, comedy of manners, and melodrama, sometimes all at once. But as soon as we turn to the humorous afterpieces, we are back in the familiar world of unsympathetic fathers, witty servants, pristine lovers, and ridiculous blocking-figures. Even the "mixed" or "compromise" afterpieces draw complacently on Menander and Plautus, exhibiting the usual comic economy of plot and character and device, though they combine the traditional with the sentimental approach to humor. The compromise technique was a means of handling the farce, short comedy, or dramatic satire that allowed the gentler spirits and finer sensibilities in the audience to be drawn into the normally rowdy pleasures of afterpiece comedy. Representing about one-sixth of the total, the mixed type includes some of the most popular afterpieces of the century, and those most closely resembling the full-length comedies of the day.

Several alloys were tried, but none of them won widespread approval. Samuel Foote combined manners satire with plots and characters usually found in sentimental comedy at least twice, in *The Author* and *The Minor*. Some writers have dismissed these, I think rather undiscriminatingly, as "sentimental." They are laughing, satirical farces with mellow endings, and the satire undercuts the sentiment. In Francis Gentleman's *The Pantheonites* (1773) and in the anonymous *Love Match* (1762), which are made from the same formula, it is the satire which is vitiated by the sententious and patriotic touches. Gentleman described his piece as a "burlesque of affected gentility"; it is a kind of *Bourgeois gentilhomme* with sentimental additions. Both here and in *The Love Match* the satire is unusually forceful, yet tainted by antagonistic elements. Satire is combined with a moral exemplum in James Townley's *High Life below Stairs* (1759), one of the more successful afterpieces of the century. *High Life* varies the plot of *The Alchemist* by having a master fake a trip out of town in order to spy on his servants, whom he suspects of cheating him. The uproarious antics as the servants ape the manners of their betters make good stage comedy, but Tom, the honest servant, is stridently moral, and the play becomes heavy towards the end.

A similar but less successful compound was that of social satire with patriotic sentiment. Robert Dodsley's *Sir John Cockle at Court* (1738), a sequel to *The Miller of Mansfield* in which the newly knighted miller comes to London and exposes the courtiers' vices and pettiness, is a moral and satirical farce that indulges in some fulsome rhetoric and fawns on the king. Foote's *Englishman in Paris* also exploits the nationalistic vein, though its mainspring is ridicule of the French and Francophiles. Tobias Smollett's *The Reprisal, or, The Tars of Old England* (1757), a patriotic farce with the accoutrements of a musical revue, mixes anti-Gallic ridicule, the humors of the Scots and Irish, and sentimental patriotism in about equal quantities.

A mixture of genial warmth with moral reform in a framework of comedy was tried by several playwrights, with results bordering on sentimental comedy. William Havard's *The Elopement* (1763, unpub., Larpent MS 223) is a two-act farce on the careless husband–neglected wife theme. Pompone, the clever servant manquée, is amusingly egotistical and malapropos, but the play is dull and occasionally sententious. One of the most successful farces of the century, David Garrick's *The Lying Valet* (1741), was similarly compounded. Virtually a condensation of *The Beaux' Stratagem,* the play misses sentimentality by an even narrower margin when, at the conclusion, the reformed hero kneels to the redeeming heroine, who raises him. Somewhat better balanced is *The Experiment* (1777, unpub., Larpent MS 429), probably written by Charles Stuart, a mildly comic drama about the simultaneous courtships of the two Warren sisters. It is interesting and fairly original (despite a slight resemblance to *False Delicacy*), but neither funny nor satirical; its sentimental dialogue and reform motif clash with the author's apparent desire to be humorous.

Most other combinations held more firmly to the laughing tradition. One of the most successful (aesthetically as well as financially) was that of the sentimental with the humorous. Much later Dickens would perfect this pairing in the novel, but on the mid-eighteenth-century stage the intensity of the sentiment was less and the bonds to traditional comic effects closer. Foote's *The Bankrupt* and Garrick's *Miss in Her Teens,* both well-known afterpieces, allow some sentimentality in a basic humors framework; in neither piece, however, is the sentiment allowed to touch the main character—another difference from Dickens. *The Absent Man* (1764, unpub., Larpent MS 239), by Thomas Hull, also illustrates this strategy.[5] The legal humor of attorney Wiseacre ("Now attend, listen & give ear!") and the comic absentmindedness of Sir William Wander remain distinct from the sentimentality of the plot of romantic reunion. The sentimental/comic afterpieces that succeeded generally kept the opposed elements in distinct compartments. Seldom or never, for example, would the writer of an afterpiece confront a sentimental character with an antisentimentalist and let them fight it out, as Hugh Kelly did with Lady Betty and Mrs. Harley in *False Delicacy*. Hildebrand Jacob went so far as to write *A Nest of Plays* (1738), three one-act comedies performed consecutively in one night. In this trilogy are *The Prodigal Reform'd*, a sentimental "test" play along the lines of *The West Indian*, featuring another benevolent incognito relative; *The Happy Constancy*, a romantic Spanish intrigue of mixed impulse; and finally a crudely erotic laughing comedy of the Restoration type, *The Tryal of Conjugal Love*. As chemistry distinguishes between compounds and mixtures (the former designating a fusion or alloy of elements, and the latter simply placement in physical proximity), we can identify compounds in Georgian drama, but as a general rule afterpieces of the compromise mode are simple mixtures.

There is, again, a difference in what is meant by *sentimental* as we move from play to play. In *The Minor* and *The Absent Man* the term denotes plot devices frequently associated with sentimental comedy—prodigal reform and reunion of long-separated relatives or lovers—though the actual handling of these devices is only partly and mildly sentimental. In other plays sententious diction mars the comic mood. Sentiment may crop up as "benevolism" (e.g., *The Lying Valet*), and in a very few afterpieces, such as Macnamara Morgan's pastoral *The Sheep-Shearing* (1754), we find the maudlin and emotional Optimism of Cumberland: manifestations of sentiment are no more monolithic in the mixed afterpieces than in full-length comedy.

But plays of this type are still the exception; mixed and sentimental afterpieces together constitute only about one-fifth of the total. The rest remain faithful to the older laughing tradition. The mellow benevolence of many comic mainpieces and of some of the afterpieces is foreign to these plays; they reject it utterly for the unfeeling toughness of traditional comedy, exhibiting the "anesthesia of the heart" that Henri Bergson found at the core of laughter.

The roughly eighty-five diverse plays in this category admit of a few tenable generalizations. For one thing, they fall into three main groups: the farce, the short comedy, and the dramatic satire. Second, they are profoundly derivative, as we would expect traditional comedy to be. Most theorists have invented some term to express how deeply comedy is set in its ways. Bergson noted a certain "mechanicality" at the root of every comic situation; Northrop Frye articulated the principle of "comic economy" by which the genre conserves and recycles a relatively small number of situations and characters. There is nothing new under the sun of laughing comedy, and this static quality is also noticeable in the afterpieces, though it takes on many guises. Not only do most of them show affinities with Greek and Roman plots as old as drama itself; many are adaptations of earlier plays or taken from countless novels, tales, essays, and actual events reported in newspapers and magazines. The evolution of new genres was not accompanied by any general feeling that new plots and characters were needed; a very little updating and naturalizing sufficed to make a Plautine comedy or a Molière farce perfectly at home on the London stage of 1750. In this respect afterpiece comedy resembled its ancestor the commedia dell'arte and its modern descendants the film farce, the cartoon, and the situation comedy. From the first scene or panel the audience already knows a great deal about the characters, their roles, the kinds of situations they will probably encounter and even, within limits, the sort of outcome to be expected. The aesthetic strength of all these forms lies precisely in our familiarity with the building materials, eliminating the need for much laborious exposition, and our interest in just what novel twist the old artificer can devise this time. The suspense, then, attaches not to the destination, which is foreseen in a general way, but to the particular route by which it will be reached. There is indeed a kind of mechanicality in the rigid tenacity of the plots and characters of these afterpieces to ancient stereotypes.

A related kind of rigidity appears in the sorts of names frequently given to characters in these farces and short comedies. Most afterpieces were modeled on Jonsonian humors comedy rather than on Shakespearean romance, and this allegiance involved the use of names calculated to divulge information about the character rather than to allow for change or depth or to achieve realism. Such labels tend to flatten character by restricting its scope; a Quidnunc, a Sir Archy Macsarcasm, or a Lady Diana Henpecker is obviously as limited in sphere as a Subtle or an Erotium, and ought to be as predictable. We feel, logically enough, that the outcome of many a comedy of humors should be discoverable simply from a careful reading of the dramatis personae, yet often eighteenth-century dramatists reversed a characterization in the last scene with scant regard for psychology, logic, or propriety. Another disadvantage is the dreary repetition of the same role-names again and again; the line of virile Franklys and nubile Harriets sometimes seems destined to stretch out to the crack of doom. Yet both of these drawbacks could be avoided by the ingenious. Charles Macklin was especially gifted in creating original though humorous names: Sir Pertinax Macsycophant, Lady Rodolpha Lumbercourt, Sir Hector Mackrafty, Betty Hint the maid, and so on. Nor did such a name have to be a cul de sac. At the end of *The Upholsterer*, Arthur Murphy quite credibly uses the humor of Quidnunc (a passion for news) to facilitate the marriage he has so long blocked. Quidnunc's rabid interest in his son's news from the West Indies simply overrides his objections, and he runs off to buy the papers, as humorous and as appropriately named as ever, but outmaneuvered by the young folk. (Sheridan, in *The School for Scandal,* exacted triple duty from the name "Surface": neither brother was what he appeared on the surface, nor was Uncle Oliver fooled by surfaces.) Thus the problem of creating a dynamic comedy of humors, however difficult, was not impossible to solve, and its handling serves as a barometer of dramaturgical skill. But it must be admitted that the glass was seldom high; the large majority of characters in the afterpieces either remained trapped within labels, or changed radically at the expense of breaking faith with a humor-name.

Only a dozen or so afterpiece comedies introduced original variants on inherited themes and character-types. At the end of *The Guardian* (1759), David Garrick allowed the "autumnal" Heartly to marry his ward Harriet, a most unusual denouement. The anonymous *Politican* (1758, unpub., Larpent MS 145) rings a change on the traditional clever servant in the person of Spy, who is atypically craven and unresourceful, and thereby creates that rarity in farce, a three-dimensional character. The most numerous variations occurred in portrayals of the classic blocking characters. James Townley's *False Concord* (1764, unpub., Larpent MS 236) allows the blocker to withdraw at the end intact and happy, presumably because he is a lord. Paul Hiffernan permits a quack doctor to emerge unscathed in order that he may continue to dupe the gullible rich in *The New Hippocrates* (1761, unpub., Larpent MS 192). A phlegmatic and ridiculous blocker is mysteriously awarded marital happiness in Charles Stuart's *The Experiment,* while *The Love Match* (Larpent MS 209) adopts the simple expedient of killing off such a character. But for the most part these are superficial innovations, varying well-worn themes in minor ways. Derivation from the comic models of the past, and close adherence to their methods, remained the rule.

Of the three main types of afterpiece comedy mentioned earlier, two of them, the short comedy and the farce, show some agreement on principles of structure. In a play whose duration is less than an hour and whose principal intent is humor, the *complicatio* or "ravelling-up" must be done quickly; most afterpieces accomplish it by means of a rather bald exposition in the first scene. A two-act play will set forth the problem by the end of the first act, so that the second act (and perhaps the last scene of the first) is available for resolution. Development tends to be scanty in farce, where a duple form, simple rise and fall, is common, but there are exceptions: Arthur Murphy's *The Upholsterer* has a long development section. The three-act play usually spends the second act on development of the comic situation, and thus is put together in a triptych, like a five-act comedy. The rarer "comedy of errors" type proceeds in a straight line of complication until the last scene, then resolves quickly. There was a tendency in both kinds and lengths to lower tension early in the play and focus on gulling the dupes, as in Garrick's *Miss in Her Teens*. Thus any attempt to distinguish farce and short comedy on the basis of structure is a critical imposition without eighteenth-century foundation. The terms were not used in that way.

Modern literature has learned to take farce seriously. In our century, due partly to Kafka and the dramatists of the absurd, farce has gained recognition as a serious and potentially profound way of interpreting experience. Bummidge, the hero-farceur of Saul Bellow's *The Last Analysis* (1965), says, "Farce follows horror into darkness. Deeper, deeper." This perception seems natural, even inevitable, in a time when politics, war, and everyday life vie with each other in farcicalization. Recent critics have been increasingly impressed with the pervasiveness of farce, its ramifying psychological depths, and its efficacy at representing reality in literature. William G. McCollom has described it as "a drastically penetrating look into disproportion and injustice."[6] Farce's time seems to have come; it is the genre for this season.

But these modern expectations are generally disappointed when we turn to the period that one critic has described as "the great age of English farce."[7] The proponents of farce as a serious art-form find scant

111

support among eighteenth-century examples, but if we examine them by the lamp of Ionesco or Beckett, we will create a problem where none existed. The Georgians looked to farce for jollity and levity, not for surreal absurdity or moral vision. What audiences desired and writers produced in the form is succinctly expressed in Joseph Reed's prologue to *The Register Office* (1761, unpub., Larpent MS 196):

> The Bard, whose hopes on Comedy depend,
> Must strive instruction with delight to blend,
> While he, who bounds his less-aspiring views
> To Farce, the Combrush of the Comic Muse,
> With pleasantry alone may fill the scene;
> His business chiefly this—to cure the spleen:
> To raise the pensive mind from grave to gay,
> And help to laugh a thoughtful hour away.

In his search for pleasantry the farce-writer was free to employ slapstick, novel incident, improbabilities, and magic; he was not encouraged to attempt serious social criticism, much less an analysis of existence, and the rare farce that gave these was an anomaly. Ordinarily, as in Reed's definition, *farce* simply designated a short humorous piece, something in the laughing tradition yet mostly devoid of the deeper comic functions, and not readily classifiable into another genre such as pantomime or comic opera.

If we hold to the terms of Reed's definition—and it is reasonably close to the Georgian standard—we find that Miles Peter Andrews's *The Conjuror* is virtually a made-to-order farce, perfectly illustrative of the eighteenth-century type. "It was received with applause" at its single performance in May 1774, wrote William Hopkins, the Drury Lane prompter, and though never published it passed into the Larpent Collection (no. 372). The prologue, whose speaker represents himself as a pander to the Muses, stresses the low level of ambition involved in writing farces; the author is working at the "bottom of stairs." In the first act Andrews sketches the problem and develops it to the point where the forces of youth and love are ready to begin their counteroffensive. A foolish alderman has bequeathed his two daughters to the joint guardianship of "boisterous Capt. Bluster and his gourmandising neighbour the Justice" Swallow, who may either marry the girls themselves, or dispose of them as they wish. Already the play is deeply indebted to

112

Plautine and Shakespearean devices, and the plot as it thickens begins to resemble Mrs. Centlivre's *Bold Stroke for a Wife*. The guardians are archetypal blocking-figures, and the timelessness of the farce is emphasized by the vagueness of the setting: it could be any country, any time, any guardians, and any girls. Of course Harriet and Maria prefer two young men, Truman and Worthy, but since the girls dwell with their guardians access is a problem. The girls, however, have an ally in their aunt, the Widow Watchem, who knows of the girls' inclinations and of their guardians' coltish yearnings, and in scene 3 she acquaints the suitors with the need for action. At the end of the act the young men hire a roguish conjuror named Juggle to help them hoodwink the old ones and bring the lovers together. Juggle is an amalgam of the clever servant of Roman comedy, the medieval Vice, and the Elizabethan confidence man (Autolycus); it is he who generates most of the *vis comica*.

Most of the second act concerns the duping. Once bought, the charlatan Juggle proves a trustworthy accomplice; he nonplusses the guardians with necromantic double-talk and binds them in a magical hoop while the lovers elope. The scene is farcical in its disregard of reality, yet has clear precedents in *Friar Bacon* and *The Old Wives' Tale*. After a brief absence Juggle reappears as a lawyer who negotiates with the guardians and obtains their consent to legal releases of their wards in exchange for freedom from the hoop. Once at liberty, they gladly withdraw (i.e., are ejected), muttering vague threats. The newly married couples then return to voice suitable sentiments, and the curtain falls on Juggle's candid explanation that virtue will be easier now that his pockets are full.

By eighteenth-century standards for light comedy this farce was good entertainment, and probably would not have died so quickly if it had not been a benefit afterpiece (customarily given single performances): there was little demand either to repeat or to print such plays. It has no sentimental taint, except possibly the diction at certain predictable points, a convention common to all comedy at the time (see chapter three). The plot conforms to one of the time-honored patterns of Western comedy, the outwitting of the *senex amans,* which is the given in the comic equation. Andrews's variable consists of doubling the usual complement of characters and introducing magic as a resolvant, but it is the atmosphere of almost prehistoric antiquity, rather than the modest changes wrought in the pattern, that gives the play its appeal. There is a classical symmetry to the cast—two guardians, two girls, two suitors, one widow, and one rogue—and the plot: two acts, one old and one young, one threatening and one comical, one climbing in tension but falling in fortune, the other just the reverse. *The Conjuror* seems to mean more than it actually says, through its connection, however faint, with ancient forms and rituals.

An equally typical farce with a different kind of plot is William O'Brien's *Cross Purposes* (1772). The first scene satirizes the humors of modish London servants who affect the fashions of their masters. It is the only scene in the play that would tie it to contemporary London, and is irrelevant to the plot; the real story begins in scene 2. The Bevil brothers, both in debt, have decided upon marriage as the best course, and it is soon obvious to us (though not to them) that they are courting the same girl. We meet her quarrelling parents in scene 3. Grub and his wife disagree about the proper suitor for Emily, as they do about the investment business and everything else. The argument carries over into act 2, where it stops when they discover that both favor a "Mr. Bevil of Lincolnshire." And Emily, as it happens, is in love with a Mr. Bevil: a third brother, of course. Discrepancies appear in each account of him, however, and all begin to worry. By this time the spectator begins to anticipate the denouement with pleasure, partly because it is so foreseeable, partly because it is a mechanical parody of life. The inevitable, nearly simultaneous entrance of the three brothers into the room is visual farce at its purest, but then the piece has spent itself. The younger brothers bow out with no provision for their future, the parents acquiesce meekly, and the eldest Bevil closes with an awkward compliment to the royal family.

Cross Purposes shares with *The Conjuror* several characteristics common in eighteenth-century farce. They both focus on amusing incidents, seek broad comic effects, ignore probability, are deficient in characterization and satire, and repeat, without interest, the convention of saturnalia. Much like the *fabliaux*, they are funny stories well told. Both are clear-cut examples of farce, which did not prevent Arthur Murphy from ranking *Cross Purposes* "with the best of our little comedies" (*Life of Garrick*, 2:98).

By 1740 some dramatists were becoming dissatisfied with farce. Both Henry Fielding and James Miller wrote short plays that were really abbreviated comedies, but it was young David Garrick who made the self-conscious pronouncement that the afterpiece might aspire to comedy, and should be taken seriously. His prologue to *Miss in Her Teens* (1747) appears in retrospect a kind of manifesto of the English short comedy:

> Too long has Farce, neglecting Nature's Laws,
> Debas'd the Stage, and wrong'd the Comic Cause;
> To raise a laugh has been her sole Pretence,
> Tho' dearly purchas'd at the Price of Sense;
> This Child of Folly gain'd Increase with Time;
> Fit for the Place, succeeded Pantomime.
> . . . .
>
> More gen'rous Views inform our Author's Breast,
> From real life his Characters are drest;
> He seeks to trace the Passions of Mankind,
> And while he spares the Person, paints the Mind.

Garrick generally agrees with Reed as to the nature of farce, but insists that he is writing something different: more ambitious and important, more sensible and realistic, more universal. Yet *Miss in Her Teens* was usually billed as a farce, and is generally so listed today. Whether or not Garrick's prologue and play had any real influence, short comedy (on the French model) flourished in London from the late 1740s to the early 1770s, its chief practitioners (besides Garrick) being Arthur Murphy and George Colman. Charles Macklin and Sam Foote also contributed substantially to afterpiece comedy in those years, but if their work is examined carefully most of Macklin's proves to be farce and most of Foote's satire.

The short comedies are what the name implies: scaled-down replicas of full-length laughing comedies. Making due allowance for the truncated form, one finds in some of them genuine humor, forthright satire, character integrated with plot, and saturnalia that is not just a mechanical reflex. But owing both to the brevity of the form and to audiences' expectations, the tendency to farcicalize traditional comic themes and characters was strong; they were often treated perfunctorily, and the situations of laughing comedy were either sketched casually or overdrawn. There was also a freedom of construction allowed in the afterpiece not acceptable in regular comedy. Playwrights were not bound by any traditional rules for propriety of action or coherent endings, though an author such as Foote who carried this freedom too far would have his pretensions to comedy denied on this score. The freewheeling approach permitted in the afterpiece resulted both in a profitable emancipation and in formless, abortive sketches. For some writers the consequences of freedom were dire; Mrs. Gardner's *Matrimonial Advertisement,* she candidly admitted, could be termed

> dance, or Roundelay—
> Or what you will.—In faith it is no Play.
> No Aristotle's rules conduct my plot,
> For this good reason—that I knew 'em not.
>   (Larpent MS 435)

On the other hand *The Kept Mistress; or, The Mock Orators* (1756), an anonymous product of the same liberation, develops an unwieldy power rare in this age of restraint, and, as it also occupies the frontier between farce and short comedy, is worth a close look (Larpent MS 125). Garrick produced the play at Drury Lane on 10 April 1756, and possibly again in October, though as a benefit piece (for Richard Yates) it was not likely to be repeated. Title and subtitle refer to two quite different and rather loosely connected plays. *The Kept Mistress* might almost have been a Restoration comedy with its rakes, belle, and casual immorality. Belladue is the "kept mistress": kept at present by old Ringworm, the *senex amans,* but originally ruined by the rake Belton, with whom she still has an ambiguous attachment. Late in the play her father, Old Belladue, arrives, comes to an understanding with each of the principals, and oversees the marriage of Belladue to Belton. What is remarkable for the period is that this is accomplished without overemphasis on moral reform. No one attempts to revise personal histories, or waxes sentimental over the obviously fallible human natures involved. Old Belladue concludes that "it is sometimes better to know how to repair a fault, than not to have committed it" (II.iii)—*o felix culpa!*—but that is as moral as the play gets. And Ringworm, an unusually clearsighted *senex amans,* decides that he has been a fool and that he will "reform" by marrying someone his own age.

His intended is the widow Lovephrase, who belongs to the other plot. As her name implies, she is caught up in the "fangled fashion of oratory"; *The Mock Orators,* a descendant of Old Comedy, is designed to ridicule the contemporary craze for elocution.[8] The principal agent of satire on the rhetoricians is Harry, Belton's servant and the main link between the two plots. Harry is employed by Belton's friend Hempton as suitor-by-proxy to Miss Lovephrase, the widow's daughter, who can be approached only by humoring her mother's foible. Harry does this by posing as an oratory master; under cover of a verbal smokescreen he delivers Hempton's love letter and obtains a reply. This letter, however, is intercepted and detained by Belton, who decides that a blooming heiress would be just the thing for his depleted fortunes, and its discovery causes a duel between him and Hempton. Belton is disarmed but unhurt, and the brush with cold steel puts him in a reflective mood. Reflective, but not repentant:

> Had I resolution to repent—nay had I shame enough to be sorry for what I have done?—Sorry I am indeed, sorry that it did not succeed— and yet this Hempton's a brave fellow, and has behaved generously to me—what then, I am like other unfortunate schemers a rogue because I am unsuccessful. This I may thank Miss Bella for, now she's even with me. I began her ruin, she has completed mine, but I must own I have deserved it,—would her father but take her into favour again, I believe he would now have no objection to my marrying her, and as my circumstances are at present, indeed I should be glad of it. (II.iii)

This decision resolves the plot by matching up the "right" couples, and also atones for Belton's crime against Belladue's honor, yet the speech is pure Realpolitik and its moral relativism pure Horner. At a standard place for a sentimental recantation, Belton refuses to gloss over his motives: he sticks to facts. And his general reconciliation with the others is believable precisely because he stays off his knees and avoids sententiousness: "You'll excuse me at present Sir, if I don't express myself as I ought to do."

Harry is a curious character, the traditional clever servant with some additional baggage and a foot in each plot. The anonymous author seems to have wished to account for his cleverness in a rational fashion, so he represents him as a gentleman born and college-educated, who has fallen out with his father. But Harry's rather mysterious references to aspirations above his present estate are never adequately explained or used in the plot, so that they come to seem a structural flaw. He does, however, demonstrate his cleverness, and not just by announcing his discovery of the author's preordained plots. His verbal sparring with the

Widow Lovephrase, as he delivers Hempton's billet-doux to her daughter, is no mean display of elocutionist doubletalk:

> Madam, I am come to syllogize from the priori to the posteriori, and through the whole converging series of investigations—mathematically, physically and metaphysically, I am, Madam, while I have an idea existing your most succumbent, and incumbent preponderating humble servant.
>
> WIDOW: Sir, I am dialectically through the whole circumference of expression, your most obliged, though unknown to command.
>
> HARRY: Unknown, no, Madam, the Goddess of Fame with her cloud-covered head has expanded her voice in your favour, her speaking trumpet re-echoes with your renown, you are the paragon of phrase, and your lips bear the blossom of eloquence.
>
> WIDOW: Sir, I am essentially your humble servant.
>
> HARRY: But where's my pupil, Madam? Suffer the retina of my eye to be depicted by the attitude of her form lest the blossom of my wishes, that budded with expectancy, and have put forth the fruit of full hopes, should be blasted by her absence, and my curiosity wither in the famine of a disappointment.
>
> WIDOW: She shall wait on you, Sir, in the forming of an argument. (I.iv)

Harry is generally farcical, as is this whole scene, but another servant is used more seriously. Belladue's maid Betty has a comment on their hedonistic way of life that is a long way from the usual world of Georgian farce:

> Well, the world may call us ladies of pleasure if they please, but they never were more out in their judgments. Our lives are no more than a drunkard's dream, and hurry all our happiness. We are just as fit to have money as sailors, get it in as many dangers, and spend it in as much folly. And yet, though I blame my mistress, I am too much like her, for this love is the devil, and we unhappy women are sure to be troubled with the evil spirit. (I.ii)

One of the minor ways in which this play violates convention is that Betty and Harry are not matched when their mistress and master finally pair off.

The most notable trait of the unknown author is the number of his characters who have insight into themselves or a realistic perspective on their situations, not just at the end of the play but all along. The just-quoted speeches by Belton and Betty bear witness to this; Ringworm and Old Belladue also prove that they know themselves. Ringworm realizes perfectly well that Belladue is cheating him, that he is a "complete grey-headed coxcomb," and that his persistence is irrational. In his confrontation with Belladue's father he neither spares himself nor feigns a guilty conscience:

> Sir, I saw your daughter, if Miss Belladue is your daughter, in great distress. I took compassion on her.—I relieved her; 'tis true I expected a return.—I did not know who or of what family she was. A man of intrigue would have a fine time on't indeed if he must consult the Herald's Office before he addressed a fine woman. . . . As to infamy, I don't find myself a whit worse than my friend. As to your daughter, you shall have her immediately. (II.ii)

It is an unusually hard-nosed speech, and one in which I suspect we learn more of how these matters were really ordered in eighteenth-century London than in a hundred more typical comedies. After this conversation Old Belladue becomes a character of some depth; love for his daughter overcomes his sense of moral wrong, as he forgives and reaccepts her without rant.

The play's final scene is rough and disorderly, a bewildering farce with only tenuous connections to the rest of the comedy. Ringworm, Widow Lovephrase, and Harry have gone to the "Inquisition," which proves to be a public exposure and purge of professional elocutionists. Here three fantastic orators run wild, Harry appears as the "Inquisitor" to match their antics, and at last a press gang arrives to chase them and catches one of the orators. The Royal Navy thus finds the unanswerable argument against unchecked rhetoric. This mad scene, almost as Kafkaesque as it is Swiftian, is one of the few eighteenth-century realizations of the potential of farce as understood today. The abyss of chaos under the smooth surfaces of comedy and society is found and briefly plumbed, and the result is catharsis. After the chase Hempton and Miss Lovephrase turn up in the gallery and induce the Widow to accept their marriage, thus superficially connecting the farce with the comedy. Ringworm, remarking, "This comes of logic chopping," pays court to the Widow and is accepted. From the stage Harry announces that he is off to seek his fortune in the Navy, and the curtain falls on a patriotic song.

This unwieldy playlet possesses several features common to other mid-century afterpieces: it blends farce with comedy, relies a good deal on stage business without losing sight of traditional comic norms and functions, possesses abundant *vis comica* and prefers satire to romance. In other respects, however, it is far from typical. The degree to which sentiment and didacticism are skirted is unusual, as is the force, if not the depth, of several characters. *The Kept Mistress* is surprisingly tough-minded about morals and motives. The general level of playwriting—scene sequence, exposition, and dialogue—is high, despite some loose ends and a general air of unruliness. Whatever its shortcomings, the play is an interesting example of what afterpiece comedy could be, and sometimes was.

The Kept Mistress is basically a two-act Restoration comedy with farcical additions; Thomas Hull's *All in the Right* (1766, unpub., Larpent MS 255) is a timeless situation comedy of the Plautine type well represented among the afterpieces. But so schematized and mechanical is its structure that the finished product seems improbable, thus farcical. Old Harcourt simply comes out and tells us the bare bones of the situation: he wants his children, Harcourt and Isabella, to wed Lady Wishwould and Old Wentworth, both his own age, and therefore opposes their inclinations for younger spouses. Little does he know they have already married Julia and Belfield. When they reveal these matches at a final assembly, Old Harcourt discloses that he himself has married Charlotte, Lady Wishwould and Old Wentworth quickly agree to wed each other, and even the siblings' servants join the parade to the altar. Inevitably with these ingredients, *All in the Right* has a warmed-over taste. There were many Georgian afterpieces in this vein, and only the playwright's skill at handling formulae and introducing twists kept an entertaining ritual from becoming tired, dry repetition.

The social-problem comedy that began to appear in the 1770s had a counterpart in the afterpiece. The anonymous *Jehu* (1779, unpub.) attacks the aristocracy with the fervor of a *sans-culotte*, though it also satirizes the influence of foreign, especially French, manners in England. Lord Jehu, a cross between his biblical namesake and Squire Western, is suitor to Lucy Gules, a commoner despite her heraldic name. As a go-between Jehu employs one Whiffle, a kind of social pimp who does favors and dirty work for the nobility in return for casual familiarities in public. The plot turns on whether Lucy will chose Jehu or Fenton, her untitled but devoted admirer. While she wittily vacillates for two acts, the playwright concentrates on his real interests: the caricatures of Jehu and Whiffle, and satire, mainly on the nobility. The prevailing tone is one of disgust with a useless aristocracy and its parasites. When Lucy seems insensible of the honor of marrying above her station and Whiffle begins to lament her leveling tendencies, the girl shoots back: "One man *usefully* employ'd, is of more real value to his country than a legion of trifling danglers upon Quality" (Larpent MS 467). Jehu's abdication in order to pursue runaway horses eventually gives Lucy and Fenton their chance, and they are wed by an unsuspecting parson. Mrs. Gules is at first angry, but when she receives an insulting letter from Jehu blaming her for the mishap and giving up the courtship, she transfers her hostility and accepts the young couple. The saturnalian close recalls the piece to comedy, and it does have amusing aspects that are lost in a summary. Lucy is a witty coquette and Jehu is a humors character with a passion for horses; the conversation with Mrs. Gules in which he is talking about a filly and she about Lucy without either noticing the disjunction is a skillfully handled stretch of cross-purposes dialogue, as well as a scathing comment on Jehu's mentality. But here the traditional comic structure is mostly a vehicle for satire, of a different and more serious kind than that of *The Kept Mistress*.

The penchant for social satire was so strong in afterpiece comedy that it could outrun the comic purpose altogether and produce the genus known as dramatic satire. Often it is difficult to say just when we pass the ill-defined boundary between comedy and satire; the Old Comedy of Aristophancs, naturalized in England by Ben Jonson, was primarily satiric, and thus satire is as much a part of our comic tradition as saturnalia. But it is sometimes possible to distinguish the two impulses with illuminating results. Charles Macklin's *True-Born Irishman*, for example, satirizes English social climbers, and his *Will and No Will* attacks lawyers, so unequivocally that both plays failed onstage, yet both have the basic structure of farce. Similarly, Arthur Murphy hits out at excessive newsmongering in *The Upholsterer* and at the vapors of the wealthy bourgeois in *What We All Must Come To*, which borrows freely from Pope and Swift, but each play owes its main allegiance to laughing comedy.

In a play such as Paul Hiffernan's *The New Hippocrates*, (1761, unpub., Larpent MS 192), however, a different set of principles is operative, though it still has links to each genre. As the subtitle *A Lesson for Quacks* suggests, this afterpiece attacks the "unqualified meddlars in physick" who practice with only a "diploma of impudence." In scene 1 Planwell and Scribbledash set out to hoodwink the dupes of London (as Subtle and Face did in *The Alchemist*). Planwell, alias Hernando, the New Hippocrates, explains blandly that the systematic neglect of "merit" (especially his) creates an obligation to retaliate. The *élan vital* here is an old one in both comedy and satire: *O tempora! o mores!* The times are infamous and stupid and deserve anything I can give them. Scene 2 introduces Lady Brainsick, the fashionable hypochondriac who is vaguely nauseated by the robust health of her country cousin. Act 2 is devoted to a sustained exposé of medical quackery and its gullible victims. Scribbledash and Planwell surround their art with all the gibberish and hocus-pocus of *The Alchemist* and Chaucer's Canon's Yeoman's Tale. But Lady Brainsick's husband Sir John Resolute returns home unexpectedly, and violence is avoided only by his and Planwell's discovery that they are old schoolfellows. Sir John therefore contents himself with having Planwell and Scribbledash describe their methods before his lady, and hearing her express shame and repentance. Then he releases the quacks to continue their purges of the foolish rich, on the grounds that they are harmless and their victims deserve to be laughed at (though they are not likely to benefit from the experience if they learn as slowly as Lady Brainsick, whose first husband died of bad medicine). *The New Hippocrates* harks back to Old Comedy in its satire of quackery and to reform comedy in its handling of Lady Brainsick, but unlike most comedy it allows the villains to emerge unscathed and go on their way, in which respect it resembles nondramatic satire.

In the second quarter of the eighteenth century a few playwrights began to produce a dramatic equivalent of the Augustan satire for which the period is best known; the dramatic satire proper was more directly influenced by the Scriblerus Club than by anything in the comic tradition. John Gay's *The Beggar's Opera* (1728) was the first of any importance, and Henry Fielding, who wrote a number of dramatic satires in the next nine years, liked to style himself "H. Scriblerus Secundus." Generally these pieces were tamer and less political after the Licensing Act—or else they were not licensed—and as a rule they were very short, usually one act. Fielding's *The Author's Farce* (1729) begot Garrick's *Lethe* (1740), one of the purest and most popular examples of the type, with 155 performances at Drury Lane in the thirty years that Garrick managed the theater.[9] The author's conceit is that once a year, on the anniversary of Proserpine's rape, Pluto allows mortals into Hades to consult with Aesop (the subtitle is *Esop in the Shades*) and drink of Lethe. The structure follows naturally: an episodic series of visits by self-satirizing humors types to the bemused Aesop, who learns about current London manners and offers wry comments. The dialogue is natural, fast-paced, and witty, while the cause of morality is paid lip-service by Aesop's terse closing admonition to "forget Vice." This concoction proved extremely agreeable to audiences, and even spawned an anonymous sequel, *The Anniversary* (1758, unpub., Larpent MS 144). Like *The Dunciad*, *Lethe* could be considered a fire—a very tepid one, being lit by Garrick—into which new fuel must be fed almost constantly; the play's satiric targets were all local, temporary, and hence evanescent. Garrick, with help from other actors and actresses, was kept busy with revisions. In 1748 the play had to be resubmitted to the Licenser for inspection, requiring a new Larpent manuscript to indicate accumulated changes. By the sixth edition in 1768 in additional character had appeared. The seventh edition (1774) lists an old man, a fine gentleman, Mr. Bowman and Lord Chalkstone, Mr. and Mrs. Tatoo, a Frenchman, and Mr. and Mrs. Riot as stage characters, in addition to a poet and a tailor who are by now "omitted in the Representation." *Lethe* evolved continually, and its success encouraged Garrick to other satiric efforts, such as *Lilliput* (1756), an expansion of the Lady Flimnap episode in Book 1 of *Gulliver's Travels*. Structurally both plays are anticomic: their denouements, contenting themselves with satiric exposure, leave the major characters steeped in their vices or follies. The same author's *Male Coquette* (1757), on the other hand, is related to the comic tradition by its ejection of Daffodil (the title character) to make way for the match between Tukely and Sophia.

Perhaps encouraged by the success of *Lethe*, John Kelly wrote a satirical farce called *The Levee* (1741) that was accepted at Drury Lane but denied a license, whereupon Kelly published it. *The Levee* is written in excellent prose for plays of this type and period, but obviously Kelly discovered the bounds of the censor's political toleration. The first act, especially, lashes out at rich, dishonest lords and their sycophantic levees, the middle-class gentry who ape the aristocracy by snubbing servants, and the servants themselves, who take out their social frustrations by hissing actors and damning plays. The second act declines, but *The Levee* is an obvious effort to pick up where Fielding had left off.

One of the more celebrated dramatic satires, and in some respects the most important example of the genre, was Sam Foote's *Piety in Pattens* (1773), which is discussed more fully in the next chapter. Coming at a time when Kelly and Cumberland had given sentimental comedy a certain vogue, *Piety* used puppets to satirize the type, and was said to have succeeded in rendering sentiment ridiculous. Foote simply inserted stupid but conventionally benevolent characters into a plot closely resembling that of Richardson's *Pamela* and let events take their course. Amid a welter of bathetic sentiments Polly (Pamela) clings to "vartue" until Squire Thirdle proposes marriage. Polly is so "sensible" of obligations to Thomas the butler that she refuses the Squire, however, and offers herself to Thomas. But he and the Squire are equally magnanimous, and the combined "delicacy" of the three principals at last prevents any comic union, diverting the play from comedy to satire. *Piety in Pattens* is the theatrical counterpart of *Shamela,* and may have dealt the sentimentalists a more damaging blow than the better-known comedies of Goldsmith and Sheridan.

Dramatic satires per se were not numerous in this period, but the satirical urge of which they were the extreme expression was almost ubiquitous in comedy, forming the hardest edge of Georgian theater. The bulk of Foote's and of Sheridan's work, for example, is heavily satiric, while Macklin had a sharp eye for certain character-types. Satire is by nature unsentimental, and eighteenth-century satirical humor was particularly hostile to sentimentalism because of its currency in the literature of the day and its periodic fads onstage. Attempts to pin the "sentimental" label on Georgian comedy must come to terms with its widespread use of satire in a more satisfactory manner than has yet been done, taking into account Sherbo's psychological and emotional definition of sentimental comedy. Just as we question the overall sentimentality of any single comedy that indulges substantially in humor and bawdry, so we need to ask whether a comic theater so given to satirical thrusts can validly be characterized as sentimental. However it stands up elsewhere, that description makes no sense when applied to the afterpiece.

PART IV
Comic Authors

The major comic playwrights of the Garrick era fall naturally into two groups, which we may loosely call "amateur" and "professional." The amateur dramatists, those who made their careers mostly outside the theater, subdivide again. On one side stand Cumberland, Kelly, Whitehead, Mrs. Griffith, Mrs. Sheridan, and Edward Moore, all somewhat sentimentally inclined; on the other are the more traditionally comic writers discussed in chapter eight: Murphy, Goldsmith, and Sheridan. Despite the numerical imbalance, this second group (of whom the first and last were sometimes quite professional) gave us the outstanding examples of comedy in the century. But among the actor-manager playwrights, the true professionals, there was agreement amounting to guild solidarity. Their ranks contain no sentimentalists—tacticians and compromisers, but not senti- mentalists—though the quality of their plays generally runs well below that of the amateurs' best efforts. Pressed for time, harried by authors and the need for box-office success, the professionals favored short forms solidly within the estimated range of audience interest and tolerance. They were artisans, not artists, and their plays, while very much of their time and thus popular, were also only of their time, and thus transient.

Reading the comedies of Goldsmith and Sheridan, and then the work of the professional dramatists of the forties, fifties, and sixties, however, one encounters the same flower-and-soil relationship as between Shakespeare and earlier Elizabethan drama. The developments were quite similar, and certainly many comedies of the eighteenth century are as deserving of attention, as enlightening about their final product, as Gorboduc *or* Gammer Gurton's Needle, *plays that we read less for themselves than for the Shakespearean milieu they represent or herald. Goldsmith and Sheridan also grew out of the comedy of their own age, as a full study of their sources will show; they can be read in the context of Georgian comedy with no sense of dislocation, though the obscurity into which those plays have fallen and their general disrepute tend to make us minimize any major writer's debts to them. After considering the most important of the second-rank writers, the gifted professionals, we will be better able to see how the finest playwrights of the age looked in their native habitat.*

We That Live to Please

Through the peculiar blight which has fallen on late eighteenth-century dramatic literature, Goldsmith and Sheridan have tended to be considered the sole opponents of the sentimental play. It is as if they, and they alone, stemmed the torrent of a weeping age and taught men how to laugh once more. As a matter of fact they were but two among a large number of others who passed on to the nineteenth century the traditions of the comedy of earlier times. In dealing with their work, therefore, the background against which they ought to stand relieved should ever be borne in mind.

—Allardyce Nicoll, *A History of Later Eighteenth Century Drama*

Whether or not a "large number" of dramatists were writing traditional comedy in the mid–eighteenth century, they were numerous enough to require selectivity here. Robert Dodsley and James Miller wrote some interesting plays near the beginning of this period, some of which have been briefly mentioned. Both Kitty Clive and Isaac Bickerstaffe made modest contributions to Georgian comedy, two of James Townley's three farces are worth a second look, and Thomas Hull was a better-than-average actor-writer. Dramatists of the indispensable third rank such as William Kenrick and Paul Hiffernan are only dim faces in the back row of these chapters. With world enough and time such playwrights might well have been included, yet the four chosen for discussion were almost without question the most successful and important of the "background" authors.

If our interest in the professionals is their fidelity or infidelity to the comic tradition they inherited and its nature as interpreted and transmitted by them, then their overwhelming preference for the short forms is significant. Of the original productions of these four authors, forty-eight are in three acts or less, while only eight are mainpieces. No such penchant existed among the sentimentalists; Cumberland and Kelly each wrote a third-rate sentimental farce, and Whitehead, one good one (*A Trip to Scotland*). The "amateur" writers of traditional comedy, especially Murphy, were more interested in the afterpiece than that, but not as much as the professionals. Their predilection for the *petite pièce* is evidence both of their allegiance to laughter and of the frenzied pace of their lives, in which brevity must have seemed a necessary virtue. Six-sevenths of their creative energies is a very high collective proportion to expend on a genre whose main characteristic was broad humor and whose usual fate was quick obscurity. The professionals wrote, in the main, without much thought of posterity, yet work of this kind can often tell us more about its day than a higher and more long-lived art. In sketches such as Foote's and Colman's we find the dramatic counterpart of Hogarth's engravings; *The Oxonian in Town* and *The Commissary* are brief chronicles of their time. Furthermore, we have here a clue that traditional comedy often resided in ephemera during this period, and that the effort of recovery will therefore lead to seldom-frequented recesses.

On the other hand, afterpiece-writing was a lucrative and relatively easy, hence alluring, proposition, and success of course encouraged a writer to neglect full-length comedy, a more exacting labor. Nor would the influence of the farces cease when a dramatist did essay a major comedy. The vitality of afterpiece comedies encouraged authors to incorporate—and audiences to accept—their tone, their devices, and their kind of action in five-act laughing comedies, a transfer that tended to cheapen the mainpieces. In the best of the afterpieces a comic tradition still lives, but it has been modified by the pressures of the form, and like all accommodations this one had its price. A Spenserian allegorist might envision Farce sheltering Comedy from the cajolery of Sentiment—on the condition that Comedy entrust its mind and soul to Sir Farce. Yet this development apparently did not alarm the professionals: for all their staunch defense of laughter, the actor-manager playwrights seem to have been generally unconcerned with the atrophy of the five-act comedy and the crumbling integrity of the comic genre. Perhaps that concern was a luxury they could not afford.

CHARLES MACKLIN (1699?–1797)

The alpha and omega of this group was the indestructible Charles Macklin, a figure of near-mythic proportions who was active in the theater long before as well as long after the other three. He was acting in Bristol and London around 1725, knew Cibber and Quin, appeared with Fielding's company at the Haymarket, and befriended young David Garrick in the days of Garrick's obscurity. It was Macklin as much as Garrick who made the 1740–41 season a watershed between the declamatory and natural styles of acting in London. In the early eighteenth century Shylock was played farcically, along the lines of Pantalone in the commedia; Macklin's more realistic approach is said to have made Pope exclaim, "This is the Jew / That Shakespeare drew" (Appleton, pp. 43–45). Macklin also introduced Samuel Foote to the stage. Following his first "retirement" in 1752 he lectured on drama and oratory (harassed by Foote), gave acting lessons, and made periodic returns to act in his own and others' plays until failing memory forced him into genuine retirement in 1789, a decade after Garrick and Foote had retired and died. Even then he was a figure to be reckoned with, stalking around Covent Garden, haunting the literary clubs—where he aroused both amusement and respect—and the theaters, where, being hard of hearing, he was apt to startle actors by roaring suddenly, "Speak up, sir! We can't hear you." Between his teaching, his own plays, and the force of his personality, the rough-edged Irishman influenced British theater from the days of the ballad opera to the dawn of melodrama.

Eight of Macklin's ten plays were comic; four of these were written in the half-dozen years preceding his 1752 retirement, and none was notably successful. *A Will and No Will; or, A Bone for the Lawyers* (1746) was the first and probably the best of this group. This two-act farce, condensed from Regnard's five-act *Le Legataire universel*, has a long dramatic "prologue by the Pit" that employs a modified rehearsal format to amuse the audience with a representation of itself. A few actors onstage, representing some denizens of the pit, wait impatiently for the farce to begin and speculate about a rumor that the prologue will be by the pit. Clearly this novelty was "given out" to lure an audience to Mrs. Macklin's benefit, yet it also has the effect of calling into question both temporal sequence and levels of reality: at the end one member of the group says that now they will see what in fact we have just seen, and then announces "so ends the prologue." Macklin was always fond of vanishing mirror-images and similar involutions, and of characters like Snarlewit, in whom truth and falsehood are curiously compounded. Snarlewit is both an emulous rival of Macklin—"Psha! A parcel of stuff!"—and the one man who knows the true nature of the piece and can thus answer anticipated criticisms of it. As in much Augustan satire, it is the reader or spectator who must supply the common and moral sense that will winnow the chaff from the grain.

The plot of the farce is archetypal, but Macklin's treatment is fresh and energetic. His two clever servants, Shark and Lucy, smoothly introduce the problem: rich old Sir Isaac Skinflint is about to die intestate, to the dismay of his needy nephew Bellair, and even if he makes a will he may name some country cousins joint heirs with our hero. Worse still, he has marital designs on fresh young Harriet, who is Bellair's inamorata. A counterattack by wit and youth quickly takes shape. Harriet amusingly convinces Sir Isaac she would kill him in bed, one way or the other, while Shark impersonates the rural relations so boorishly that they are cut out of the will. The strain of these encounters throws Skinflint into an apparently mortal fit, but Shark saves the day by impersonating the old miser before the lawyers and making an irrevocable will favorable to Bellair—with some goodly morsels for Lucy and himself. When Isaac revives, the principals brazen it out and emerge with what they wanted, though the old man threatens litigation. By turns funny, shocking, and licentious, but never prurient, *A Will* contains some good stage comedy: Harriet's terrorism of Sir Isaac and Shark's three impersonations. The manufacture of laughs out of the foolish old man's death-like trance may be (and may have been) too strong for some, but Macklin does emerge in the play as one of the few eighteenth-century playwrights whose approach to comedy was hard-nosed and unsentimental from prologue to epilogue.

Macklin's second farce, *The New Play Criticiz'd; or, The Plague of Envy* (1747), mentioned earlier, was a *pièce d'occasion* in response to the tremendous success of Benjamin Hoadly's *The Suspicious Husband* earlier the same season. A mildly satirical sketch of attitudes toward the popular comedy and drama in general is loosely embedded in a conventional romance plot, mainly by having Canker, an unsuccessful playwright, serve both as chief critic of *The Suspicious Husband* and as an unacceptable suitor blocking the love-match of Harriet and Heartly. It is Canker who is plagued with envy of Hoadly, although the poets Plagiary and Grubwit agree with him that the play is "mere incident . . . a pantomime, a thing stuffed with escapes, pursuits, ladders of ropes and scenes in the dark; all a parcel of pantomimical finesses such as you see every night in Rich's entertainments. Ranger is really the Harlequin and Mr. Strictland Col-ombine's husband" (Larpent MS 64). Lady Critic, on the other hand, Harriet's mother and formerly a supporter of Canker's suit, has a high opinion of the play. Harriet and Heartly capitalize on this disagreement so that he is cast from favor, and Harriet even induces Canker to renounce her by insisting that he attend and praise *The Suspicious Husband* as a token of his love. Macklin thus adapts the traditional comic furniture to the purposes of theatrical satire.

The exact direction of that satire, however, is left in shadow; at the end one is unsure whether *The Suspicious Husband* or its detractors have been hit harder. Macklin adroitly balances praise and blame, undercutting both at different times. Most of the play's supporters are fools, but all of its opponents are knaves. Lady Critic and Sir Patrick Bashful alienate us by preferring Hoadly's "regularity" to Shakespeare's "incorrectness"; Canker offends by his pedantry used as a cloak for ill-nature. Like Snarlewit in the prologue to *A Will*, he sometimes hits the mark with his strictures, and one seems to hear Macklin's voice. But most of the time Macklin is cultivating the audience through Heartly's reasonable, bal-anced observations (as Heartly is cultivating Lady Critic by his favorable attitude towards the play), and he finally leaves Heartly and the pro-Hoadly forces in possession of the field, though with scarcely an argu-ment left intact. Clearly the playwright was too shrewd to oppose the public's choice openly if he disagreed with it.

The farce concludes with another involution reminiscent of the pro-logue to *A Will*. Heartly suggests that Lady Critic write up the events of the last hour into a farce called *The New Play Criticized*, and that she have it end with her giving Harriet to himself. Dazzled by his suavity, she agrees, and all the principals go off to meet Dr. Hoadly. Macklin persistently toyed with the idea that his stage was really a drawing room full of theatrically-minded characters, or, to put it another way, that his audi-ence was onstage.

Macklin's third farce, *The Club of Fortune-Hunters; or, The Widow Bewitched* (1748), is something of an embarrassment. William Appleton describes it as a negligible though "laughing" play on the theme of the biter bit (p. 87), and Robert R. Findlay calls it "even more caustic" than *A Will* and *New Play*.[1] But J. O. Bartley has argued that the play *The Fortune-Hunters* published in London in 1750 is demonstrably not Macklin's. Indeed, Bartley insists that Macklin's farce was not printed and does not exist in manuscript.[2] Until these objections are answered and the differences among Macklin scholars resolved *The Club* will remain a bibliographic puzzle.

Covent Garden Theatre; or, Pasquin Turned Drawcansir (1752: ed. Jean Kern for the Augustan Reprint Society) was intended as a Fieldingesque satire of the rehearsal type; the title evidently alludes to both the novelist's burlesque *Covent Garden Tragedy* (1732) and to his *Covent Garden Journal*. It is possible that Fielding himself had a hand in it (Findlay, p. 402). Despite these props the play—nearly plotless and heavily censored—was a failure, and Macklin, discouraged by his inability to catch the public's fancy in four tries, quit the theater to teach oratory and keep a tavern. When he decided to return to playwriting after seven bumpy years, he immediately scored his first and most lasting success. *Love à la Mode* (1759) was so popular that it was Macklin's main source of income in the last forty years of his life (Appleton, p. 122), and Sir Archy Macsarcasm became his most celebrated role, at least until *The Man of the World* twenty-two years later.

The farce as it stands has two acts, though it is said to have been condensed from five on the advice of Arthur Murphy (Bartley, p. 25). Various other debts have been proposed—to Fielding, to Garrick, to Thomas Sheridan, one may as well add to Shakespeare—but the question of influence is relatively superficial here; in this play Macklin touches certain archetypes of comic theme and structure which have served a number of comic writers. The plot is classic in its simplicity and symmetry: Charlotte's four suitors are consecutively exhibited and tested. The first three appear during act 1, "an hour before dinner" in the London house of Sir Theodore Goodchild. His ward Charlotte is solicited first by Mordecai, a Jewish beau with a foppish humor, then by Sir Archy Macsarcasm, with his proud humor and waspish tongue, and finally by Sir Callaghan O'Brallaghan the military man. As each is displayed he deprecates the others, which brings about a brief sword-fight between the Scot and the Irishman that demonstrates the latter's good temper. O'Brallaghan, more Othello than Falstaff, comes off the best of the three, Mordecai the worst. The part of Macsarcasm, one of Macklin's own favorites, gave free rein to his acidulous temperament and talent for dialect—not, of course, his own (O'Brallaghan, suspiciously enough, speaks remarkably standard English).

Act 2 opens with the arrival of suitor number four, the horsey Squire Groom. His account of the York race is ample demonstration of Macklin's ear for colloquial speech.

> It lay between Dick Riot and me. We were neck and neck, madam, for three mile, as hard as we could lay leg to ground—made running every inch—but at the first loose I felt for him, found I had the foot—knew my bottom—pulled up—pretended to dig and cut—all fudge, all fudge, my dear—gave the signal to pond, to lay it on thick—had the whip hand all the way—lay with my nose in his flank, under the wind—thus, (*Here Squire Groom imitates all the postures and motions of a rider in a severe struggle to win his match*) snug, snug, my dear, quite in hand—while Riot was digging and lapping right and left—but it would not do, my dear, against foot, bottom and head; so within a hundred yards of the distance post, poor Dick knocked up stiff as a turnpike, and left me to canter in by myself, madam, and to touch them all round—for I took all the odds, split me! Ha? wasn't I right? ha? took the odds! Aye, aye, took all the odds, my dear.
>
> (Bartley, p. 67)

The set piece of the act has O'Brallaghan courting Charlotte with a song while the others hide and eavesdrop *à la Twelfth Night*. After the spies depart, Charlotte requests her Irish gallant to engage to give up the army for her if they marry; when he refuses (in patriotic speech), they are apparently finished. Then Sir Theodore and Charlotte spring their trap, acting a charade of their financial ruin. All the suitors quickly back down except Sir Callaghan, whereupon Sir Theodore blesses the union and announces that the fortune is intact. The outwitted and discredited suitors withdraw, and O'Brallaghan concludes that "the whole business is something like the catastrophe of a stage play." Besides betraying its author's national origins, *Love à la Mode* purveyed traditional laughing comedy of the humors variety and proved eminently actable.[3] Neither ambitious nor original, it succeeded and succeeds very well within the limited and familiar bounds Macklin chose.

The School for Husbands (1761, produced as *The Married Libertine*) has usually been dismissed as a boring sentimental flop, but it deserves a second look. In the first place it was not a failure: it ran nine nights against personal and political opposition by Scots who had been offended by Sir Archy Macsarcasm. Second, it is misleading to label *School* "a sentimental comedy"; it is a reform play which uses some sentimental devices without adopting the sentimental style (Bartley, p. 25). As for the charge of boredom, *School* is doubtless too long by a couple of acts—there are signs of padding from act 3 on, mainly in the form of sententious moralizing—and one "H.F." of the Middle Temple wrote Macklin an interesting letter that suggested cutting out some passages of turbid dialogue (such as Angelica's in act 4) and concentrating on comic action. We do know that various cuts were made after the first night; unfortunately they have not survived, though a modern director could make an intelligent guess at them.

The situation at the opening curtain is reminiscent of that in Cibber's *Love's Last Shift:* Lady Belville chafes at home while her husband errs. She and Townley, his nephew, agree that action is necessary both as revenge for his illicit conquests and as instruction that may yet reclaim him. Townley articulates the *élan* of reform comedy: "I would not expose him; but if by a private shame we can make a friend reflect, and see a folly that injures his fame and fortune, I think it is the greatest service we can do him" (I.i, Bartley, p. 131). But from this familiar course Macklin launches out on his own. A houseful of conniving females—Lady Belville, Harriet, and Angelica—gathers to stage an elaborate farce whose purpose is to humiliate and dissect Lord Belville. Anticipating John Fowles's *Magus,* they subject the aging rake to their own "God-game," which they carry to such destructive lengths that our early dislike of the man is almost turned to sympathy. As it develops the comedy stresses the consequent gulling of Belville, rather than the emotion attendant upon his reform; the scene in act 3 where the peer is duped and frightened witless has the striking verisimilitude characteristic of Macklin's best writing. His single plot moves on at a good clip and develops a powerful centripetal quality as it hurries toward a foreseen but desired conclusion, where Macklin's and Belville's sins overtake them. Fear seems psychologically inadequate as a motive for renewed love and lasting reform in a man "infatuated with the itch of intrigue," but the plot requires a resolution, and Macklin, after all the "probing to the quick," is content with a conversion under duress.

When the plot is finally exposed, Macklin gives it the kind of twist we have come to expect from him. Harriet says: "Every person you have seen to-night in this house . . . have been as rank cheats as yourself. We have all been acting a sort of comedy at your expence" (p. 191). The remark, being equally true of the real and the feigned stage action, tends to dissolve the proscenium of suspended disbelief that customarily separates players and audience. Stage and society momentarily become one, an effect more ritualistic than theatrical, and rarely achieved in the eighteenth century outside of Macklin's work.

The True-Born Irishman was first performed in Dublin in 1762, and, as the title suggests, is a celebration of the Irish spirit that pleased audiences there. It is also virulently anti-English; when revived in Dublin in 1910 the play was hailed as "surprisingly up to date" and "quite topical of the moment" (Bartley, p. 81). For himself Macklin wrote the part of Murrough O'Dogherty, a reasonable nationalist, and an even more favorable portrayal of *homo Hibernicus* than Sir Callaghan O'Brallaghan at a time when the conventional stage Irishman was a fool. The plot concerns the troubles O'Dogherty has with his young wife after she returns from the coronation of George III with a bad case of Anglophilia: she loathes everything Irish, speaks mincingly, insists on being known as "Diggerty," lusts for a title and cultivates London vices and vapors. Eventually her husband, brother, and servant combine to reform her (much too cursorily) and to expose the hypocrisies of her pretty English beau. The flaw is that the central device in shaming her—the sexual presumption of Beau Mushroom—does not arise entirely from her own conduct, but has been systematically encouraged by her husband, so that we cannot see how she would have reacted if left to herself. Basically the piece exists to satirize those Irish who ape English manners, and, to a lesser extent, to attack the source of the corruption as well.

Just how and why Macklin thought he could stage this play in London is not clear; it was a quixotic gesture, as if Macklin's sense of theatrical realities had for once failed him. He did make some alterations—an occasional prologue, a new and quite lively opening scene in the streets of Dublin, a partial shift of satiric fire from England to France, and a new

135

title, *The Irish Fine Lady*—that were shrewd as far as they went. The London title changes the focus to Mrs. O'Dogherty, another Irish fool, the geographical references are Anglicized, and a description of the coronation is added as a crowd-pleaser. One might also imagine that the audience would have found Macklin's equation—Ireland is to England as England is to France—thought-provoking, at least. But he did not remove, for example, Mrs. O'Dogherty's affected London accent, and too much else that was offensive remained in *The Irish Fine Lady*. This most outspokenly Irish of Macklin's plays was withdrawn after a single performance at Covent Garden in November 1767.[4]

The same pattern was repeated, up to a point, in the development of *The Man of the World*, Macklin's last and by consensus his best comedy. The earliest version, in three acts, was *The True-Born Scotsman*, which was well received in Dublin in 1764. In this case the title was ironic—the "true-born" Scot is a corrupt political manager—and while the anti-Scots bias was an asset in Dublin, and would not have hurt the play much in London at this time, it did make licensing in England a problem. Macklin's first try, in 1770, was "thought unfit to be licensed," and his second was likewise rejected in 1779 as dangerously incendiary. That the rejection was due more to the inflamed political atmosphere of the time than to anything in the play itself is shown by the fact that a slightly altered third revision was approved in 1781.[5] When *The Man of the World* did finally open in London, with the eighty-two-year-old Macklin in the lead role, it enjoyed a great success, and has had its share of revivals.

The plot possesses a certain amount of high seriousness. At the house of Sir Pertinax Macsycophant near London, we find the owner on the eve of a great stroke: marrying his son Egerton to Lady Rodolpha Lumbercourt, thus completing a twenty-five-year scramble onto Lord Lumbercourt's shoulders in order to place his son in the Ministry. But there is an obstacle: Egerton loves Constantia, the ward of Lady Macsycophant. Sir Pertinax is enraged at his son's independence and at his liberal politics; and he has already disinherited his other son, Sandy, for patriotic and reformist leanings. In act 3, when Egerton and Lady Rodolpha finally confer, each confesses alienated affections (she loves Sandy!), so they agree to oppose their fathers. Egerton duly informs his father that the match is off, but then Betty Hint the maid brings Egerton an apparent billet-doux from Constantia to one "Melville" that momentarily throws all into confusion. Fortunately Melville turns out to be the long-lost father of the "orphan" Constantia, and Egerton promptly marries her. Sir Pertinax disinherits them and breaks with his wife for supporting the match, but accomplishes his design by marrying Sandy to Lady Rodolpha. Luckily Egerton's fortune is independent.

The Man of the World has been described both as a sentimental comedy and as ranking behind only *The Beaux' Stratagem, She Stoops to Conquer,* and *The School for Scandal* in its age. The difficulty is that the play defies generic labels and transcends such Georgian categories as "laughing" and "sentimental." There is, indeed, little or no humor, and the moral sententiousness of Egerton and Constantia is somewhat reminiscent of Steele's followers. But one encounters little benevolist sentiment either, and reform is conspicuous by its absence: Sir Pertinax remains unregenerate and unscrupulous. There is also a great deal of obviously sincere satire on the political venality of the period that alarmed the Examiner by its directness. Macsycophant's "principles" and his burr point directly at Butite ministers and indict the court by association. As much satire as comedy, the play might seem another throwback to Fielding, except that it lacks his energetic high spirits, and possesses an almost Victorian earnestness that foreshadows the serious dramas of the middle of the next century. In either case *The Man of the World* has little in common with the "artificial comedy," whether Restoration or Georgian. Even the traditional happy ending is compromised by Macsycophant's obduracy and unchecked power: he is not so much ejected as allowed to continue at large, a threatening figure of worldly evil. In fact the weakest aspect of the play—the one in which it most closely resembles melodrama—is that Sir Pertinax is too completely its villain (though he is sometimes right), Egerton too virtuously its patriotic hero. Macsycophant's exit line, "My vengeance leeght upon ye aw together," recalls Malvolio's, but Macklin has allowed his protagonist to become flat, playing Mr. Worldly-Wise to Egerton's Christian. It is chiefly this flaw, and stretches of insipid dialogue, that relegate the play to the second rank of major comedies.

If Macklin's best comedy does not quite make the inner circle, he was a talented playwright nonetheless, a practitioner of the comic tradition during its most attenuated days as well as a formidable dramatic satirist. Probably we should not judge him on *The Man of the World,* his "big" work; some of his less ambitious plays are much more nearly perfect of their kind. Macklin, like other writers of his day, could not rid himself of the itch to write a full-length comedy, but when he limited his material, as in *A Will and No Will* and *Love à la Mode*, he was generally in better control and more successful with his audience. In the short plays he has a distinctly individual style: often dark, as Findlay says, sometimes involuted, almost always convincingly colloquial. Macklin's best writing possesses the energy and realism to "bounce" his audience into acceptance of the action, in E. M. Forster's phrase: the quality that has been called *enargeia*. He could take a conventional scene, as of raking and exposure in *The School for Husbands*, or social-climbing in *The True-Born Irishman*, and give it life and freshness. If Macklin's legacy to comedy is modest, it is also estimable.

DAVID GARRICK (1717–1779)

In the annals of eighteenth-century theater, no name is more eminent than that of David Garrick, actor extraordinary and manager of Drury Lane for thirty years. His contemporaries were extravagant in their praises. The wit Bonnel Thornton compared his voice to a double-keyed harpsichord, a deaf admirer found his face "a language," and William Whitehead, the Poet Laureate, exclaimed of his managership, "A nation's taste depends on you." To all he was "the English [or "the little"] Roscius." When Garrick finally ended his famous series of farewell appearances in 1776 with a performance of *The Wonder*, a weeping audience broke all precedent by refusing the afterpiece, and the adulation continued after his death. George Colman, Hannah Cowley, John Pinkerton, and Arthur Murphy were among the later eighteenth-century writers who testified to his support of legitimate drama and credited him with having staved off the deluge of theatrical "junk" that swamped the stage after his departure. Murphy, who did as much as anyone to establish his reputation, averred that after the contemptible age of Cibber "dramatic poetry retrieved its honour" with Garrick.

Until about 1960 it was rare to find dissenters from Murphy's view, but the boom in Georgian theatrical scholarship of the past twenty years has tarnished Garrick's image considerably. Kalman Burnim, in 1961, argued that Garrick's concessions to public taste led to an increase in spectacles or "raree shews."[6] Noting that throughout his career, especially after his Grand Tour (1763–65) and the arrival of de Loutherbourg (1771), Garrick was increasingly preoccupied with scenery, Burnim discovered that he actually spent more on lights, scenes, and costumes than Covent Garden, which was notorious for extravaganzas (p. 83). In 1962, George Winchester Stone, Jr., concluded that Garrick equalled the infamous John Rich in attentiveness to scenes and machines (*The London Stage*, pt. 4, 1:cxix). Leo Hughes described Garrick's attitude towards spectacle as "exasperatingly ambivalent," and his attempt to champion legitimate drama versus pantomime as a failure (*Drama's Patrons*, p. 108). And Cecil Price has pointed out that many of the complaints about the difficulty of getting new plays acted at the time were directed at Garrick (*Theatre*, pp. 151–54).

But if for the moment Garrick's managership is under a cloud, his work as an actor, a director, and an arbiter of public taste still has more substance than do his own plays. Only about half of his dramatic output is both original and "legitimate," the remainder being alterations and spectacles. Most of his comedies and farces are unexciting and highly derivative, though generally clever and "stagey," and even his most popular plays now seem rather pallid. With certain reservations we can call Garrick an upholder of the laughing tradition in comedy, but there was nothing staunch or clear-cut about his position. George Kahrl describes him as "caught . . . between his preference for the older comedy and high tragedy and the current fashion for sentimentalism in both."[7] The only hard edge in his work was a penchant for satire of the Horatian variety: throughout his career he satirized, chiefly, manners, sentimentalism, and his audiences, whose tendency to annoy him was thus sublimated and returned, under the guise of a general satirical purpose.

In this predilection for topical satire Garrick was most in tune with the literary temper of his times. When he took his famous walk with Dr. Johnson from Lichfield up to London in 1737, already stage-struck, Pope was working on *The Dunciad*, Swift's major works were current, *The Beggar's Opera* was still a great favorite, and Fielding's political satires at the Haymarket were just then being suppressed. In this atmosphere it is not surprising that Garrick's first play, *Lethe; or, Esop in the Shades* (discussed in chapter six), was a dramatic satire of a distinctly Fieldingesque hue. Produced in 1740 as Garrick was beginning to act (but not published until 1749), the play's early versions "contain episodes which form a sequel" to Fielding's *An Old Man Taught Wisdom; or, The Virgin Unmasked*[8]; *Lethe* also resembles his *Author's Farce* and *Eurydice* in some respects. The twenty-three-year-old Garrick had written a popular play, albeit of only one act, on his first try, and it held a place in the repertoire throughout his career.

The year of Garrick's sensational debut in *Richard III* also witnessed the production of his second play, a two-act comedy called *The Lying Valet* (1741). More ambitious than his first, it seems to be that rare bird, a sentimental afterpiece—and a popular one at that—but it raises nice problems of interpretation. Sentimental clichés are presented so baldly as to suggest either a gross lapse of taste or a parody of sentimental comedy; it is easy to imagine a modern director playing it as a subtle spoof of the genre. The fact that Garrick never wrote in quite this vein again compounds the difficulty of ascertaining what he wanted to do with sentimental materials here (*The Guardian* [1759] being a much more obvious case of self-satirizing sentimentalists).

The plot is reminiscent of *The Beaux' Stratagem*. Aimwell becomes Gayless, a needy gentleman who has been "cut off" by his father for "extravagance." His Archer is Sharp, a witty valet in the Roman tradition. Their Dorinda is Melissa, beautiful, virtuous, and rich. Gayless is half-tempted to make a clean breast of his wretched condition and throw himself on the lady's mercy, but Sharp convinces him to machinate: marry first, then tell all. Their designs are opposed by Kitty, Melissa's clever servant, who suspects Gayless' poverty. She arranges a wedding-eve party at his house that is certain to expose him. Meanwhile, Gayless' father, learning of the situation and knowing Melissa's character, has written her a letter: he will consider marriage to her such an indication of his son's reform that he will restore his fortune. The knife in the back, as it were, cuts out the cancer. Melissa resolves to teach her fiancé a lesson before extricating him, and consents to attend the party in disguise. Given the balance of forces, it is not difficult to defeat Sharp and Gayless, but when the penniless and harassed pair has been publicly humiliated, Melissa is induced by the gentleman's first word of apology to declare: "His tears have softened me at once (*aside*).—Your necessities, Mr. Gayless, with such real contrition, are too powerful motives not to affect the breast already prejudiced in your favor—you have suffered too much already for your extravagance; and as I take part in your sufferings, 'tis easing myself to relieve you: know, therefore, all that's past I freely forgive." She then gives him his father's letter; he kneels, and she raises him, at once a redeeming angel, a fairy godmother, and an object of erotic desire. Sharp and Kitty indulge in some off-color banter, and Gayless pronounces the moral tag: "Virtuous love affords us springing joy, / Whilst vicious passions, as they burn, destroy."

Neither Gayless nor Garrick seems to realize that this is not the point. He has not been a rake—his passion, while expedient, was always virtuous—and he has nothing to repent except the deception of his fiancée, which he does not mention and which she forgives rather too facilely. Here the play resembles *Love's Last Shift* more than it does *The Beaux' Stratagem*, in that the protagonist does not actually repent until he has been exposed and has nothing to lose by "reform." Farquhar's more impressive procedure, followed by Goldsmith, was to have his hero act upon feelings of benevolence while they might still be inconvenient. And Melissa's easy reacceptance of Gayless, after his desperate plot on her fortune, is not a great improvement on the spirit of Cibber's Amanda. The moral noises made by *The Lying Valet* are unconvincing because Garrick does not appear to understand that Gayless, so far as we know, has erred not in the ways he suggests, but in others. Also, the plot is fortuitous, using the father's letter as a *deus ex machina*. But these imperfections did not deter Georgian audiences from welcoming numerous performances of the play over the next twenty-five seasons.

By the time his next play was produced Garrick was, at thirty, half-owner and manager of Drury Lane, and in the forefront of the acting profession. Moreover, *Miss in Her Teens* (1747) is of its kind as nearly perfect as anything Garrick ever wrote, from its confident, manifesto-like prologue (discussed in chapter six) through its ejection of blocking figures to its classic saturnalia.[9] "Miss" is sixteen-year-old Biddy Bellair, whose lover "Rhodophil" (alias Captain Loveit) went off to war after a brief courtship. Now he returns to find that she has three suitors: the effeminate Fribble, the swaggering Flash, and his own father Sir Simon. But Biddy's heart has remained sound, and with the aid of two intriguing servants and the sympathy of Biddy's aunt, the Captain has little real difficulty obtaining the lady, her fortune, and his father's consent. In fact the most striking characteristic of the play is its extreme lightness; it has the early lowering of tension frequently found in eighteenth-century comedy, especially in the afterpiece. At the beginning of act 2, the lovers' problems (such as they were) having been brought under control, comedy stands aside for farce and we sit back to enjoy the satirical exposure of imposters. Here is some of Garrick's best comic dialogue, especially between Biddy and Fribble, which he played himself:

> FRIBBLE: You must give me leave to make you a present of a small pot of my lipsalve; my servant made it this morning—the ingredients are innocent, I assure you; nothing but the best virgin's wax, conserve of roses, and lily of the valley water.
> BIDDY: I thank you, Sir, but my lips are generally red, and when they an't, I bite 'em.
> FRIBBLE: I bite my own, sometimes, to pout 'em a little, but this will give 'em a softness, colour, and an agreeable *moister*.—Thus let me make an humble offering at that shrine, where I have already sacrificed my heart. (*Kneels and gives the pot*.)
> BIDDY: Upon my word that's very prettily expressed, you are positively the best company in the world—I wish he was out of the house. (*Aside*.)

Miss in Her Teens is said to have laughed out of society the strutting coffeehouse officers and pretty gentlemen of the day, just as Molière's comedies (it was claimed) rendered *précieuses ridicules* and *femmes savantes* unfashionable. Garrick was always fond of French sources; the idea for *Miss* came from D'Ancourt's *La Parisienne*. Despite its derivativeness, the play was breaking new ground in England: it was virtually the first true short comedy, on the model of the French *petites comédies*. As the prologue says, farce and pantomime (it might have added satire) had hitherto monopolized the afterpiece, but after 1747 the formula of condensed comedy plus farcical accompaniment recurred often. Garrick deserves credit for providing the first English example of the short comedy and helping to usher in its heyday.

The early years of managing left Garrick little spare time for writing plays, though he did alter several and put his name to *The Chinese Festival*, a scenic spectacular, in 1755. The following year he produced his satiric farce *Lilliput*.[10] Like *Lethe*, it uses an outlandish setting as a safe means of spoofing English manners; a sturdily middle-class Gulliver is amusingly juxtaposed with Lady Flimnap's *bon ton*. Restoration licentiousness is banished to Lilliput, while British virtue is ironically praised. Thin but entertaining, and sometimes clever, *Lilliput* was acted by boys and girls to give the town novelty, an old trick known to Hamlet. In the prologue to this "dramatic entertainment" Garrick first took the sarcastic tone with his audience that later became almost habitual:

> Beware you lay not to the Conjuror's charge,
> That these in miniature, are you in large.
> To you these little folks have no relation.

He learned to be less heavy, fortunately, but almost every one of his original plays from then on could have been subtitled *A Lick at the Town*. Perhaps the animus stemmed from the kind of work he felt the public was forcing him to stage in order to keep afloat. In this period (1754–56) he was producing his controversial alterations of Shakespeare: *Florizel and Perdita* (from *The Winter's Tale*), *Catherine and Petruchio* (from *The Taming of the Shrew*), and the operatic version of *The Tempest*, among others. Against such tamperings must be set, of course, his constructive efforts to restore other texts and various revivals, notably his production of an abridged *Antony and Cleopatra*.

Garrick was still in a testy mood when he wrote the prologue to *The Male Coquette* (first produced as *The Modern Fine Gentleman*, 1757). He plans to expose each "modish Vice," but the audience may relax: "His female Failings all are Fictions: / To which your lives are contradictions." Behind the strained smile Garrick is up to the familiar business of exposing a fop. Daffodil is a male coquette who, out of mere wanton disregard, steals hearts and befouls reputations without ever coming to performance. Among his targets are two cousins, Sophia and Arabella. Tukely, Sophia's admirer, enables her to see for herself how false Daffodil is to her and everyone, and by the halfway point they have reached their understanding; all that remains for act 2 is the elaborate roasting of Daffodil. Structurally, it is *Miss in Her Teens* all over again, with Daffodil as a slightly less effeminate Fribble. At the climax, the male coquette is lured to a midnight tryst at Rosamond's Pond, where "Incognita" (Tukely) induces him to slander his reputed harem, all hiding in the bushes. Sophia, disguised as Incognita's husband, arrives to frighten Daffodil, who is duly laughed off the stage. Insomuch as it follows no one literary source, *The Male Coquette* is "original," yet one catches echoes from Shakespeare and Addison, not to mention Garrick's own work, and Murphy stated that the play was based on an actual incident at a village in Surrey (*Life of Garrick*, 1:308). The play is supposed to have succeeded in rendering the Daffodils of the time contemptible to society, which is perhaps why an observer of the theater in 1760 singled out Garrick's and Foote's plays from the "heap of little wretched pieces which have appeared for some years past," Garrick's especially, "because they answer all the ends of comedy, commixing use with entertainment."[11]

In 1759 Garrick adapted *The Guardian* from Fagan's *La Pupille*, supposedly as a benefit piece for Kit Smart.[12] It can be thought of as a two-act prototype of *False Delicacy*, in that the sentimental refinements of a gentleman and lady too delicate to declare their feelings furnish the plot-dialectic. Without their reticence and the monumental conceit of the coxcomical Young Clackit, there would be no complication and no story, so that manners satire is inherent in the action. Admittedly Harriet and Heartly have some cause to hesitate, for she is his ward, but we are shown from the first that she loves him anyway and that an *éclaircissement* is needed, whatever problems it may cause. Harriet, however, is too shy to declare, and Heartly too scrupulous and short-sighted to see how things are until the very end, mainly because he thinks she favors Young Clackit. At the final assembly she rejects Clackit, and Heartly, who can no longer doubt, at last conquers his reticence and falls to his knees to spare Harriet, who accepts him. Given the difference in ages, these could be the materials of serious, even high comedy, but Garrick's handling is superficial: there is virtually no preparation for Heartly's declaration of love, unless we count his several "muses." Garrick chose rather the path of satiric comedy of humors, with a variety of "sentiment" as the humor. The play is unusual, yet also has a few good theatrical scenes in well-worn grooves, such as Harriet's dictation of the ambiguous love letter to Heartly. Normally, of course, comedy would frown upon a ward-guardian match, but Garrick took care to describe Heartly as "young" to be Harriet's guardian, and also (perhaps with May-December jokes in mind) as merely "autumnal." Garrick himself was then forty-two.

In the same year Garrick also wrote and staged *Harlequin's Invasion*, the anti-pantomimical pantomime discussed in chapter four. It is symbolic of his dilemma that the call to Shakespearean arms took the form of a harlequinade, which in itself contributed to the growing ranks of irregular drama, as did *The Enchanter* (1760), a miniature Italian opera. *The Farmer's Return from London* (1762) is a one-act verse interlude of less than 100 lines giving a rural perspective on the coronation of George III. Garrick then broke away from his responsibilities for a Grand Tour that lasted two full seasons (1763–65.) His hopes that the public would welcome him back were borne out fully, and he responded with one of his bursts of playwriting activity. In 1766–67 he was associated with half a dozen new or altered plays: *The Country Girl*, an emasculation of Wycherley; *Cymon*, all music, procession and spectacle; *The Narrow Escape; Linco's Travels; A Peep Behind the Curtain;* and, the most popular and substantial, *The Clandestine Marriage* (1766), an uncertain collaboration with George Colman. Earlier critics gave Colman the lion's share, but recent studies have argued that Garrick's contributions were at least equally important.[13] He was apparently responsible for much of the lively dialogue, for the part of Lord Ogelby, and for the comic denouement, an unusual "final assembly" in the herione's bedroom in the middle of the night. Whether this is equal to Colman's involvement remains a matter of debate, but it is a very fair share of one of the most important comedies of the century, and includes some dramatic writing of a reasonably high order. The smooth expository dialogue in act 1 and the *double entendre* interviews in act 4, if they are Garrick's, do him credit, while the character of Lord Ogleby, the humane and goodnatured aristocrat, is surprisingly three-dimensional in terms of prevailing conventions. The final scene is rich in both dramatic action and comic turns of character. But because the play as a whole has the feel of Colman's work, I have chosen to discuss it in his section of this chapter.

Garrick's individual efforts of this time are comparatively slight. *The Narrow Escape*, better known as *Neck or Nothing*, is virtually a translation of Le Sage's *Crispin rival de son maître*. It generates a few good laughs—mainly as the clever servant Martin attempts to impersonate his master—but is all roguery and plot: there is neither development nor character. *Linco's Travels* (1767) consists, in Murphy's words, of "manners satire on various nations" (2:47). It is a plotless interlude written for the benefit of Thomas King, who had played Linco in *Cymon*. A more considerable play than either of these, *A Peep Behind the Curtain* is subtitled *The New Rehearsal*; according to tradition, it was Garrick's success as Bayes in Buckingham's play that prompted this effort. An interesting prologue complains that in these "nicer times" few write farces: "All now are comedies, five acts, or two." Theatrical affairs have come full circle since Garrick denounced the hegemony of farce in the prologue to *Miss in Her Teens* twenty years earlier. Here he exaggerates, but around a kernel of truth. The short comedies were booming, and their influence on Garrick's "farce" is obvious, for he builds a plot of romantic elopement into his theatrical burlesque. The Drury Lane rehearsal of a new burletta by Glib provides the occasion for Wilson to run off with Miss Fuz, an heiress whose father has retained money rightfully belonging to Wilson's deceased father. Wilson sees this as poetic and financial justice, while Miss Fuz, a novel-fed maiden linking Colman's Polly Honeycombe with Sheridan's Lydia Languish, is just sentimentally in love with the idea of elopement.

But all this is beside the main point of satire on the new playthings of the theater—burlettas and grandiose machines—and the patrons who demand them. Garrick hedged his bet cleverly, however: the portrait of a Drury Lane rehearsal would have had the pleasures of familiarity and satisfied the craving to know more of the inner workings of the craft, as well as pricking "all these new vagaries" that infuriate the carpenter. It is also difficult to say whether the presentation of Glib's burletta in act 2 was more sop or satire: probably some of each. Certainly Garrick's satiric purposes were broader than Buckingham's, embracing the manners and morals of audiences, represented by the tasteless, meddling Sir Toby and Lady Fuz, as well as the vulgarity of those who peddle variety and novelty, represented by Glib and Sir Macaroni Virtu. Many a spectator's smile must have grown stiff as he saw his portrait in *A Peep*, though Murphy says it was "for several successive nights a favourite entertainment" (2:51). Perhaps the very breadth of the satire saved it. The relationship between Garrick and his public was strange, a mixture of esteem and opinionated egotism on their side, flattering accommodation and barely concealed hostility on his. In many of his direct addresses to the audience a polite or jesting surface has been allowed to form thinly over cold contempt.

In 1769 Garrick involved himself in controversy and unfavorable publicity by producing a Shakespeare Jubilee at Stratford-on-Avon. Garrick obviously wanted to cement the connection of his name with Shakespeare's, but critics such as Samuel Foote were quick to point out that the ceremonies featured a great deal of Garrick and very little Shakespeare. To recoup his financial losses Garrick brought the festival procession—embedded in a slight plot satirizing the Stratfordians—to Drury Lane in October as a spectacular entertainment called *The Jubilee*, a bathetic denouement to an enterprise begun as homage to the Bard.[14] Stung by the resulting criticism, he refrained from placing original work before the public for three years. *The Irish Widow* (1772), adapted from Molière, is a slight though traditional farce written to give Mrs. Barry an Irish part. The plot, which in Garrick's version shows the same early lowering of comic tension as his other plays, has been defended as "more kindly, moral and logical" than Molière's (Stein, p. 98). The following year Garrick produced a revision of his carefully moralized 1747 alteration of Thomas Tomkis's *Albumazar* (1614–15); its prologue, trading on the recent success of *She Stoops to Conquer*, attacks sentimental comedy sharply, as if Garrick really did prefer the traditional variety, and was, typically, just waiting for a safe moment to say so. *The Meeting of the Company; or, Bayes' Art of Acting* (1774) is a one-act burlesque of the rehearsal type. Bayes visits Drury Lane in his capacity as an author and makes himself obnoxious, but the satire is spread liberally over actors and audiences as well as dramatists. There is no plot, only transient sketches embodying commentary.

In *Bon Ton; or, High Life above Stairs* (1775), his last and one of his most popular plays, Garrick mixes laughing comedy with a strong dose of patriotism and bourgeois morality. The play preaches that "good morals are English," but does so comically, within the framework of a farce of sexual intrigue. The plot is thin enough. Lord Minikin's household has profited from a year on the continent by growing luxuriously decadent: Milord, the main proponent of French morals, is carrying on with Miss Tittup, his country cousin, while Milady is besieged by Colonel Tivy, Miss Tittup's mercenary fiancé. Into this hotbed of cynical iniquity storms Sir John Trotley, Miss Tittup's uncle, who hates London—and "innovation"—so much that he hasn't been to town for twenty years. Sir John serves as critic of the city and moral touchstone, but is himself such a testy misanthrope as to make sympathizing with him difficult; railing at the times and manners is his humor. In the darkness and confusion of the final scene he stumbles across the intrigues of the house, spews reproaches, and dispenses justice. The Colonel is turned away; Sir John "gives a paper" to Lord Minikin, predicts ruin and exile for him, and departs for the wholesome air of the country with the two erring ladies on his arm. Though the Anglophilia is a bit heavy at times, the brisk pace of the action and some lively dialogue carry the play through. One would not go to any great lengths to recommend *Bon Ton* as a reading play, but it does demonstrate that Garrick, at the end of thirty-five years as a dramatist, still had a sure sense of what would prove effective onstage. His rather didactic brand of nationalism certainly did him no harm with audiences on the eve of war with the American colonies.

Garrick's last plays tell us little about him we did not already know, and nothing reassuring. *The Theatrical Candidates,* a musical prelude, was written to mark the opening of a renovated Drury Lane for Garrick's last season in September 1775. Figures representing tragedy and comedy debate their claims to audiences' favor, while Harlequin speaks for pantomime. Then Mercury announces Apollo's decision: tragedy and comedy should remain in their own realms (i.e., no tragicomedy or sentimental comedy) except when united by Shakespeare. Pantomime is admissible as a sideshow only if music and farce fail to entertain the audience. Like *Harlequin's Invasion* sixteen years earlier, *The Theatrical Candidates* deals rather with what ought to be than what was, and with what Garrick professed rather than what he practiced.[15] The play was published along with *May-Day; or, the Little Gypsy,* a "musical farce" (or pastoral operetta) of one act that Garrick wrote to introduce seventeen-year old Harriet Abrams to the stage. The plot is a traditional trifle. Thomas A. Arne, Miss Abrams's teacher, composed the music to the nine songs.

Garrick's career is a patent instance of chiaroscuro in its mixture of lights and shades. He was an actor of undoubted brilliance in what then seemed a naturalistic style, yet who was criticized for exaggerated and stylized effects. He was a manager who championed regular drama but staged pantomimes and processions, and during whose tenure the *il-legitimi* began to dominate the repertoire. If the Laureate's dictum, "A nation's taste depends on you," is to be taken seriously, we may give qualified praise to Garrick's good offices during his career, but must also record that as soon as the teacher left the schoolroom pandemonium broke loose. As a dramatist he seems to have preferred laughing comedy but flirted with sentimentalism, and his theoretical allegiance to legitimate drama was compromised by the spectacular entertainments he wrote. In order to maintain one's respect for Garrick's work in this area, it is necessary to concentrate on his eight or ten unpretentious contributions to the comic tradition. Garrick's performance was radically ambivalent, and his position in Georgian theater very nearly that of Pope's Man:

> Created half to rise, and half to fall;
> Great lord of all things, yet a prey to all;
> Sole judge of truth, in endless error hurl'd:
> The glory, jest, and riddle of the world!

SAMUEL FOOTE (1721–1777)

Although the Licensing Act of 1737 had a constricting effect on London drama, the decade of the forties was lively and productive of important new talents. David Garrick began to act, wrote three popular plays and took over as manager of Drury Lane; Charles Macklin presented his revolutionary Shylock and two interesting farces; and one of Macklin's apprentice actors set up shop on his own. This was Samuel Foote, a fat, bright-eyed and cruelly witty mimic whose acting career was earthbound until he started performing his own material, based on the eccentricities of particular people and the social follies of the town. To the fallow decade of the fifties Foote contributed four actable comedies, and by the time he retired he had written about twenty. His short-term impact on early Georgian theater was second only to Garrick's, yet posterity has generally snubbed him. One reason for this, perhaps, is that he was a rakish *bon vivant*, a notable eccentric even by eighteenth-century standards, and a formidable wit who left behind two volumes of table talk. Such traits apparently made it difficult to take him seriously as a dramatist, and they still constitute a tempting distraction from his plays.[16] Another reason he has been forgotten—and he was repeatedly warned of this fate at the time—is that his plays were almost all extremely topical and hence evanescent. When their specific targets had passed away, ran the argument, they would be of no further interest; and to a large extent this has been the case.

Yet Foote deserves to be taken seriously. It was principally he who continued the work, begun by Fielding, of developing the *petite pièce* into a satirical weapon of some value. That he profited by this, that it was his livelihood, that he could be malicious does not detract from the legitimacy of the satires which he produced in greater abundance than any other Georgian dramatist. He wrote scarcely anything else, and this singleness of purpose, during a career of nearly thirty years, says much for the sincerity of his claims to have been a genuine scourger of vice and folly. He was serious about his work, if about nothing else. In 1775, when *A Trip to Calais* was banned at the urging of its satiric object, Foote, instead of backing down, wrote to the Lord Chamberlain. "Between the muse and the magistrate," he argued, "there is a natural confederacy; what the last cannot punish the first often corrects" (quoted by Trefman, p. 238). The ban was not lifted, and Foote had to alter the play. He may have been, as is often said, the "licensed jester" of the period, but it was not, at least in the beginning, a safe license from the Examiner of Plays. His contemporary portrait would tend to corroborate the view of Foote as a kind of dramatic magistrate. The eyes, though mild, are serious, even reflective, the mouth looks equally ready to laugh or bite, and there is a slight but surprising resemblance to George Washington.

One of Foote's eighteenth-century nicknames, "the English Aristophanes," was quite apt, within the limits set by the Licensing Act and the depth of his talent. To recreate on the London stage the topical satires of Aristophanes and Old Comedy in general was Foote's explicit desire and principal achievement. Yet he has frequently been castigated, by those who would not and will not take him on his own terms, for doing just what he set out to do: it is reasonable to say that he has been misunderstood. A typical Georgian critique runs as follows:

> The rational end of comedy, which is the reformation of folly, cannot take place in personal ridicule. . . .Mr. Foote's works will aptly exemplify the matter; in which, the fund of genuine comedy, derived from happy strokes upon the manners of the times, and uncommon, but not entirely singular characters, will secure a lasting admiration, when the mimicry which supported the parts of Squintum [in *The Minor*] and Cadwallader [in *The Author*] is despised or forgotten.[17]

Twentieth-century criticism has based its generally low estimate of Foote on roughly the same grounds, viewing his plays as farces, since they subjugate plot to caricature, and denying him comic character. Such objections, by ignoring Foote's repeated explanations of his artistic principles, simply decline the challenge as he gave it; they insist on judging him by the irrelevant canons of New Comedy, and thus end by condemning him for failing to achieve what he never attempted. To take Foote on his own terms, we must examine these inherited notions of his defects in the light of his stated convictions about comedy. Probably the earliest clue we have to his principles is a definition of the purpose of comedy, in *The Roman and English Comedy Considered and Compared* ... (London, 1747), as "the Correction of Vices and Follies of an inferior sort," teaching us by "a Representation of fashionable foibles, and particular extravagant Humours, to shun Ridicule and Absurdity" (p. 6). The drift of these remarks is confirmed by the new prologue to *Tea,* dated January 1748, which praises the personal satire of Aristophanes as a public good and an inducement to virtue (see Trefman, p. 29), and by the "Dedication to Frances Delaval" prefaced to *Taste* (1752), virtually a manifesto of the satirical short comedy. Here Foote asserts that "the follies and absurdities of men are the sole objects of comedy," and declares himself "a Rebel to this universal Tyrant [love] who, not contented with exciting all that is pitiful or terrible in human Nature, has claimed the privilege of occasioning every thing that is ridiculous or contemptible in it; and thus ... is both *Tragedy* and Comedy subjected to the Power of Love."[18] The reason for this rejection of the favorite emotion of sentimental and New comedy is that only thus can he "confine the Eye to the single object of [his] Satire." Admittedly Foote did not always practice precisely what he preached here; several of his plays have prominent love-plots, and some have even been called sentimental. But satire is usually present too, and generally he stood by his theory. In a pamphlet of 1760, replying to a critic of *The Minor,* he defined comedy as "an exact representation of the peculiar manners of that people among whom it happens to be performed; faithful imitation of singular absurdities, particular follies, which are openly produced, as criminals are publicly punished, for the correction of individuals, and as an example to the whole community."[19] As criminals are publicly punished. No wonder Foote's comedies, as dramatic gallows, appealed to the audiences who still made street theater of the road from Newgate to Tyburn. Apparently he took the confederacy of the Muse and the magistrate literally. Finally, the Preface to *The Comic Theatre* (1762), which may be by Foote, gives a view of the history of comedy that certainly coincides with his previously expressed ideas:

"The original purpose of comedy was to expose particular follies for the punishment of individuals, and as an example to the whole community" (p. v). The operative word here is again "particular." Criticized for satirizing individuals, not types, Foote retorted that that was exactly what Aristophanes did, with Socrates, for example, and as for Molière: "The original of the principal character in almost every piece was thoroughly known to the audience" (p. xii). To be sure, Foote took liberties with Aristophanes, sometimes invoking him with ulterior motives, but he worked sufficiently by the lights of Old Comedy so that responsible criticism must judge him accordingly.

It is not Aristophanes, however, but the commedia dell'arte that seems the correct frame of reference for his first dramatic entertainment, *The Diversions of a Morning*, in the sense that the written text or scenario is treated as a mere starting point for the actors' improvisations.[20] In its earliest form *Diversions* probably consisted of one act of *Rehearsal*-like burlesque, called "Tragedy à la Mode" and featuring a critic named Puff (Fitzgerald, p. 285), followed by an act of topical satire and mimicry (Trefman, p. 27), but the material was too evanescent to be described confidently; "formless and ever-changing, [it] can scarcely be accorded the name of drama."[21] And *Diversions* was fugitive in more senses than one: since Foote had no patent, he was put to constant shifts to evade the restrictions of the Licensing Act as applied by the Examiner of Plays. He would charge for refreshments and offer the play gratis, play noontime matinees to avoid conflict with the patentees, change the name of the entertainment: *A Dish of Tea*, *A Dish of Chocolate*, *The Auction*, *The Auction of Pictures*, *The Virtuoso*, and finally *Taste*.[22] Foote's retreat, though steady, was orderly; it was, on the whole, the most successful skirmish fought by any dramatist against the Examiner during the Garrick era.

In 1752 this most Protean of plays finally acquired the shape of print. *Taste* is a Jonsonian exposé of London's purveyors of fake antiquities, then a flourishing trade. In the prologue we can recognize material from *The Auction of Pictures;* it is spoken by an auctioneer who is afraid the play will hurt his art business. His boast is that he encourages modern British art by having "antiquities" made in the Strand, and he turns the barb against the audience: "They'll thrive as Ancients, but as Moderns starve." In the play proper we encounter Puff, from act 1 of *Diversions*, now an entrepreneurial dealer in "'antique art" who runs an "old master" factory in London. His head painter is Carmine, whom he dragged out of the mud as a starving wretch and set over assistants such as Varnish, Brush, and Scrape. In the manner of Subtle and Face they hoodwink citizen Pentweazle and his lady, Lord Dupe, Novice, Squander, and others. When at the end Puff is detected impersonating a German baron at an auction, he is the one who laughs at the dupes, and casts off the treacherous Carmine. Foote once described the play as his "favorite offspring," and he continued to tinker with it: in 1758 he submitted a new *Diversions* to the Examiner (Larpent MS 149), and in 1761 a new *Taste* (194). The 1758 version shows how freely Foote worked; it consists of the Lady Pentweazle scene from *Taste* set in a new frame, sans Puff, with a second act containing the burlesque rehearsal—act 1 of the original *Diversions*. There are two added characters, the virtuous, rusticated Manly, and the quasi-Restoration rake, Freelove, who mouths Milton: "Hail wedded love, mysterious law, / Delicacy and innocence, haw, haw, haw." This version of act 2 approximates that printed by Tate Wilkinson in *The Wandering Patentee* (1795, 3:237 ff.).

In 1749 Foote wrote and acted in *The Knights*, his first regular play if we consider the volatile condition of *Diversions* at the time, and already the traits that mark most of his later work—strong satiric characterization, weak plots, and a seminal effect on the major dramatists—are visible. The story concerns Hartop's attempt to discharge his mortgage to the miserly Sir Penurious Trifle by marrying his daughter Sukey, a scheme that is spoiled when Hartop's disguise is discovered. But by this time Foote's purpose—to satirize two knights, Trifle and Sir Gregory Gazette—has been achieved, and he is so indifferent to the outcome of the plot that he leaves matters dangling there, with Hartop's fate still in doubt. Despite its truncated ending, *The Knights* was an influential play. Murphy is said to have based Quidnunc in *The Upholsterer* on Sir Gregory, though other models were also available; Fitzgerald thought that Goldsmith borrowed Tony Lumpkin from Timothy Gazette, Sir Gregory's lubberly son, and Hastings from Hartop (pp. 275–76), and both he and Mary Belden saw a resemblance between Mrs. Malaprop and Penelope Trifle (Fitzgerald, p. 283; Belden, p. 191). Influence-hunting is always speculative work, but the recurrence of such parallels suggests that Foote was near the comic center of Georgian drama and attuned to its vibrations, whether he was their source or not.

At about this point Foote inherited a fortune—his third, according to tradition—and dashed off to France to spend it. He was away from the stage for three years, but soon after his return transformed some of his experiences abroad into a dramatic success. *The Englishman in Paris* (1753), however, although its satire maintains a nice balance between French manners and the stupid rejection of them by English boors, is not one of Foote's better plays; it lacks wit, the patriotic vein is too strong, and the denouement is disastrous. Squire Buck, 200 percent British, has been sent by his father to Paris for polish. There he is having a wild debauch, hating France all the while, and is well on his way to marrying Lucinda, a woman of the town, through the machinations of the conniving Subtles, when his father, guided by the faithful tutor Classic, arrives to overhear, expose, and reclaim. But in a heavy and unexpected turn, Lucinda has last-minute qualms of conscience about the scheme in which she has just participated with such verve, and it is discovered that she is the long-lost daughter of Sir John Buck's best friend. The intrusion of this device from romantic fiction destroys the unity of satiric tone that the play has so far possessed. Lucinda is taken into the family and Buck is allowed to hope for her hand if he reforms. Foote rarely acted in this play—he is said to have known it was dull—and the cast was usually dominated by the three Macklins, to whom the author dedicated it.

Three years later Foote produced a sequel. *The Englishman Returned from Paris*, which was popular for several seasons, forms a rather neat complement to the earlier play: the British brute has become a Gallic coxcomb, whose open-mouthed admiration of everything French is now the satiric target. Here Foote was on well-trodden ground; his foppish Buck—now Sir Charles Buck—is the man of mode, down to a smattering of French and a Continental entourage. Buck is inexplicably accompanied by Lord John, a sensible young nobleman who shows an immediate interest in Lucinda, which she requites. This is a complication, because Sir John Buck's will, which left some property to Lucinda, also stipulated that she marry Buck; she will inherit less if she refuses him. On the other hand if Buck refuses Lucinda, he must settle twenty thousand pounds on her. Disliking both marriage and forfeiture, Sir Charles declines to refuse formally (no time limit was stipulated), but offers the lady what he considers a Parisian choice: either live and die a spinster, or become his mistress and keep the money. The enraged Lucinda "poisons" his tea, and while Sir Charles is under the illusion that he is dying he is persuaded to cast off his French frippery and renounce Lucinda, who is thus freed to marry Lord John. Sir Charles is then persuaded that he has not been poisoned, and the lovers are betrothed. This hardly constitutes "reform," a convention often scanted by Foote. His greatest problem, however, is Lord John, whose grave, sententious conversations with Lucinda contribute to the tedious length of act 1, and whose association with Buck is never accounted for. The play improves on its predecessor in one respect: it gives a wider berth to sentimental twists of plot, and thus remains true to itself.

Foote's last play of the fifties, *The Author* (1757), was another big success and is said to have influenced Sheridan. Sometimes described as "sentimental," it does use a favorite device of sentimentalists, the benevolent incognito relative, but the handling, until the rather mellow conclusion, is in the laughing tradition. The recently retired ruler of a British colony, Governor Cape, returns to London after a long absence to see his son and test if he be worthy of an inheritance. He has allowed Young Cape to think he (as well as the mother) is dead, educating him under the guise of a foreign friend. Robin, Governor Cape's servant, has sought out the young man and finds him a poor but virtuous author. Some affinities of this plot with the Sir Oliver– Charles Surface portion of *The School for Scandal* are obvious, and indeed Sheridan's debt to Foote has long been recognized. The relationships of Stockwell and Belcour in *The West Indian* and of Sir William and Young Honeywood in *The Good-Natured Man* are also similar to Foote's story, but here the differences are more significant; "the English Aristophanes" plays the situation mostly for laughs and satire. A long scene in Young Cape's chambers exposes the miseries of Grub Street and introduces the principal object of satire, Cadwallader. This eccentric was supposedly based, down to specific mannerisms, on one Mr. Apreece, who eventually applied to the Lord Chamberlain to have *The Author* suppressed. In the play Young Cape is courting Cadwallader's sister, the heiress Arabella, and needs his consent. Though his stratagems are finally blown up, the author is saved by his father (who feels his principles have passed the test) and the customary saturnalia ensue. What put the play across, apart from Foote's recognizable mimicry of Apreece, was the witty dialogue, a definite improvement over the *Englishman* plays.

Foote did not write again for three years, but *The Minor* (1760), a popular and controversial play, began a series of six mostly successful comedies in as many seasons. The popularity and the controversy seem to have been connected. "Squintum" was a take-off on George Whitefield, the Methodist preacher, whose sermons Foote attended in order to parody them; and "Mother Cole" the bawd, played by Foote, was a cruel portrait of a particular convert to Methodism. *The Minor* became the most discussed of Foote's plays, bringing out the Jeremy Colliers of the day. The *Remarks, Critical and Christian, on "The Minor"* elicited a reply from Foote, mentioned above, and *The Theatre Licentious and Perverted, or a Sermon for Reformation of Manners . . . partly occasioned By the acting of a Comedy, entitled, "The Minor,"* by James Baine, reached a second edition in 1770. These gentlemen had neither the talent nor the success of Collier, however, and *The Minor* became a staple of Foote's repertoire.

The plot's connections with earlier and later drama have struck many readers. A possible influence on *The School for Scandal* has often been proposed: Young Wealthy finds himself in a situation similar to Charles Surface's, and Little Transfer inevitably suggests Little Premium (Belden, p. 191; Fitzgerald, pp. 192, 279–80). On the other hand Foote himself may have borrowed some of his minor characters from Joseph Reed's *The Register Office* (1761), which could have been circulating in manuscript (Trefman, p. 118). But the parallels with Terence's masterpiece *The Brothers* (also used by Cumberland) are equally close; Sir William and Richard Wealthy, the aristocratic gentleman and the merchant, resemble Demea and Micio in that their opposed values are projected onto and tested by a younger generation, here George Wealthy. Like Terence, Foote preserves a balance by having both fathers' schemes of education fail, yet there are also many differences. Though the plan announced by Sir William at the outset—"George, as I have contrived it, shall experience all the misery of real ruin, without running the least risk"—aims at the kind of managed reform of a prodigal favored in sentimental comedy, the father is clearly no benevolist, and again Foote demonstrates his interest in social satire. In act 1 Shift, Sir William's factotum, recounts how he rose from link-boy via a talent for mimicry that enables him to impersonate an auctioneer and a usurer, Smirk and Transfer. In acts 2 and 3 Foote played all these parts and that of Mother Cole (a portrait of Jennie Douglas, also satirized by Hogarth), a symbol of the religious zealot and superficially saved but unregenerate sinner. She explains that she became a Protestant because the Catholics would have forced her to leave off "business"; her conversation moves easily from religion to whoring and back with the aid of Methodist imagery: ejaculations, enthusiastic endeavors, and so on. Foote avoids a sociological perspective that might see her as a victim trying to escape from a miserable life, yet in act 3 he does introduce a pathetic character of the same class. Lucy, who has been ruined by Methodism and the mercantile system, suddenly forces us to consider how a girl becomes a Mother Cole, and the comedy turns sentimental. George, hitherto a fop and a rake, is moved by the girl's plight and promises aid. Shift determines to shift sides, informs George of the contrivance against him and unmasks the players, including the father. Amid a general sense of relief, Lucy is betrothed to the reclaimed prodigal.

Fitzgerald thought *The Minor* Foote's best play, though lacking plot (p. 184). On the contrary, it has too much. This was the first time Foote had essayed three full acts, and for once he overplotted. Usually his plots are thin and cursory, mere skeletons for the satiric flesh; *The Minor* has the customary full-bodied satire, plus enough story for a five-act comedy. In the melee Foote lost control of the tone. After asking us to laugh at sharpers and follies for two acts, secure in the knowledge that Geroge's straits are artificial, he suddenly gives us a character, Lucy, who is in real trouble and requires immediate sympathy and assistance. The comic law of "no consequences" is rudely violated. Ridicule and outrage are unexpectedly displaced by pathos, and the play becomes emotionally incoherent. *The Minor* comes as near to Cibber's type of sentimentality as anything Foote wrote.

The play has an unusual dramatic introduction in which Foote expounds his comic principles for some theatrically minded gentlemen. His three "Don'ts" are surprising: no personal satires, no national portraits, no topical satire. The first and third are expecially unconvincing in view of the play to which they are prefaced; Squintum, Loader, Smirk, and Mrs. Cole all had known topical referents. Foote was, however, less guilty than most of spoofing national types. On the positive side, he names affectation as "the true comic object," and ridicule as "the only antidote" against social evils and abuses. To this thoroughly traditional conception of satiric comedy he adds a characteristic personal twist: "Where then can we have recourse, but to the comic muse; perhaps, the archness and severity of her smile, may redress an evil, that the Laws cannot reach, or reason reclaim." Nearly fifteen years of writing satires had not modified his theoretical position any more than the subsequent fifteen would, but the experience of *The Minor* seems to have confirmed Foote in his notion of what he was doing; he articulated his critical position most fully at about this time.

The Lyar (1762) is anomalous for Foote both in being an adaptation—of Lope de Vega, says the Prologue; of Corneille's *Le Menteur* or Steele's *Lying Lover,* say modern scholars (Trefman, p. 121; Belden, pp. 188–89)—and in being virtually without topical satire. Young Wilding is the extravagant humorist of the title who compulsively lies his way into and (almost always) out of difficulties until the final assembly, when everyone gathers to prove his falsehoods and laugh him off the stage. Many of his desperate prevarications, however, are highly comical (Foote played Young Wilding) and even the conclusion does not treat him harshly: the way is left open for him to marry his sweetheart Miss Godfrey if he reforms. The situation of one character courting as two different persons also occurs in *The Rivals,* and the conversation of the Wildings on courtship, marriage, and duty parallels that of the Absolutes on the same subject. In the prologue Foote undertook a somewhat confusing defense of farce on the grounds that modern comedy was a reduction of the Attic variety which had become disjoined from humor and satire. As a rule he called his plays "comedies," but apparently he was conceding that this play was a farce. Either way, it contains sufficient humor to place it within the laughing tradition.

Later in 1762 Foote produced a much more characteristic play. *The Orators* is so topical that only by a wholly Aristophanic definition could it be called comedy. It has no plot in the conventional sense, only a series of sketches satirizing the current vogue of oratory. Originally, it is said, Foote intended to ridicule Samuel Johnson in the play, but Johnson scared him out of the idea (Belden, p. 25), though the trial of the Cock-Lane ghost in act 2 may be a survival of the first scheme. As it stands the play is directed chiefly against Thomas Sheridan, Richard Brinsley's father and unofficial dean of the orators. In his first appear-ince, for example, Foote is a speech teacher who is called "Foote" but delivers a long harangue full of hypocrisy, backbiting, wild schemes, and the mannered speech of the professional elocutionist; the bald pitch for students that closes act 3 would certainly have been understood as a reference to Sheridan. *The Orators* must have been amusing entertainment in its own day, but it holds little for posterity, and shows Foote at his most petty and venial.

The Mayor of Garret (or Garratt), Foote's contribution for 1763, is said to have been his most popular work, yet now it seems one of his thinnest productions. The play's raisons d'être are the humors of Major Sturgeon (a *miles gloriosus* played by Foote), which are not very funny, and the satire on the caprices of the campaign for the mayoralty of the rustic village of Garret. This quaint and colorful ritual (which Foote, with Garrick and Wilkes, had attended in 1761) serves as a background to the action and evidently appealed to the first audiences, but today the topical allusions merely clutter the text and require explanatory footnotes. Before this tapestry Foote erects a slight though many-faceted plot. At its center is the good-natured mayoralty candidate Jerry Sneak: henpecked by his wife, possibly cuckolded by the present mayor, and loved by playgoers. Around him gather the amusements of the election, the candidates, their managers, and the voters. There is Major Sturgeon, a whimsical new kind of braggart who boasts lightly and doesn't take himself too seriously; Matthew Marrowbone, a ridiculous Methodist; Sir Jacob (meant for the Duke of Newcastle); and Bruin, the "great man" who pulls the strings, and his wife-berating son. And there is the malapropping "Heel-Tap" who manages the election, discredits "Matthew Mug," and is finally appointed by Sir Jacob to be Sneak's deputy when that worthy is chosen mayor. Sneak suddenly develops a German accent and tries clumsily to scold his wife; then they are superficially reconciled, and a dance ends all. Much of *The Mayor* seems irredeemably foolish in print, but with broad acting of the rude mechanicals it pleased the London theatrical public.

Foote maintained his one-a-year pace in 1764 with *The Patron*, which he considered his best play to date. Based on one of Marmontel's *Contes moraux*, *The Patron* was thoroughly Anglicized in order to "expose the frivolity and ignorance of the pretenders to learning, with the insolence and vanity of their superficial, illiberal protectors." This Foote does with such abundant energy that satiric purpose outruns dramatic organization by farther than usual, discarding characters unceremoniously once their absurdities have been revealed. At the top of the infamous heap is the title character Sir Thomas Lofty, a portrait of George Bubb Dodington (Pope's Bubo) and perhaps the namesake of Goldsmith's Lofty in *The Good-Natured Man*. Flattery is as vital to him as air, and the best scenes are those that show the various sycophants soothing him up; "Nothing new today from Parnassus, Sir Thomas?" (ii.ii) But Foote's satire ranges as widely as ever; the patron, a kind of static picaro, rather than traveling upwards through society has all levels of society come to him. An antiquarian (Rust), a West-Indian nabob (Pepperpot) and his chaplain, a poet (Dactyl), a publisher (Puff), and a stuttering orator (Sir Roger Dowlas) all parade through his drawing room. Naturally the procession becomes a bit disorderly (not since *Diversions* had Foote taken such broad aim) yet *The Patron* is structurally sound. What holds it together is young Bever's pursuit of Sir Thomas's niece Juliet Lofty, also courted by Rust and Pepperpot. Bever finally earns the girl by publicly acknowledging authorship of an execrable play about Robinson Crusoe, which is hissed off the stage. Its actual author is Sir Thomas, and as a reward for keeping his secret he gives Bever his niece. Thus the satire neatly serves the purposes of the comedy.

In 1765 Foote scored another success with *The Commissary* and reached the peak of his career. He had become something of a London institution despite his irregularities, but in 1766 he would suffer a serious setback and not write again for three years. *The Commissary* deserves study because of its special position in his career, at the far edge of bloom, as well as for its intrinsic merits. It gives in the compass of three acts a selection of the best Foote had to offer. Basically a free-swinging satire on war profiteers, the play keeps several other topical irons in the fire, while maintaining greater coherence in a more elaborate plot than was usual with Foote. Its forte is careful observation and recording of contemporary manners. Foote's plays do not hold the mirror up to Nature or Man, but the men and women of Georgian London can be seen and heard in them. Heard, especially: the reproduction of colloquial speech, of which Foote considered himself a student, is the chief ornament of the play. *The Commissary* is the dramatic equivalent of an Elizabethan "cony-catching pamphlet," feeding the public curiosity about "how it's done" while claiming the moral function of an exposé.

Foote even allows Mrs. Mechlin, his shady lady of all trades, some didactic speeches against the vices and follies of her victims; and though they ring false to most moderns, *The Dramatic Censor* (1770) has a long, extravagant eulogy on the improving tendencies of the play, applauding particularly the lashing it gives to rapacity (1:299 ff.).

All of the action transpires on the questionable premises of Molly Mechlin (i.e., Macklin: perhaps a dig at the actor). This engaging confidence woman wears many hats, all stolen; she is a bawd and a marriage-broker, a dealer in smuggled and faked goods, and the bilker-general of solvent dupes. A fast opening scene catapults us into the middle of this household without so much as a prologue. The double set of stichomythia between her servant Jenny and Simon serves the purposes both of exposition and ironic humor:

JENNY: . . . to be sure, though now and then to oblige a customer, my mistress does condescend to smuggle a little—

SIMON: Keep it up, Mrs. Jane.

JENNY: Yet there are no people in the Liberty of Westminster that live in more credit than we do.

SIMON: Bravo.

JENNY: The very best of quality are not ashamed to visit my mistress.

SIMON: They have reason.

JENNY: Respected by the neighbours.

SIMON: I know it.

JENNY: Punctual in her payments.

SIMON: To a moment.

JENNY: Regular hours.

SIMON: Doubtless.

JENNY: Never misses the sarmant on Sundays.

SIMON: I own it.

JENNY: Not an oath comes out of her mouth, unless, now and then, when the poor gentlewoman happens to be overtaken in liquor.

SIMON: Granted.

JENNY: Not at all given to lying, but like other tradesfolks, in the way of her business.

. . . .

SIMON: Hey-day! why where the deuce have I got, sure I have mistaken the house; is not this Mrs. Mechlin's?

JENNY: That's pretty well known.

SIMON: The commodious, convenient Mrs. Mechlin, at the sign of the Star, in the parish of St. Paul's?

JENNY: Bravo.
SIMON: That commercial caterpillar?
JENNY: I know it.
SIMON: That murderer of manufactures?
JENNY: Doubtless.
SIMON: That walking warehouse?
JENNY: Granted.
SIMON: That carries about a greater cargo of contraband goods under her petticoats than a Calais cutter?
JENNY: Very well.
SIMON: That engrosser and seducer of virgins?
JENNY: Keep it up, Master Simon.
SIMON: That forestaller of bagnios?
JENNY: Incomparable fine.
SIMON: That canting, cozening, money-lending, match-making, pawn-broking—

This exchange, exhibiting the symmetrical design of much good theatrical farce, prepares us for the motley parade of visitors: Mrs. Loveit, "the old liquorish dowager from Devonshire Square," in quest of a young husband before the old one has been in the earth for a month; Paduasoy, the "Spitalfields weaver," who, like Puff and Carmine in *Taste*, is a domestic manufacturer of "foreign goods"; Young Loveit, seeking a rich old wife to repair his fortunes; and the train of teachers who earn a living by trying to make a gentleman of the commissary, Zachariah Fungus. The principal of these maestros, whose antics occupy act 2, are Mr. Gruel the orator (Thomas Sheridan again) and Dr. Catgut the musician (Thomas Augustine Arne); Bridoun the riding master appears in act 3.

The object of their attentions, the commissary, went off to the Seven Years' War "very little better than a driver of carts," but came back from Germany with "a whole cartload of money," which he is anxious to spend in acquiring the accomplishments of a lord and "a seat in a certain assembly." Foote compares his ill-got wealth to an Indian Governor's— seven years later he would satirize nabobs in another play—and is generally less tolerant than Molière of *le bourgeois gentilhomme*, as the name Fungus indicates. Zachariah is particularly susceptible to the sin of pride; he is mad for a noble wife, and Mrs. Mechlin, with whom he lodges, just happens to know Lady Sacharissa Mackirkincroft, "the hundred and fortieth lineal descendant from Hercules Alexander, Earl of Glendowery, prime minister to King Malcolm the First." As Zachariah puts it, "Zooks, she has a pedigree as long as the Mall . . . with large trees on each side, and all the boughs loaded with lords." This lady, however, is better known as Dolly Mechlin, a "beggar's brat" whom Mrs. Mechlin took in and calls "niece." Following a "slip of her youth" (with Dr. Catgut) she turned strolling player and acted for two years in Edinburgh, where she acquired the accent for her present role. Mrs. Mechlin hopes that management of the Zachariah-Dolly match will shortly make her "easy for life," as the risks of her trade are so great and its problems so onerous that she begins to think of retirement: "Time has been, when a gentleman wanted a friend, I could supply him with choice in an hour; but the market is spoiled, and a body might as soon procure a hare or a partridge as a pretty—" *Enter Dolly*.

The comic and satiric center of the play is the tutoring of Zachariah. When his fencing-master does not appear, he undertakes to show his brother how he has learned to quarrel, has a bout with Mrs. Mechlin, and is outclassed. Mr. Gruel the oratory-master then arrives to hear Zach recite his speech on the importance of trade. But when he gets to the passage about the "languid, but generous, steed" who "capers through a whole region of turnpegs" his riding-master is announced and he has to rush off in pursuit of still another accomplishment. Gruel's exit is a fine bit of farcing, and as good an illustration of Bergson's remark about the mechanicality of comedy as one could wish: he becomes a robot, a talking machine who has to be pushed out of the room and down the stairs. Mrs. Mechlin is momentarily afraid she has hurt him, but no, she can "hear him going on with his speech" below. Bridoun the riding-master has Zachariah practicing on a wooden horse, which throws him. "When," asks Zach, "do you think I may venture to ride a live horse?" Bridoun's answer is satisfyingly obvious: "The very instant you are able to keep your seat on a dead one." Dr. Catgut does not actually teach Zach to sing; he "quitted that paltry profession" some time ago. Now (like his original, Arne) he has taken to writing libretti for comic operas, of which he gives a stultifying sample. The whole portrait of Catgut/Arne is slanderous; it represents "the meagre musician, that sick monkey-face maker of crotchets" as a philanderer, an "eternal trotter after all the little draggle-tailed girls of the town." Arne did not prosecute, but Foote had stretched his Aristophanic license to the limit and was living on credit; another time he would not be so lucky.

163

Nothing about *The Commissary* is more Footian than its conclusion, or rather ending, for it is characteristically truncated. The plot to marry Zach to Dolly is exposed when Jenny switches sides and brings Isaac on the run, but Molly Mechlin produces a marriage contract stipulating that a stiff penalty must be paid for breach of promise. At this point Foote, his satiric purpose achieved, appears to lose interest; he simply leaves Zachariah dangling on the dilemma of whether to marry Dolly or pay the forfeit-money. The problem, he seems to say, is the character's, not mine: why should I solve it and get him off the hook? From the standpoint of satire, the ending as it stands is both just and artistic; it is only when the play is viewed as comedy that the lack of resolution creates problems. On the whole *The Commissary* is one of Foote's most satisfying plays, an asset to the laughing tradition which challenges the idea that he never developed or matured.

At this promising juncture Foote was vitimized by what the *Oxford Companion to the Theatre* terms "ducal horseplay." Some waggish aristocrats at the Duke of York's estate goaded the actor into riding a spirited horse; it threw him, and his leg had to be amputated. Foote was at first despondent, but soon he talked the conscience-stricken duke into obtaining a summer patent for him at the Haymarket Theatre, and in six months he was acting once more, throwing in jokes about his wooden leg. When he next wrote, two years after the accident, it was of hobbling heroes—a devil on crutches and a one-legged lover—whom he could play with "decorum." Neither *The Devil Upon Two Sticks* (1768) nor *The Lame Lover* (1770) is impressive next to *The Commissary*, but the wonder, as Johnson said of the dancing dogs, is not that they perform poorly, but that they perform at all.

Devil, adapted from Le Sage (Trefman, p. 166), is a mannerist play; it begins in the Spanish intrigue genre and then violates all our expectations for this kind of drama. Two fugitive lovers (Harriet and her mercantile paramour Invoice) hide in a chemist's house in Madrid, where they release a devil imprisoned in a bottle. This proves to be Sam Foote on crutches; he calls himself Cupid, or the Devil of Fashion, and reveals that Lucifer is now a nobody. Since the lovers are in imminent peril of detection he spirits them away to England, where in the last two acts he stages for their edification a satirical parade of doctors and lawyers. At last "Cupid" returns to Spain, and the lovers go to work for

Foote at the Haymarket. More than ever, Foote now played himself onstage, and the public loved it (Trefman, p. 170). Plot and sense are overwhelmed by satire and ridicule in *Devil*, but it was received for what it was: a courageous comeback.

Even flabbier is *The Lame Lover*, which has little story and less character, being simply an off-beat vehicle for mimicry. Foote played the title role, Sir Luke Limp, whose humor is a perverse vanity in having lost his leg, of which affliction he insists on making a conspicuous virtue. He is a social-climbing lord-hunter who permits himself no affection except for what is in his interest, a vulgarian up to his armpits in whatever is new. Fitzgerald held the view that Lofty, the blowhard villain of Goldsmith's *The Good-Natured Man*, was modelled on Sir Luke (p. 278), which is just possible, though Lofty is more amusing and less odious than Foote's character. This piece of bombast lodges in the house of Sergeant Circuit, a veritable law-machine—even his family's love affairs are tried "in court"—and casts eyes at both the sergeant's wife and daughter. Young Charlotte will have none of it: she warns her father to look to his honor, and interests herself in the languishing Woodford. Sir Luke continues to play loose with Mrs. Circuit, an aspiring clublady, and after the comic climax, the mock trial of act 3, he confesses to having cuckolded Circuit. But Mrs. Circuit denies everything and demands apologies, whereupon Sir Luke announces that his confession was just a device to disqualify himself as a suitor to Charlotte. This seems thin enough, yet is accepted all around, and the official verdict is "slander." Sergeant Circuit even apologizes for his suspicions. Evidently Foote thought that he had sufficiently exposed legal chicanery at this point, and was probably tired of limping around. It is the old story: once the satire is complete, any huddled-up finale will do.[23]

After these two advertisements for himself Foote hit his stride again, so to speak; *The Lame Lover* is the first of a string of seven comedies that he reeled off in the last seven years of his career. The second was *The Maid of Bath* (1771), a clever adaptation of current events to the old *senex amans* framework, and a great success. Elizabeth Linley, the belle of Bath who later became Mrs. Richard Brinsley Sheridan, appears in the play as "Miss Linnet." Both were singers—Elizabeth being the daughter of Thomas Linley the musician—and the objects of almost universal gallantry. Miss Linnet is particularly sought by the old miser, Solomon Flint, who is desirous of an heir, but Major Rackett, one of her rakish admirers, decides to prevent the wedding and "save" Miss Linnet. To this end he, Sir Christopher Cripple (Foote) and Billy Button, an ex-suitor, agree to win over Flint's friends and cure him of his colt's tooth. In act 2 Flint makes a ridiculous figure courting Miss Linnet, but the wedding is set for the morning. In act 3, however, the trap is sprung, commencing with the traditional comic terrorization of the old dotard by the hale young beauty: "You are a bold man!" It is unsuccessful, however, and Flint makes an ill-advised attempt to bed her first, then pay Button to marry her. Miss Linnet's demurrals are loud as well as virtuous, and all assemble to face down the villain. Flint is threatened with "ridicule by Foote" if he persists, whereupon he exits breathing defiance. Sir Christopher Cripple offers a dowry of two thousand guineas if Miss Linnet will marry Rackett (Button interjects: "Please your worship, I'll accept her with half"), but she is not interested: she prefers to remain a singer as long as the public continues its kind protection. The slightly sentimental tone of the last speech is reinforced by Cumberland's epilogue, which describes Flint as "that *monster*—an unfeeling man," and rhapsodizes characteristically: "Speak hearts for us! To them we make appeal: / Tell us not what you think, but what you feel." The ending, which eschews New Comedy saturnalia in order to remain true to life, also moves away from satire by inviting us to sympathize with the victory of virtue over vice in the manner of the melodramas. But the moment is short, and the comic mood is not destroyed. *The Maid of Bath* is Foote's most genial play, obviously written to capitalize on Elizabeth Linley's popularity.

Of quite another stripe is *The Nabob* (1772), perhaps his most vicious attack on a contemporary social abuse. It is essentially a satiric portrait of Sir Matthew Mite, the nabob, in his various roles as vulgar materialist, *nouveau riche* antiquarian and unprincipled destroyer of families. The plot is only a vehicle to show the nabob's unscrupulousness: he has maneuvered Sir John Oldham into his debt for some ten thousand pounds in order to render his suit for Sophy Oldham irresistible. When the proud Oldhams refuse him anyway, Sir Matthew threatens to foreclose; but Sir John's brother Thomas, a city merchant, pays off the debt, saves the family and betroths his son to Sophy. This rather trite and facile denouement has caused some critics to see the plot as sentimental, but the Jonsonian ridicule of Mite is the core of the play, if *ridicule* is the word. Sir Matthew remains a dangerous force up to the very end: he is viewed as a real threat to society against whom there is little defence but the better qualities of the English middle class. In Boswell's familiar anecdote, a party of nabobs felt so affronted by the play that they called on Foote to take him to task; of course he charmed them and they ended by staying to dinner. Foote's play was only one item of a whole anti-nabob literature, which both reflected and aroused feelings that culminated in the Hastings trial of the next decade. In the nabob Foote had one of his most promising targets for satire, but a good play did not emerge from the onslaught; only a sketch was needed, and all but the sketch seems incidental.

In 1773 Foote staged two interesting plays, *Piety in Pattens* and *The Bankrupt*. *Piety* was something of a *cause célèbre* in its day—a pre-Goldsmith assault on sentimental comedy—but remained unpublished and obscure until 1973.[24] Back in 1769 Foote had wanted to ridicule Garrick's Shakespeare Jubilee procession; perhaps remembering how Fielding had used puppet-shows to spoof *Tea*, he planned to use "Garrick-size" puppets (Fitzgerald, pp. 304–6), and puppets were once again brought to his attention in November 1772 when he went with Goldsmith to see the Italian *fantoccini* perform. Goldsmith admired the cleverness of the mechanism and envied the smoothness with which these "actors" were manipulated, but Foote was struck by the "general stiffness and absurd gravity" of the puppets, which he thought could be "an additional comic element" in a satire (Fitzgerald, pp. 320–21). Realizing that puppets would be beyond or beneath the Examiner's Office, he must have set to work almost at once, for *The Primitive Puppet-Shew* was performed with partial success in February, after weeks of newspaper advertisements emphasizing that Garrick would be taken off by a puppet named Dubois. A revised version caught the public fancy in March, and was presented (by human actors) during the summer and on numerous occasions for the rest of the decade.

The spring production naturally cut into the patent theaters' audiences, but apart from this and a passing reference or two *The Primitive Puppet-Shew* does not appear to be aimed at Garrick, despite the huckstering. Of course Foote may have added in performance satirical bits not in the manuscripts—Bogorad's edition demonstrates how much more there was to a Foote production than the bare text—but it is more likely that Foote, who could seldom confine himself to one object of satire, stumbled across better game than mere mimicry, and followed it. His nobler quarry was sentimental drama and fiction. Everyone recognized allusions to recent sentimental comedies and comic operas, as well as the general resemblance to *Pamela* (or *Shamela*) that most modern readers apprehend, and shortly *Piety in Pattens* was hailed as the precursor of one greater than itself. The *Morning Chronicle* for 19 March 1773 asserted that "the ridicule aimed by Foote, at what has for some time past been received as comedy by the town, aided in establishing . . . *She Stoops to Conquer*," while both Arthur Murphy and Thomas Davies in their biographies of Garrick went so far as to credit *Piety* with bringing sentimental comedy "into disrepute" (Murphy, 2:52, Davies, 2:140–41). *Piety* may have been instrumental in ending a transient fashion; it obviously did not overthrow the sentimental tradition, still flourishing as Murphy and Davies wrote, though it did thrust home.

The Primitive Puppet-Shew falls into three sections: an "Exordium" spoken by Foote, *Piety in Pattens* itself, and some concluding by-play wherein the puppets are arrested. The text of the first section was printed by periodicals and collected from them by theater historians; it consists of a sham history of puppet-shows, followed by unflattering comparisons between puppets and the live actors of the town. Foote boasts of having "a theatrical manager upon stilts made out of the mulberry tree" (Bogorad, p. 19). Garrick had had souvenirs made out of Stratford mulberry during the Shakespeare Jubilee, but Foote was also a "manager upon stilts," and not above pointing to his own leg as he spoke. After a good deal more in this vein Foote announced "a sentimental comedy" entitled *The Handsome Housemaid, or, Piety in Pattens,* and the curtain rose on the smartly-costumed puppets.

At this point *Piety* proper begins. The piece may be generally understood as a takeoff on *Pamela,* but its humor cannot be fully appreciated without the intermediate term, Isaac Bickerstaffe's *The Maid of the Mill* (1765). In Bickerstaffe's musical version of *Pamela* Squire B— becomes the virtuous Lord Aimworth, betrothed to Theodosia Sycamore but in love with Patty Fairfield, a miller's daughter, who, however, is plighted to Farmer Giles, Finally, in a burst of sentimental generosity, Lord Aimworth offers old Fairfield a thousand pounds for his daughter's dowry, plus the expenses of her wedding to Farmer Giles. Foote takes these characters, adds a dash of stupidity and a pinch of self-interest, accentuates their benevolence and sets them a-jerking. Lord Aimworth becomes Squire Thirdle ("Spindleshanks"), who reached the fourth form in Westminster School and has since grown rich as a nabob. Patty is now Polly Pattens (i.e., high wooden shoes), his handsome and "vartuous" housemaid, whose honor is threatened by his designs and whose peace is marred by the insults of his proud stewardess, Mrs. Candy. Polly is also apprehensive of the intentions of Thomas the butler, her self-proclaimed friend, who has a way with a sentiment: as he warns Polly, "The Woman who loses her Virtue, from that very instant all her Chastity's gone." Polly, impressed by this and other admonitions, decides to pack her bundle and flee at once. "Never mind your Bundle, my Dear," counsels Thomas. "Beauty when join'd with Innocence, tho' naked will find out Admirers." In act 2 the Squire attempts to prevent her departure by offering her "a thousand Pounds a Year" for life to become his mistress in London. Polly admits to a liking for him, but is also drawn to Thomas's offer of lawful matrimony. The squire is stunned by the prospects now opening before him:

> Her Tears as the Play says, would soften Rocks, & bend the knotted Oak, & am I made of tougher Materials than they?—rise, Child, & let me consider.—Her Virtue astonishes, Whilst her Beauty inchants me. what, if I should make her my Wife? ah! can I bear to be a Butt for the Finger of Scorn. I, who am a Delatanti, a Macaroni, a Savoir vivre? to take up with my House Maid. can I after that shew my Face at Arthurs, Boodles, or Almacks? but what of that? shan't I have me dear domestic Delights, what are Nights consum'd in Pharoah, Hazard, Quintz, to stirring the fire, rocking the Cradle, or warming the Pap at my own House in the Country. illusive & desultory all. Reason is Victor. Vain World adieu. come then to my Arms, my dear Polly, there Cling & climb, just like a creeping Grape round the tall Elm, my ever destin'd, my acknowledg'd Wife.[25]

The housemaid's dream has come true, but now Polly, reflecting that she owes the preservation of her "Vartue" to Thomas, calls him in and accepts his offer instead of the Squire's. Thomas, however, with equal magnanimity refuses to stand in the way of Polly's "Preferment," and steps aside. It is the Squire's turn to posture, and he replies with all the snobbish condescension of the benevolist:

Matchless Pair! & shall these poor people, little better than Peasants, the one just able to write, & the other not able to read, shew such dignified Sentiments, & shall I, who reach'd the fourth Form in Westminster School, jade & tire in the Horserace of Glory? no. down love, up Honour. ye noble minded Pair approach, & let me join those Hands, whose Hearts so exactly agree. I will stock Nettle Bed Farm, which is Ten Pounds a Year, & settle it on you for both your lives.

"Exalted generosity," cries Polly, politely forgetting his recent offer of a thousand a year for carnal knowledge. Not to be outdone, she announces that, as the merits of her suitors now appear equal, she cannot justly reject either, so she will marry—neither. The Larpent MS ends here, with all three in a benevolist's ecstasy, uttering spasmodic cries of delight: "Oh! oh! oh!" The Folger MS, truer to the idea of parodying comic opera, has each character sing a doggerel couplet or two, importing his or her return to business as usual. At this point the show is broken up by the constable; Foote has some exchanges with his plants in the audience, and *exeunt omnes*.

Considering the quality and quantity of satire packed into his obscure playlet, the large claims that were made for it are not surprising. Foote anatomizes the stock situations, characters, and speeches of sentimental drama, and he is never more the Hogarthian caricaturist than in exaggerating these conventions to bring out inherent contradictions and dualities of motive. The sentimental heroine, the reforming rake, the benevolist, the "friend" are understood, mocked, flayed, and dissected; the dramatic sentiment is given the gentle nudge required to topple it into nonsense or bawdry. The use of puppets is perhaps the most brilliant stroke. Sentimental comedy did turn its characters into virtue-machines, producing, or operated by, the correct sequence of sentiments, and Foote saw the comical side of this mechanicality as clearly as would Henri Bergson. *Piety* is a satisfying riposte to the Muse of the Woeful Countenance, more forceful, accurate, and unalloyed than any work by Goldsmith or Sheridan.

The Bankrupt, however, produced later the same year, is widely held to be as sentimental as anything Foote ever wrote, and is certainly a surprising successor to *Piety*. The diction and characterization of Sir James and Lydia, the pathetic use of filial devotion, the cozy anticipation of a domestic idyll at the end, and perhaps the fortuitous introduction of bankruptcy, seem to belong to the school Foote had just attacked. Yet the bankruptcy theme is employed partly to expose Pillage and Resource and to bring about the self-ejection of the villainness, functions associated with traditional comedy. On this side of the ledger, too, are the satiric hits at Grub Street through Margin the printer and the central humors portrait of Sir Robert, not to mention Robin, the valet who "has by him . . . a genteel comedy of one act, that is thought to have a good deal of merit." *The Bankrupt* has the framework of laughing and satiric comedy, but the serious and sentimental touches, and especially the softer mood at the close, do considerably vitiate the comic spirit. Thomas Holcroft used some of its material in his 1792 melodrama *The Road to Ruin* (Belden, p. 190).

The purpose of *The Cozeners* (1774), was, according to Garrick's prologue, "to chase a smuggling crew, who law deride"; Foote had not given up trying to help the magistrate. As "Captain Timbertoe," he spoke these moral words self-consciously:

> Dramatic writers were, like watchmen, meant
> To knock down Vice—few answer the intent.
> . . . .
> When wanted most, the watch a nap will take—
> Are all our comic authors quite awake?

It is a return to the topical mood of *The Commissary;* there are allusions to Chesterfield's letters, to Fox, and to Arne again, besides the type-portraits (Fitzgerald, pp. 331–32). *The Cozeners* is also one of Foote's best-constructed plays, largely because it follows *The Alchemist* so closely. In act 1 Flaw and Mrs. Fleece'em (reminiscent of Simon and Mrs. Mechlin), after an initial falling-out, practice a series of subterfuges on various gulls: O'Flannagan, Moses Manasses and Mrs. Simony. In the best Jonsonian tradition, the satire simultaneously exposes the vices of the knaves and the follies of their dupes. Flaw tries to swindle the rustic Aircastles in act 2 by marrying their son Toby to a black girl, though Toby hankers for his pregnant country wench, Betsy Blossom. This owes a good deal to the Hardcastles, Tony Lumpkin, and Bet Bouncer in *She Stoops to Conquer*, though Mrs. Aircastle's seduction by Colonel Gorget is certainly out of the Goldsmithian mood. In act 3 the great scheme is just coming to a head when all the dupes return at once, bent on vengeance.

Flaw bolts, Colonel Gorget dispenses advice and poetic justice, and Mrs. Fleece'em warns us pointedly that criminals far more highly placed than she could equally well be in Old Bailey. *The Cozeners* is solidly in the tradition of Old Comedy, and one of Foote's most purely Aristophanic efforts. Laughter is plentiful, character is static (in the manner of *Lysistrata* and *The Alchemist*), and sentiment is nonexistent.

Foote's art had always depended on the sufferance of his victims, and in 1775 his luck finally ran out. *The Trip to Calais* satirized the notorious Duchess of Kingston as Lady Kitty Crocodile, and she succeeded in having the Lord Chamberlain forbid its performance. Foote's "Muse and magistrate" letter availed nothing; he had to alter the play (to *The Capuchin*, 1776), omitting Lady Kitty. But the damage was done: the Duchess allowed her deputy, the Reverend Jackson (portrayed in *The Capuchin* as Dr. Viper), free rein and unlimited funds to smear Foote, which he did chiefly by reviving old rumors of sodomy. Although Foote was eventually cleared of the charges, he felt so harried by the anonymous newspaper paragraphs and the pressures of the public trial that he sold his theater to George Colman in January 1777, and upon his acquittal collapsed hysterically. Within the year he was dead.

Artistically the experience was not fruitless: the revision considerably improved the weak and wandering plot of the original play. In *The Trip to Calais* Jenny Minnikin flees to France to marry Dick Druggett, her father's apprentice. The Minnikins' hot pursuit prevents the marriage, but once they appear the plot diffuses into general Gallophobia, featuring Luke Lapelle, in a rerun of *The Englishman in Paris*. In act 2 French Catholicism is satirized through the Capuchin O'Donnovan and the Abbess, but then we take a new direction via Lady Kitty Crocodile's lugubrious and hypocritical lamentations for her dead husband, and her tyranny over the virtuous Miss Lydell. The Minnikins are introduced to Lady Kitty, who is persuaded to try recalling Jenny to her duty. In the end, the upright Colonel Crosby exposes Lady Kitty's character and is affianced to Miss Lydell; Lady Kitty is made the guardian of Jenny (it being felt they deserve each other), while Dick Druggett drops quietly from sight. In no other play is his plot such an obvious embarrassment to Foote, so patently a mere vehicle for satiric laughter and ridicule.

The enforced revision replaces Lady Kitty and Lapelle with Sir Harry Hamper, who discharges Lapelle's function by his boorish admiration of all that's French, and Lady Kitty's through his designs on Jenny. He is aided by O'Donnovan (played by Foote), whose part is expanded, and by Dr. Viper (the Reverend Jackson), who is only mentioned in *Trip*. Foote's portrait of the man who finally ruined him has a morbid interest. Persuading Sir Harry to rape Jenny (who has gotten herself to a nunnery), Viper muses, "To be sure—a rape, and upon a nun too . . . it will shew a noble contempt for decency, religion, and virtue, and can't fail recommending you to all people of spirit." But this is prevented, and at the end Jenny appears likely to marry Druggett after all. Miss Lydell is also cut, and Colonel Crosby might as well be; his belated appearance to help unravel matters is clearly superfluous. These changes unify the plot by focusing the satire on rogues and confidence men allegedly hiding under the cloth.[26]

In Foote's final account, both the debits and the credits are characteristically extravagant. He was the principal dramatic satirist of the Garrick era, an upholder of the oldest Western comic tradition during the doldrums of the fifties, and a major contributor to the development of the *petite pièce*. For the most part Foote's work is unsentimental or even antisentimental, and he completely eschewed writing in illegitimate forms. On the other hand, he made his living from unsparing mimicry, often of particular people; he gives us caricatures for human beings; his plots are negligent, and his endings truncated. He spoke with a forked tongue of the moral dimension and the general reference of his satire. To call most of his plays "comedies," as he insisted on doing, is a bit of pretension; they are such sketches of people and manners as a night-club comedian might give. But Foote's desire to be "the English Aristophanes," though it does not excuse his failings, puts these objections in a different light. For him, "a comedy's being local or temporary is so far from being a moral or critical fault, that it constitutes its chiefest merit" (*Letter from Mr. Foote . . .*, 1760). And the dramatic satirist is naturally more concerned with content than with form. Then too, the Licensing Act first forbade Foote an outlet in regular drama—a plot would have made his early entertainments illegal—and audience response bade him continue in that vein. What he might have become had he not been made a dramatic outlaw we can only speculate. As for his plays not being "real" comedies, they correspond well enough to Old Comedy and to what Henri Bergson calls "light comedy," exaggerating the "natural rigidity in things," or comedy of wit: "a gift for dashing off comic scenes in a few strokes."[27] Foote would probably have liked the term "corrective comedy," with its implications of moral utility. For all his posing, he enriched and enlivened the traditions of earlier comedy for transmission to better playwrights.

GEORGE COLMAN (1732–1794)

George Colman the Elder, youngest of the professional group, produced a body of comic work more substantial than Macklin's or Garrick's and more heterogeneous than Foote's, though he backed into the theater. Until 1764 Colman expected to be a leisured gentleman, but the early death of his uncle and patron, William Pulteney, Earl of Bath, disappointed his hopes of patronage and left him to seek his own livelihood. Since several of his plays had already been successful, he chose a theatrical profession; from 1767 until his death he was usually managing either Covent Garden or the Haymarket. It was when he became a professional that Colman's work began to exhibit its heterogeneity. Up to that juncture he had written three afterpieces and a mainpiece, all either spoofing sentiment or holding firmly to the laughing tradition; afterwards he wrote six mainpiece comedies mixing sentiment with laughter, three farces, and about a dozen *illegitimi:* burlettas, "preludes," and the like. Prior to 1764 he resembled Foote or Murphy as a dramatist—a traditional *farceur* and satirist—but then he began to sound like Garrick: the careful compromiser, willing to purvey what the town wanted. This shift was the easier for him to make because, being less of a public figure than Garrick or Foote, he had not been called upon (nor was he inclined) to proclaim his dramatic aesthetics. Colman did not put himself forward as a critic until late, and the collection of his *Prose on Several Occasions* (1787) is a quiet commentary on theatrical fashions; it tells us little of his principles, except that he espoused "nature" and "variety."[28] In all likelihood Colman simply realized in 1764 that now he "must please to live."

In 1760, when his first play was produced, no such exigency constrained him; he was a bright young lawyer, his expectations were reasonably great and the town was his oyster. If true stage comedy was languishing, that dearth might be supplied at the expense of its rivals by a man of talent. Thus *Polly Honeycombe*, "a dramatic novel in one act," let off a spirited blast at the sentimental novel and, by implication, at its cousin the sentimental comedy. In the prologue Colman billed himself with a becoming lack of modesty as the new Cervantes, prepared to treat novels as the Spaniard had romances, while mounted on a steed of moral alarm:

> And then so *sentimental* is the Stile,
> So chaste, yet so bewitching all the while!
> Plot, and elopement, passion, rape, and rapture,
> The total sum of ev'ry dear—dear—Chapter.
>   'Tis not alone the Small-Talk and the Smart,
> 'Tis NOVEL most beguiles the Female Heart.
> Miss reads—she melts—she sighs—Love steals upon her—
> And then—Alas, poor Girl!—good night, poor Honour!

But this moralizing (repeated in the epilogue) is not an accurate description of what happens in the play. Polly does not lose her honor, only her suitor, and she is a more sympathetic and less ridiculous character than her descendant Lydia Languish. We are even forced to take her part against the representatives of the non-novel-reading world who oppress her: Mr. Ledger, her 'Change-Alley beau, and old Honeycombe the heavy father, with his tag line, "Hark ye, hussy!" Colman seems unable to decide whether his heroine is more benighted or heroic. When she informs Ledger that he is "more tiresome than the multiplication-table," and her father that "you would dispose of your daughter like a piece of merchandise," we see her point. Yet we learn at the end that Polly is being hoodwinked by her other suitor, Scribble, who, like Beverly in *The Rivals*, observes all the romantic forms for the young lady's sake. If we were shown early in the play that Polly's propensity for sentimental fiction has made her an easy mark for the machinations of Scribble and his aunt (Polly's nurse), we would be more inclined to take the purported moral seriously. The novels themselves are played for laughs; their art furnishes the matter with which Polly confronts every crisis of her life. After she has dismissed Ledger, it is "Ha! Ha! Ha!—I have outtopped them all—Miss Howe, Narcissa, Clarinda, Polly Barnes, Sophy Willis, and all of them. None of them ever treated an odious fellow with half so much spirit.—This would make an excellent chapter in a new novel.—But here comes papa—in a violent passion, no doubt.—No matter—it will only furnish materials for the next chapter." The conclusion, which leaves everyone dangling, is in the manner of Foote; the satire prevents the fulfillment of the comedy, so there are no winners. Unlike Foote, however, Colman leaves us in moral confusion. Are we to approve Honeycombe's diatribe against circulating libraries? True, novel-reading turned Polly's head, almost betrayed her to the clutches of a scoundrel, and broke up the match her parents had arranged. But would marriage to Ledger have been a comic ending? And would Polly have had the spirit to resist it without the examples of Clarissa Harlowe and Sophy Western? Even when all is out Polly finds Scribble the better suitor, as we do. Colman's light satire seems finally to touch everyone, and every position. Moral there is none.

The play was so successful that in 1761 Colman decided to attempt a full-length comedy, and aided by Garrick produced *The Jealous Wife,* an adaptation of *Tom Jones* with additions from *The Spectator* and Terence's *The Brothers.* Colman retained a good deal of the plot and spirit of Fielding's novel, but embellished it with characters of humors such as Sir Harry Beagle, Captian O'Cutter, and Mrs. Oakly, the titular heroine. Sir Harry combines Squire Western's love of venery with Blifil's role as the unwelcome rival suitor; evidently Colman felt that the character of Blifil was not suited to stage comedy. Captain O'Cutter provides maritime color along the lines of Ben in *Love for Love,* and is rather awkwardly made the agent of an important development when he delivers the wrong letter. Mrs. Oakly's jealousy is only a patina covering warm love for her husband, which he reciprocates. Excessive love is in fact the Oaklys' only real marital problem; it accounts for her jealousy and his lack of firmness. As Major Oakly tells his brother, "Mrs. Oakly would make you an excellent wife, if you did but know how to manage her." The misunderstandings, *éclaircissement,* and reconciliation of the Oaklys make up the original half of the plot.

The rest is recognizably *Tom Jones*. Mr. Oakly corresponds to Fielding's Squire Allworthy, though he has a wife and a legitimate son, Charles (Tom), in love with Harriot Russet (Sophia). Disappointed in Charles and pressed by her father to marry Sir Harry Beagle, she flees to the dubious protection of her kinswoman Lady Trinket in London, whither she is pursued by her father, Beagle, Charles, and his parents. In the city,

Harriot's honor is assaulted by Lord Trinket (Fellamar) and Lady Freelove (Bellaston), who cleverly turns Mrs. Oakly's jealousy against Harriot. Now the girl has no refuge. After Charles saves her from rape by Lord Trinket she runs to her father's lodgings, where she has to reject Beagle's importunities. Discouraged by this setback, Sir Harry now trades his rights over Harriot to Lord Trinket in exchange for a horse. Eventually Charles is allowed to take Harriot under his protection after a rather fulsome reform, the only sentimental scene in the play; Harriot exacts a much fuller measure of confession and contrition from him than Sophia ever did from Tom. When old Russet finally discovers Lord Trinket's designs he wearily awards the girl to Charles, Beagle retires happily to the saddle, and Lady Freelove and Lord Trinket withdraw with polite aristocratic noises. It only remains for Oakly to confront his wife, which he does; a renewal of their vows, and a pledge never to be jealous again, follow in due order.

We do not know how much or what kind of assistance Colman received on *The Jealous Wife*, but certain of its features are redolent of Garrick. Where *Polly Honeycombe* had opposed the sentimental novel and employed an original plot and characters, the mainpiece is derivative and admits some sentiment: the reform of Charles, and the generally mellow tone of the individual relationships and characterizations. Some compromise with sentiment was, however, expected in mainpieces, and the pathetic tendencies are kept in perspective by Lady Freelove's barbs: "Where's the difference between truths and untruths, if you do but stick close to the point?" The overall effect is that of an intrigue comedy in the laughing mode, with a genial atmosphere and one sentimental scene. Garrick's influence need not be doubted, yet, given the skill of *Polly Honeycombe*, Colman was clearly capable of writing most of the comedy himself.

The Musical Lady, a two-act farce of 1762, may afford some idea of how Garrick edited *The Jealous Wife* if, as Eugene Page claims, the farce consists of material cut from that comedy.[29] The plot bears a close resemblance to *Polly Honeycombe* in that a penurious lover wins the lady by donning a disguise of affected manners to humor her foible. George Mask, a law-student, hopes to wed the pseudo-musical Sophy before his father comes to town. Aided by his friend Freeman's purse and his own amusing imitation of Italian musical fashions, he does achieve his conquest, but then his father arrives and disabuses Sophy concerning George, who readily admits the ruse. All three men join in a concerted attack on Sophy's foreign tastes; they finally laugh her into acceptance of plain British George and life in Merrie England. The strain of patriotic sentiment carries over into the epilogue:

> For arts and arms a Briton is the thing!
> John Bull was made to roar—but not to sing.

A few such notes aside, the play is a laughing farce of the "festive reform" type, with the musical lady as the humors character who leaves off her foibles. The well-sketched background and competent exposition of the first scene promise something higher than afterwards transpires; characters do not develop and some of the satire is silly.

Colman's best play of these years, a two-act farce called *The Deuce Is in Him* (1763), returns to the attack on sentiment. Taking the well-worn device of the lover who insists on testing his beloved—which had appeared in Ovid and Chaucer and would reappear in Sheridan—Colman turns it to ridicule. Colonel Tamper is the uneasy spirit who must make certain that Emily loves him for his essential self, so he feigns the loss of an eye and a leg. Colman associates this morbid restlessness with the sentimentalists: Emily describes her story as "quite a little novel," and Colonel Tamper admits self-consciously, "There is an excess of sensibility in my temper [which] . . . must be assured that she will . . . retain her affection for me." Major Belford remains a welcome voice of reason and the playwright's spokesman. "Most precious refinement, truly!" he exclaims to Tamper, ". . . picked up in one of your expeditions to the coast of France, I suppose." (In the Advertisement Colman admits founding the piece on two of Marmontel's *Contes moraux*.) Belford has no more sympathy for Emily's talk of a "pure and disinterested passion" abstracted from person or fortune, and finally convinces her that passion may be rational. Together they maneuver Tamper into repentance and a request for forgiveness, no sooner asked than conventionally given. *Deuce* is interesting chiefly in that it shows how comfortably the afterpiece was now discharging the old comic functions.

Colman's only dramatic activity in the next two seasons was a moralized alteration of *Philaster*. He was chiefly occupied with his translation of Terence's comedies in blank verse, and the upheaval that the death of his patron represented for him.[30] The "gentleman-in-training" woke up suddenly to find himself a *bourgeois malgré lui*. Hitherto he had been semi-dependent on the Earl of Bath; now he was a professional, fully dependent on the public, with all that implied for his work. It was a radical change of outlook: no wonder a concern with the relationship of the aristocracy to the bourgeois runs obsessively through five of his last six mainpiece comedies.

The first of these was *The Clandestine Marriage* (1766), another collaboration with Garrick, treated here because its class-consciousness is more typical of Colman. The earlier assumption that most of the work was Colman's has been challenged by Frederick L. Bergmann and more recently by Ann T. Straulman as mentioned earlier; she divides the credit about equally, attributing to Colman "the serious romantic aspect of the main plot," the satirical details about social climbing, and the development of a substantial plot. Garrick is supposed to have created Lord Ogleby, polished the dialogue, and composed the riotous nocturne that concludes the action. A story attributed to Catherine Clive sounds rather like Garrick at work: that the piece was such a thing of the theater that actors' and actresses' names were used for the various characters as it grew.[31] Whatever the truth about the respective shares, *The Clandestine Marriage* was certainly the most important play with which Colman was ever involved; Page calls it "the most representative comedy of its day" (p. 125).

In working up the story Colman may have drawn on James Townley's *False Concord* (1764, unpublished), a farcical short comedy now extant only in the Larpent Collection (MS 236), which tells how Miss Sedley and Miss Johnson contrive to avert Miss Sedley's marriage with Lord Lavender, a *senex amans*, so that she can wed her cousin Raymond, whom she loves. They have the support of Mr. Sedley, but are opposed by the villainess, Mrs. Sedley, who is mad to have a title in the family and play the aristocrat: "Oh! I shall take a prodigious deal of pains to be easy—Then I will be near-sighted and rude, and know nobody." Trimmer, the lawyer who stands to gain by the match, is naturally one of her party, but Miss Johnson defeats them both simply by announcing that Miss Sedley has eloped with Raymond. Though the information is false, Lord Lavender betrays his indifference by leaving for London without further ado. Mrs. Sedley, her eyes opened, accepts Raymond as a son-in-law, and a happy Mr. Sedley closes the play with a warning against "intermar-riages" between trade and nobility:

> 'Tis linsey wolsey tack'd to satin,
> False Concord!—as we say in Latin.

The Clandestine Marriage is less class-conscious than this, and its tension is not as great because the young lovers are safely married throughout, but otherwise the plots are roughly parallel. Fanny Sterling has been secretly married for four months to Lovewell, her father's clerk, and is pregnant. They have hesitated to reveal the match to her mercenary father, but now that Sir John Melvil and Lord Ogleby are arriving for the marriage of Sir John to Miss Sterling, Fanny's older sister, there is light at the end of the tunnel: Ogleby is a relation of the timid Lovewell, who hopes to secure his approval and protection. Before he can say anything, however, both of the visiting nobleman fall in love with Fanny, confess their feelings to her and open negotiations with her father. Mr. Sterling would do anything for money, and when Sir John offers to reduce the dowry by thirty thousand pounds if he can switch daughters, the consent of the crass tradesman is assured. But Miss Sterling and her rich Aunt Heidelberg veto the change and impugn Fanny's character. The couple's wishy-washiness about revealing their condition, while sometimes comi-cal, prolongs the action painfully. At last Miss Sterling thinks she hears Sir John in Fanny's room one night, preparing to elope, and she rouses the house, but in the ensuing melee the visitor proves to be, of course, Lovewell, and the secret is out. Lord Ogleby surprisingly comes to his kinsman's defence and convinces Sterling to accept the couple, though Sir John quite rightly tells Lovewell that he could have spared himself a great deal of anguish by confessing earlier.

This last remark goes to the heart of the main critical dispute about the comedy. Ernest Bernbaum called it a "surrender to the popular taste," which he took to be sentimentalism. (p. 218). Eugene Page takes the more moderate view that the play was "a compromise between the old and the new" (p. 112), a delta of the tributary modes (p. 125). I would go further and call it, on balance, a laughing comedy. Bernbaum found *The Clandestine Marriage* "sentimental in its main plot and chief characters" (p. 218), meaning Lovewell and Fanny, but he seems not to have noticed what the authors were doing with them. The theme is the familiar one of *false* delicacy: the distresses of the lovers, which arise ostensibly from their precarious financial position, in practice result from their silly conversational fumbling and blundering, and thus become comical, even farcical. Fanny's languishings before Lord Ogleby, intended to dishearten him, come across as coyly encouraging, drawing out her distress and making a difficult task more so. And if we sometimes sympathize with her, we can only laugh at her husband's feebleness; his interview with Lord Ogleby is a tissue of *double-entendres*, mistaken meanings and untruths. The couple's reticence even allows Sir John to believe he still has a chance. By the end of act 4 Fanny has two suitors, a husband, and four-ninths of a baby. As in *False Delicacy* and *The Guardian,* satire upon sentimental reticence is inherent in the plot, but nowhere in eighteenth-century comedy are two sentimental lovers made to look more ridiculous; *sentimental* becomes here a synonym for *ineffectual.* Sterling, the *bourgeois gentilhomme* and archetypal blocking figure; the senile rake, Lord Ogleby; Mrs. Heidelberg's mispronunciations; the legal humor of Flower; and Betty, the amusingly scatterbrained maid, provide further links to traditional comedy.

The modern reputation of *The Clandestine Marriage* is respectable enough to place it in the occasional anthology as "typical" of the period, but no one has ever accused it of profundity. It is rather a decent piece of social art, dramatizing a wealth of historical information about Georgian bourgeois, especially how they viewed themselves and the classes above them. Sterling is especially interesting as the representative of city money, set deliberately against the titled folk from the other end of town. His soliloquy on social fortunes (III.i) is an essay in sociological analysis, and it is a fine touch of character that he attributes Sir John's shift of affections to fickleness and indifference to money rather than to love (III.ii). His daughter Miss Sterling is not ashamed to aspire higher than the title of "cit's wife," and even Fanny is not oblivious to money. At times the play seems less an outgrowth of *False Concord* than a parody of *The London Merchant,* and it is probably here that we see Colman's hand. The aesthetic side of social art is the generally competent standard of dramaturgy. In act 1, for example, the first exclamations of the play smoothly explain the fact of the title, and at the end of the act the remarks of Lovewell and Miss Sterling communicate very neatly the idea that Sir John's passion is for Fanny. Lapses do occur—as when Lovewell

181

begins telling Fanny what she already knows—but they are exceptions to the rule. Not the least of the play's accomplishments is the way it circumvents the eighteenth-century ban on risqué scenes. At the opening of act 5 Lovewell is in Fanny's bedroom at night, and sex is just under the surface. But it is a safe titillation, or at least a lawful one, for they are husband and wife, though they meet as clandestine lovers. This shrewd piece of evasion, now thought to be Garrick's work, has no counterpart in *False Concord*.

Although Eugene Page describes *The English Merchant* (1767) as "by far Colman's most sentimental comedy," he notes that the changes Colman made in Voltaire's *L'Écossaise*, his source, tended to augment the elements of straight comedy in it (p. 131). These do not amount to much. Only the ridiculous characters of Spatter and Lady Alton, who are ejected, at all lighten the serious atmosphere of troubles and benevolence created by the emphasis on reunion and sententious reform. Amelia is an allegory of Virtue in Distess, Lord Falbridge of Insulting Wealth Reformed. Sir William is tearfully reunited with his daughter in the centerpiece of act 3. And Freeport, the unusual merchant-benevolist—eccentric, forthright, and above social custom—is given a translation of Terence's famous sentiment to mouth: "I am a man myself; and am bound to be a friend to all mankind" (*homo sum: humani nil a me alienum puto*). *The English Merchant* seems an instance of "cross-Channel feedback": the sentimental idea, which had crossed to France from England earlier in the century and had struck sympathetic vibrations there, was now returning so amplified that many Englishmen did not recognize it, and, like Colman, ascribed it to Gallic extravagance.

The Oxonian in Town (1767) is a strange afterpiece, laughing but not traditional. One Oxonian in town on a spree (Knowell) finds another (Careless) endangered by a gang scheming to ruin him at cards and marry him off to a whore. He saves Careless by insinuating himself into the confidence of the gamblers and forcing the woman, by threat of arrest, to change sides and turn state's evidence. His reward is Careless' sister. The mildly didactic attitude to gaming and the sympathetic treatment of Lucy the whore are strangely juxtaposed with full-blooded and licentious scenes at the card tables among the ladies of pleasure. The play reads badly, especially the gibbering merriment of Careless and the moral tag by Lucy, but may have staged better; it was Colman's first independent original work since *Polly Honeycombe,* and he seems unsure what he wants to do with his independence.

Colman's efforts for the next several years were diffuse and mostly insubstantial. In 1768 he altered *King Lear* less unacceptably than his predecessors, and produced Goldsmith's *The Good-Natured Man* at Covent Garden, but also began increasing the proportion of operas and pantomimes in his repertoire. His *Man and Wife, or, The Shakespeare Jubilee* (1769), attempts to capitalize on the Stratford fiasco and its profitable sequel: Garrick's procession of Shakespearean characters at Drury Lane. The plot is a harlequinade of disguises, "business" and deceptions, set against the frenzied background of the Jubilee. Colonel Frankly and Charlotte are the lovers who require uniting; they are opposed by her two rival suitors and two quarrelsome parents, Mr. and Mrs. "Cross," the title-couple. The four feuders offset each other, negating their own opposition, and the lovers find their way to marriage. In act 3, after a "pageant of Shakespearean Characters," confusion arises over who is to meet whom in a purple domino—one can imagine Danny Kaye making a good job of this—and the action becomes a smoke-screen of masks, cross-purposes, and counter-intelligence. At the end both suitors and parents, pleased that their rivals have been checked, join in accepting the match, and Mr. Cross points the badly needed moral: a family must maintain its unity. Set against Colman's earlier plays, *Man and Wife* suggests a deterioration, yet it was another five years before he wrote anything else even as legitimate as this. The interval was given mostly to writing and producing burlettas such as *The Portrait* and spectacles such as *Mother Shipton* (both 1770), although Colman did stage *She Stoops to Conquer* in 1773.

The Man of Business (1774), Colman's first mainpiece in seven years, almost defies generic labels; it is a "comedy" only insofar as it ends happily for the principals. A few passing touches of sentiment come to nothing, and the theme of reform loses itself in a welter of financial dealings during the last act, leaving a residue of fiscal responsibility and bourgeois ethics. Colman evidently wanted to resume the discussions of social class problems he had begun in *The Clandestine Marriage* and continued in *The English Merchant,* but more directly this time, without the interference of farce or sentiment or "character." The plot centers on the misadventures of Beverley. This young middle-class man of affairs has taken to mixing with aristocrats, a development viewed with alarm by his mentor Fable: "What has a man of business to do with men of pleasure? Why is a young banker to live with young noblemen?" It is *The London Merchant* revisited, with Beverley as George Barnwell, and Fable ("Regularity and punctuality are the life of business") as Thorowgood. But Fable also suggests Freeport, the English merchant-benevolist: he stages a fictional "ruin" of "the House" to frighten Beverley into mending his ways, and later, when the counterfeit ruin becomes real in act 4, involves himself in dubious business ethics in order to extricate his protégé. The conclusion thus vindicates Fable as much as it does Beverley, who is given the boss's daughter as a reward for returning to the straight and narrow. For all its shortcomings as entertainment, the play radiates a genuine concern with the real-life problems of the bourgeois element in the audience, making it finally more a drama than a comedy.[32]

The Spleen; or, Islington Spa (1776, produced at Drury Lane) is a light farce that employs familiar devices to satirize the new suburban spa at Islington and its attendant quacks and hypochondriacs. The plot in part suggests *The Clandestine Marriage*: Merton, a gentleman of slight fortune, has secretly married Eliza Rubrick, and is looking for a propitious moment to announce how matters stand. Unfortunately her parents intend her for old D'Oyley, a retired businessman much addicted to vague diseases and new remedies. A group of bright young people leagued with Merton, chiefly his cousin Laetitia, bring off a scheme to cure D'Oyley of his foible, slander Eliza, and thus induce him to renounce her; he even bribes Merton to take the girl off his hands. The young man then announces the marriage to the pleasure of all except D'Oyley, who vows to leave off his follies. What with young love and old obstacles, manipulation by wit, ridicule, and saturnalia, the play could hardly be more traditional, and it is, significantly, an afterpiece, Colman's last in the comic genre. However experimental his mainpieces became, Colman kept his afterpieces within the laughing tradition. As the prologue to *The Oxonian in Town* put it: five acts for sentiment, two for us.

Colman's last comedies were all mainpieces. The first was *The Spanish Barber; or The Fruitless Precaution* (Larpent MS 436, 1777), which, as the name suggests, was adapted from Beaumarchais's *Le Barbier de Seville*, then popular at Paris. Colman's story, which follows its well-known source too closely to need recitation, belongs to the Spanish intrigue genre; the venerable character-types include young lovers, a *senex amans* and a witty servant. Through Lazarillo, the rogue-servant-barber-doctor, it is also recognizably related to picaresque fiction, while the disguises, ladders, dropped letters, and secret visits of the lovers' intrigues add the pleasures of pantomime to this hodge-podge (as Macklin had observed of *The Suspicious Husband* forty years earlier). For good measure it also wears the hat of musical comedy, by virtue of several songs.

Neither *The Spanish Barber* nor Colman's two subsequent comedies were published; as summer fare at the Haymarket they were not taken too seriously by anyone. Yet *The Suicide* (Larpent MS 450, 1778) is a serious play, almost a *drame*. Everything about it is unusual, from its length—four acts—to its particular combination of laughing, sentimental, and problem comedy. Colman touches the reform motif, the "good hearts" aspect, and the fake suicide lightly, while a romantic love match, humor characters, wide-ranging satire and exposure of imposters relate the play to the comic genre. The "suicide" is Tobine, the profligate son of a deceased mercer, and at present partner in the business with Tabby, a cheerless bourgeois. Tobine, however, represents the antithesis of all Tabby's mercantile values, and he is rapidly coming to the end of his rake's progress: money is running out, he has given up his beloved Nancy Lovell because of his unworthiness, and now contemplates suicide. It seems he would rather give up life than pleasure, though his version is that he would rather not hurt anyone else by his prodigality. In a desperate attempt to save him, Nancy has donned men's clothes and become his boon companion "Dick Rattle"; together they drink and duel. Tobine keeps asking for poison, so Nancy obtains a painful but ultimately harmless cordial that she represents as the real item. In the strange scene at the end of act 3 they stage a ritual suicide in a tavern, with Tobine adapting speeches from *Hamlet* and *Romeo and Juliet* as he sinks. The unpleasantness of the potion and the opportunity for reflection make Tobine heartily wish for life again, and when he awakes he is amenable to reason and persuasion. Nancy, again a woman, confesses all and puts herself at his disposal. Tobine does not dwell on his previously expressed desire to reform, but we are left to assume that he will do so, and be reclaimed by Nancy and her fortune.

Colman's refusal to sentimentalize this action is notable. He pulls no punches on the reactions of Tobine's friends to his suicide; they worry about the unfavorable publicity, their own futures, the reputation of the inn where he "died." Tabby is huffy: no decent "cit" commits suicide. That is a vice of west end aristocrats (Dr. Truby has earlier made the point that Tobine's raking is understandable as aristocratic behavior, but pretentious folly in a merchant). In two respects the writing is strongly reminiscent of another tough-minded dramatist, Charles Macklin. The first scene, of a London household beginning to stir as Tobine and company return from a revel at dawn, is as convincingly lifelike as any of Macklin's efforts at verisimilitude. And for an eighteenth-century dramatic precedent to the dark humor of the suicide, which has numerous echoes in modern literature, one would have to go to Macklin's *A Will and No Will*. It is a bold stroke to allow Nancy, a lost sheep from Elizabethan romance, into this world, but Colman brings it off remarkably well. *The Suicide* is Colman's most impressive play after *The Clandestine Marriage,* and on his own.[33]

Separate Maintenance (Larpent MS 490, 1779), a somewhat brutal four-act comedy of London manners, is another instance of new wine in old bottles, though neither as original nor as successful artistically as *The Suicide*. But Colman's last original comedy is an interesting application of traditional comic devices to current social foibles, here (principally) the practice of "separate maintenance" for modish wives in London society. In this case the separation is absurd, for Lord and Lady Newberry love each other; they are victims of fashion, pride, and the machinations of Milord's "friend" Leveret, who has designs on Lady Newberry. Lord Newberry is vaguely aware of the scheme, but such trifles are supposed to present no problem between men of this world; as Leveret remarks to him, "No conversation, except criminal conversation, is worthy the attention of people of quality." A reaction to all this is gathering: neither of the principals is happy with the arrangement, and Milady's parents, the rusticated Oldcastles, are in town, alarmed by rumors of divorce and railing against modern times (most of the worthier characters in the play join them in condemning the excesses of the present debased age, and agree that England is not what it used to be). In the finale Lady Newberry and Miss English, her sister, wrap Leveret in swaddling clothes, lay him on a sofa between them, and tease him for the amusement of the assembled company, which includes Lord Newberry. Seeing his wife's honor, his love and better nature are stirred; he asks a reconciliation and is quickly accepted. The comic spirit is triumphant, and the ridiculous Leveret slinks off after his denouement. The strength of *Separate Maintenance* is its scenes of routs, balls, and intrigues, which are well drawn and rife with topical satire.

Colman's career leaves in its wake a number of problems and loose ends. Like his early mentor Garrick, he was strongly inclined to collaboration and borrowing; only three or four of his thirteen comedies are genuinely original. In the prologue to *The Man of Business* an angry dramatist charges Colman with having plagiarized from six authors in his play, and in the dedication Colman freely admits to four. The epilogue to the same play purports to settle the dispute by defining "invention" as "retailing from a wealthy hoard / The Thoughts which observation long has stor'd, / Combining images with lucky hit, / Which sense and education first admit," but obviously does not address itself to the substance of the question seriously enough to be of value. An adequate answer would contain at least two parts: one admitting that Colman, no less than many other Augustans and Georgians, made a merit of creative and moderate eclecticism in the arts; the other pointing out that on occasion (e.g., *Polly Honeycombe, The Suicide*) Colman showed himself capable of conceptions as original as any of his contemporaries', though this inventive power, whether from innate weakness or disinterest, was seldom displayed. Three more lines from the epilogue to *The Man of Business* summarize Colman's defence of his position: "Who, borrowing little from the common store, / Mends what he takes, and from his own adds more, / He is original." Few would dissent, but then the matter would never have been raised if Colman had always adhered to this principle in practice.

Colman also resembles Garrick in his mixture of styles and genres; in this respect both may be distinguished from Macklin and especially Foote. Colman wrote sentimental comedy (*The English Merchant*), satire on sentiment (*Polly Honeycombe*), and plays in which laughter and sentiment are mixed (*The Clandestine Marriage*). In the 1770s he composed dramas that ended happily without being quite comedies. He wrote and defended legitimate drama, yet half his plays were cast in "illegitimate" molds. Like Sprightly in *New Brooms!* Colman held "regular Tragedy and

Comedy" to be "the main body of the stage entertainments," but he also shared Crochet's opinion that ordinary plays "will never be able to make a stand against opera and pantomime" unless enlivened by music, dance, and scenery. Pure drama could no longer pay for itself, therefore (Sprightly again) "Opera and Pantomime," "Show and sing-song" must be admitted "as garnish." And if a manager were going to produce "garnish," it would be prudish to refuse to write it as well.

The social theme in Colman is likewise inconsistent, the only apparent pattern being a gradual drift from positive to negative statements. *The Clandestine Marriage* presents two rather attractive aristocrats while the bourgeois are either weak or servile or grasping, but *The English Merchant* and *The Man of Business* portray merchants favorably. *The Suicide* is negative about the characteristics of both classes, and *Separate Maintenance* castigates upper-class vices without providing any alternative. Thus Colman seems finally to give up and leave the question nearly where he found it. But though he produced no position paper, his concern with the class question is evident, and it must be acknowledged that he was one of the very few Georgian dramatists to bring onstage problems of real social importance and treat them seriously. That service, on the eve of the Revolution, deserves equal billing with his role as an occasional retainer of the laughing tradition in comedy.

True-Born Irishmen

The major Irish dramatists—Murphy, Goldsmith, and Sheridan—who wrote the best-known plays of the Garrick era belong to the latter half of that period. Their work extends from Murphy's first effort, *The Apprentice* (1753–56), to those crepuscular comedies of 1777, *Know Your Own Mind* and *The School for Scandal,* with *The Critic* as a burlesque coda in 1779. Thus each of them, by the time he reached his peak, had been exposed to some of the comedies of the professionals discussed in chapter seven, as well as to other Georgian plays, and drew substantially, though of course to differing degrees, upon the comic drama of his own century. They constitute a less homogeneous group than the dramatists of the previous chapter because, although associated with the theaters in various capacities at different times, they kept other irons in the fire, and were more often dispersed outside than included within the close-knit family of the London stage. Yet broadly speaking, each found his own way to the "classical" English laughing tradition, and consciously worked within it according to his own lights.

ARTHUR MURPHY (1727–1805)

By far the least of the triumvirate in modern repute, Murphy was rated more nearly on a par with Goldsmith and Sheridan by their contemporaries. In sheer dramatic output he was the most productive of the three, and his talents were varied if not deep: political journalist, literary critic, biographer, banker and lawyer, as well as playwright and (briefly) actor. A Dubliner, his acquaintance among the London literati became wide. In the mid-1740s, while still in his teens, he met Foote, then

Collins, Smart, and Fielding; after settling in London in 1751 he came to know Garrick, whose biography he would later write, and eventually Burke and Johnson. Generally regarded as industrious, skillful and competent rather than original or profound, Murphy nevertheless developed a voice with a recognizably individual accent, almost independent of passing fashions.

A classicist in theory and practice, Murphy was a consistent proponent of the older comic traditions of laughter, manners, and farce. This was the eighteenth-century opinion, and twentieth-century theatrical historians have generally concurred.[1] Writing in 1775, William Cook digressed from his denigration of farce to admit that, for the "last twenty years," farces have been "improving" to the point of becoming "petite pieces of comedy, which, however they may want the full extent of the *vis comica*, are many of them, far from being deficient in outline, humour, and observation." Cook credited Murphy with leading this development, acknowledging the "real merit" and "warm reception" of his plays, which "bid fair to lead the present stock of acting farces."[2] The quality of Murphy's plays is of course debatable—"farcicality" is his weakness—but there is no debating the school to which he belonged. His own criticism, scattered through prologues, prefaces, and essays, is thoroughly traditional, leaning heavily on Horace and Aristotle. The "Business of Comedy," he wrote, is to make "striking Exhibitions of inconsistent Circumstances," to "display Foibles and Oddities," mixed with "a fine Vein of Ridicule," in order to "excite ... Laughter" and a "gay Contempt," of the sort that makes us "despise and laugh at an Object at the same time."[3] There is no concession to sentimental drama here, and Murphy's theoretical conservatism applied also to the *illegitimi:* he argued against both pantomime and tragicomedy.[4] Murphy wrote neither burlettas, nor spectacles, nor comic operas, and though he sometimes associated with Foote he hung back from the excesses of satirical farce, the "monsters for ill-judged applause" that he disavowed in the prologue to *Know Your Own Mind.* To a greater extent than any comic playwright of the period except perhaps Macklin he kept within an inner circle of saturnalian laughter and shunned its dangerous periphery.

The commencement of Murphy's stage career was halting enough to have discouraged a less determined man. In 1753 he wrote a two-act farce called *The Apprentice,* which despite his theatrical connections was not acted until 1756. Meanwhile he tried his hand at acting, but had no great success and gave it up after a couple of seasons. By that time he had fallen out with Foote, his first playhouse acquaintance and the man who had suggested that he take up acting. In 1754, it is said, Murphy "sketched plot and characters" for a sequel to Foote's *The Englishman in Paris* "and then confided the scheme to his friend. Foote immediately appropriated the ideas—and produced the sequel himself" (Belden, p. 69). Murphy's own version, *Englishman from Paris,* was ignored after one performance, and he vented his spleen in *The Triple Revenge; or, The Spouter* (1756), a satire that he chose to omit from his 1786 *Works.*

Despite this quarrel, the influence of Foote is felt in the sketchy construction and satiric content of Murphy's earliest plays, the farce as well as the sequel and the satire. *The Apprentice* uses the bourgeois love-story of Dick Wingate and Charlotte Gangle to mock the "spouting clubs" then popular among the amateurs of the theater. Dick, a stage-struck apprentice to old Gangle, is neglecting business for histrionics. He elopes with Charlotte and is arrested for debt, but when his avaricious old father accepts the marriage (for the sake of the dowry) he is released, and vaguely promises to give up the stage. As in many of Foote's plays, however, a plot-summary totally obscures the raison d'être of the piece. Romance is tied onto satire like a tin can to a cat's tail; the idea that Dick's eligibility as a suitor depends at all upon his giving up "spouting" is farcical. Elsewhere the play gestures at social realism: Wingate is not only the traditional unsympathetic father but a coarse, insensate Georgian merchant, wholly out of touch with his son's world; Dick, with his laced waistcoats, is both a fop and a *Hamlet*-spouting, starry-eyed young theatrical aspirant. The Spouting Club scenes in act 2, which are humorous and effective onstage—the Scot has acted in "the Reegiceede" at Endinburgh, while the Irishman burns to succeed in "genteel and top comedy"—are said to have helped end the craze. The two halves of the plot most nearly mesh in ii.ii, where the Spouters "beat the Watch" and assist the elopement. Dick's insistence on using a ladder, which mars the plan, is represented as a theatrical folly; it also foreshadows the passion of Polly Honeycombe and Lydia Languish for correct form in these matters. *The Apprentice* is unquestionably a farce—its dialogue and dramaturgy are often crude—but it is a respectable first play.

The Upholsterer; or, What News? was, like *The Apprentice,* produced at Drury Lane (1758) by Garrick, who gave it an unusually brilliant cast; Kitty Clive, Mrs. Yates, Richard Yates, Palmer, Woodward, and Garrick himself—half a dozen of the best comedians in eighteenth-century London—all took part. It is no wonder that after a slow start the play caught on as a favorite in the repertoire, or that Murphy dedicated the first edition to Garrick. This prefatory epistle gives the theme as a "vicious Excess of a propensity to Politics," the source as Addison's *Tatlers* 155 and 160 (Murphy could have added *Spectators* 403 and 568), and the genre as farce: "In the principal Character I considered myself rather describing a *Passion* than a *Man*; and this you remember is mentioned by an excellent Critic [Bishop Hurd], to belong to the Province of Farce." But when Murphy goes on to protest that his purpose is "not to inscribe a Farce to you, for neither of us thinks so highly of these matters," he is posturing. Garrick's casting and Murphy's four revisions are sufficient comments on this pose, even without bringing in the evidence of care in the original composition. *The Upholsterer* rises above most farces of the time in conception and dialogue, moving toward the short comedy Murphy would soon achieve. The frenzied political obsession of the upholsterer Abraham Quidnunc ("What News") is farcical in that it is carried to improbable extremes, but besides furnishing most of the play's laughs it forwards the love story of his daughter Harriet and Bellmour in which it is partially embedded. Quidnunc is both the blocking figure (the interfering father of New Comedy), and a humors portrait, the butt of the Old Comedy. And when the problems are resolved, the union and reunion achieved, he is still the same passion, still appropriately named: "What are the Spaniards doing in the Bay of Honduras?" His follies are abetted by Razor the barber and Pamphlet, "the best political writer of the age."

The love plot has one notable fortuity: Rovewell proves to be Quidnunc's son Jack. This turn of events, sketchily prepared in the first scene, has been taken as a sentimental touch, but its kind is equally at home in farce or romance, and it is not handled sentimentally in the acting manuscripts. For his readers, however, Murphy added to the printed version (1758) the effusion quoted at the end of chapter two.

The play does have an ostensible didactic purpose as suggested by its roots in the moral essay, and this didacticism tended to recur in his later plays, as their very titles show: *The Way to Keep Him, No One's Enemy But His Own, Know Your Own Mind*. But here the lesson is cursory, and Murphy abbreviated it even more in his 1763 alteration.[5] It should be noted too that Quidnunc owes as much to Foote (Sir Gregory Gazette in *The Knights*) and to Fielding (*The Coffee-House Politician*) as to Addison; some of what passes as moral purpose is really satiric humor, and half the rest is dust in the eyes. The moral tag is given to, of all people, the malapropping maid Termagant, an egregious flibbertigibbet and natural daughter of Mrs. Slipslop. Murphy was then still a comic farceur, albeit a prudent and derivative one.

With *The Way to Keep Him* (1760), however, Murphy took his own direction and brought the "petite comedy" up to a new level of maturity and sophistication. Obviously he was seeking to transcend farce; in pursuit of higher seriousness he had adapted Voltaire's tragedy as *The Orphan of China* (1759), and also wrote *The Desert Island*, a three-act "entertainment," as the mainpiece to accompany *The Way*. Though he owned Swift and de Moissy as sources, Murphy reworked his materials into an original "*English* comedy" that dealt almost adequately with the familiar erring-husband theme: less pruriently than *Love's Last Shift*, less histrionically than *The Careless Husband*, more realistically than *The School for Husbands*. The widow Bellmour, an amiable and virtuous "other woman," was greeted as a novel character on the London stage. It is she who states the theme of wife-amelioration that is Murphy's new twist on the venerable motif of rake-reform: "It is much more difficult to keep a heart than to win one," she warns Mrs. Lovemore. And in addition to pointing out to the wife that she had erred by failing to exert her charms upon her husband, the widow is also a prominent participant in the climactic embarrassment and reclamation of the raking Lovemore. Around this scene, one of the clichés of eighteenth-century comedy, cluster the play's most serious problems: the unacceptably cavalier treatment of Mrs. Lovemore by her husband when it is he who has just been caught out, her submission to it, and a rather stridently moralistic tone that insists on reproving everyone. *The Way to Keep Him* is not a funny play—in his eagerness to avoid farce Murphy almost threw out the baby with the bathwater—and is a comedy only because the cast learns its lessons in time. But it *is* a comedy within the compass of the afterpiece, with one manageable plot, a modicum of realism, and a quantity of action appropriate to three acts, and this was an achievement.

The play was so popular that Murphy reworked it into a five-act mainpiece for the following season.[6] This was an unusual procedure (though numerous mainpieces were slimmed down to "curtain-droppers"), but the convention that a real comedy had to be in five acts died hard, and Murphy was not without ambition. His principal altera-tion was to add a surprisingly good subplot. The tale of Sir Bashful Constant and his wife is fitted so smoothly into the original action that it seems integral, furnishing another instance of Lovemore's roguery and pointing a second but related moral: if in fact you do love your spouse, show it, and let the town laugh. Another change, the addition of one sentimental touch, is further evidence that audiences expected more sentiment in mainpieces. In iii.i (ii.i in the afterpiece), the widow tries to ascertain the object of Mrs. Lovemore's inquiry: "May I beg to know who the Gentleman is?" Here the two texts diverge: 1760 has Mrs. Lovemore answer simply, "You have such an Air of Frankness and Generosity, that I will open myself to you." In the mainpiece that line also occurs, but only after this exchange:

> MRS. LOVEMORE: The story will be uninteresting to you, and to me it is painful. My grievances—(*Puts her handkerchief to her eyes*)
> WIDOW BELLMOUR: (*Aside*) Her grief affects me. (*Looks at her till she has recovered herself*) I would not importune too much—

The afterpiece, while didactic, had avoided sentimentality, but Murphy knew that the audience would accept, perhaps even expect, a pathetic moment or two in a full-length comedy. And he did not miscalculate: the new, longer *Way to Keep Him* displaced the original version in the reper-toire, and held the boards for over a century.

Some influential modern critics have been inclined to rank *The Way to Keep Him* above *The Rivals*. One may grant Murphy's play tighter con-struction and more unified tone but still find the judgment difficult to accept. *The Way to Keep Him* has no character as entertaining as Lydia Languish or Mrs. Malaprop, and its dialogue, though graceful and sometimes witty, never scintillates. Like Murphy, Sheridan had a satiric object, but he kept a much lighter hand on the didactic stop. *The Rivals,* moreover, gives off a Georgian fragrance; *The Way to Keep Him,* especially the mainpiece version, has the musty odor of historical comedy. The former seems to spring from direct observation of real people, the latter to operate at one remove from experience. *The Way to Keep Him* is a clear attempt to recreate the worlds of Restoration comedy and polite Augustan poetry. The related plots of upper-class intrigue and foolish bumpkinry in fashionable London, the confusion over billets-doux, the double-entendre stichomythia between Lovemore and Sir Bashful (IV.ii) call up echoes of Molière and Wycherley, while the widow Bellmour, who reads Pope aloud, is a patent combination of Arabella Fermor and Martha Blount. In short, the play is a stylish piece of secondary art, a bit of nostalgia for manners at least a generation old.

All in the Wrong (1761) strengthens the suspicion that Murphy was setting up as an eighteenth-century Molière and finding the strain too great. Taken from *Le Cocu imaginaire,* a slight farce by Molière, *All in the Wrong* draws out its source into five acts of improbable incident. What the Frenchman had dashed off Murphy appears to take seriously, with unfortunate results. In a brief farce situation is usually enough; in a full-length comedy we expect character. Murphy invites these expectations by the amount of time he spends on his principals, but he disappoints us by settling for masks and types. The plot is a comedy of errors whose mainspring is the mutual and ill-founded jealousy of the Restless family. Sir John is seen by Lady Restless comforting Belinda Blandford, who fainted after a scene with her father; rushing to the spot, Lady Restless seizes a picture of Beverly dropped by Belinda, and is discovered by Sir John admiring it. From these two events and various efforts to clarify them, plus the involvement of a second young couple whom Murphy added, spring complications that occupy 100 of the 106 printed pages. By the end of act 4 all seven principal characters are mutually at odds and the situation is so fantastically complicated that resolution seems hopeless, yet only a general assembly is needed to prove that all the right people love each other and that the only villain is misinterpreted circumstances. Any regard for realism of character would have destroyed the plot, but this consideration never arises, except in the reader's or spectator's mind. In farce it should not arise even there, of course, nor does it in Molière or in the other, more decorous and satisfactory Georgian adaptation, James Miller's *The Picture; or, Cuckold in*

Conceit (1745). But the length of *All in the Wrong*, the seriousness of the romances, the echoes of Congreve and the natural dialogue, put a dress of manners comedy on the body of farce. The play furnishes an extreme example of eighteenth-century comedy's penchant for exalting situation over character, which was Murphy's personal nemesis; a weakness for overly ingenious plotting betrays him in all of his mainpiece comedies except *The Way to Keep Him*.[7]

During the busy year of 1761 Murphy also comanaged with Sam Foote during the summer season at Drury Lane, where one of their productions was a new farce by Murphy, *The Old Maid*. Its general type and its affinity to *All in the Wrong* are indicated by Captain Cape's remark, "I see through this: it is a comedy of errors, I believe." The plot turns on a simple case of mistaken identity. Clerimont has seen two women at Ranelagh and is smitten with one. Learning that they are a Mrs. and Miss Harlow, he naturally assumes that his idol is Miss Harlow and pays court accordingly. He is wrong, but his wooing is so circumlocutory that his error is not discovered for two acts. The play may be taken as a satire on the forms and language of eighteenth-century courtship; the scene in act 1 where Clerimont bashfully courts Mrs. Harlow has interesting similarities to Marlow's first interview with Kate Hardcastle in *She Stoops to Conquer*. The farce also ridicules the amorous inclinations of the autumnal Miss Harlow cruelly. "You may go and bewail your virginity in the mountains," (cf. Judges 11:37–38) says Captain Cape sternly to the lady. Her only error was that she misinterpreted the ambiguous words of Clerimont (who made far more mistakes himself), but her colt's tooth has been revealed, and "while, fond soul! she weaves her myrtle chain, / She proves a subject of the comic strain," according to the moral tag spoken by Mrs. Harlow. Humor and romance dissipate in the satire; *The Old Maid* is hard-core situational comedy, impervious to the blandishments of the heart, wherein Miss Harlow is viewed not as a human being but as the type of the superannuated beauty, such as Lady Wishfort, or Lady Pentweazle in Foote's *Taste*. The device of having a vain old lady construe a young bachelor's addresses to a younger woman as meant for herself, a Georgian favorite, reappears in *The Rivals*.

For the next half-dozen years Murphy concentrated on afterpiece comedy. *The Citizen*, another farce produced during the summer of 1761, was followed by the alteration of *The Upholsterer* in 1763, *What We*

All Must Come To and *No One's Enemy But His Own* in 1764, and *The Choice* in 1765. The first and last were popular, but none takes a new direction, and all confirm Murphy's bent for situational laughing comedy. *What We All Must Come To* (called *Marriage à la Mode* in 1767 and *Three Weeks after Marriage* in the 1776 revival) discusses the problem of bourgeois-aristocracy alliances that would shortly recur in *False Concord* and *The Clandestine Marriage,* lashing both upper-class vapors and the pretensions of the parvenus. Druggett, a wealthy retired merchant with a taste for fantastic gardening, has married one of his daughters to Sir Charles Rackett and is about to give the other, Nancy, to another aristocrat, Lovelace. Nancy prefers Woodley, a commoner, who lacks the hypocrisy to compliment Druggett on his abominable taste. But when the Racketts visit Druggett and he sees how intensely they quarrel over trivia such as bridge, he gives Nancy to Woodley. Druggett was borrowed from *Guardian* 173 by Pope, and the Londoners' cardtable talk is reminiscent of Swift, but the class tension is thoroughly contemporary, and Murphy's approach to his subject is along the lines of Foote in *Taste* and Colman in *Polly Honeycombe*. The most insistently satirical of all Murphy's plays, *What We All Must Come To* was shouted down after one performance. In the Advertisement he disclaims particular satiric targets, and it is possible that the hostility was political or personal.

No One's Enemy But His Own, a three-act farce, is a failure, but an interesting one, and certainly the most significant of Murphy's other productions in this period. The enemy of himself is the rake Careless, who cannot, despite the warnings of Blunt, keep quiet about his affairs and prospects with Lucinda and the Widow Hortensia, not even to his rivals, respectively Bellfield and Wisely. After a series of turns and reversals, Careless is publicly exposed courting Sir Philip's "wife" (really Lucinda disguised), and is laughed at and rejected. The couples pair off, with Careless left out in the cold. Murphy's attempt to bring off the farcical protagonist as villain fails chiefly because of the repulsive stupidity of Careless, a member of that populous Augustan genus Imprudent Young Man. His nearest ancestor would be Young Wilding in Foote's *The Lyar,* who is more comical and less offensively ridiculous. The ostensible purpose of the play is to teach the gabblers discretion by laughing the title-character off the stage, and Murphy keeps his dramatic lesson appropriately moral, though never sentimental. Actually he seems here to retreat from direct observation toward another essay in the Restoration mode. The names of characters, the illicit affairs, the gossip and the wit-duels of belle and beau (Lucinda and Bellfield) are small genuflections to Etherege and Wycherley.

By 1767 Murphy's ambition had revived, and he produced a five-act laughing comedy, *The School for Guardians*. His debt to Molière is even greater than appears from the title; most of the incidents from three of the Frenchman's comedies are included, and consequently the play reads like a garbled index to that playwright. How this came about is explained in the Advertisement, a fair introduction to eighteenth-century dramaturgy. Murphy set out to alter *The Country Wife*, but found it too obscene and decided to go straight to Molière. *L'École des femmes* proved "too thin of business" (i.e., incident), however, so he interwove parts of *L'École des maris* and *L'Étourdi*. Derivation, moralization, situation: Murphy's watermark, though not his alone.

In this composite, the action necessarily proceeds and complicates at a pace that soon becomes farcical. The guardian-ward-lover triangle of *L'École des femmes* is doubled and complicated, the two groups being made interdependent. Murphy's intent throughout is clearly laughter—Belford's romantic languishings are constantly ridiculed—but by act 4 one is laughing at Murphy as much as at Belford, though the hustle-bustle stages better than it reads. When he digresses from Molière and strikes off on his own, Murphy's handling of dialogue and stock situations is quite satisfactory, and the manners are unmistakably Georgian, but some other changes are less fortunate. He discards the romantic reunion and providential motif of Molière in favor of an emphasis on material fortune, and adds a gratuitous moral (by Brumpton) to the effect that a happy marriage is built on esteem. On the other hand several scenes are direct translations of Molière, and the Frenchman's use of parallel scenes to produce symmetry is heightened to the point of extreme artificiality. The hearkening of eighteenth-century comedy to earlier—especially French—models was never carried further than in *The School for Guardians*.

Know Your Own Mind (1777) seems to have been written during the seventeen-sixties, and finished by 1768.[8] Its composition thus spanned much of Murphy's career, and we must speak even more hesitantly than usual about influences, yet one cannot help being struck by recurrent similarities to other comedies, early and late. The law of comic economy states that the same plots, devices, and character-types which have sufficed comedy from time immemorial will continue to appear, but *Know Your Own Mind* is a compendium of clichés above and beyond the dictates of this law, and no mean transmitter of the entire comic tradition. A detailed summary would challenge Mnemosyne and make tedious reading, but a few examples from the plot will illustrate the point. Sir John Millamour and Bygrove are, especially in their opening conversation, opposed much like Demea and Micio in Terence's *The Brothers,* one of many influences. Dashwould's satirical sallies upon London recall half a dozen beaux of Restoration drama, though his name and character recall another type (Witwou'd) and his function in the play is that of Ranger in *The Suspicious Husband*. He was widely seen at the time as a portrait of Foote, and certainly his hits at the Frenchified Englishman Beverly (end of act 1) are straight out of *The Englishman Returned,* yet the very next scene, of a weeping orphan in distress and a tyrannous relation (Miss Neville and Mrs. Bromley, II.i), is lifted from sentimental comedy and melodrama. Malvil's gravity and aversion to raillery, as well as his name, are obviously reminiscent of Malvolio, but his hypocrisy recalls Tartuffe and his "musty sentences" foreshadow Joseph Surface. Whims and vacillations such as those of Lady Bell and Millamour were a comic subject as old as Theophrastus and as recent as Destouches's *L'Irrésolu* (1713) and Henrietta Pye's *The Capricious Lady* (1771, unpublished). Mrs. Bromley resembles Lady Kitty Crocodile of Foote's *Trip to Calais* in some respects. And so on. With a writer like Murphy on the scene one clearly need not go back a century source-hunting. The comic legacy is not so much a linear continuum as a natural cycle, from which Murphy drew sustenance and to which he contributed.

    John Pike Emery, Murphy's modern editor, has compared *Know Your Own Mind* favorably to *The School for Scandal* (p. 334). It is true that Malvil and Dashwould and Lady Bell, at least, still make effective stage characters, that the satire is witty and the laughs reasonably frequent, and that the play is freer from sentimental touches than Sheridan's. But *Know Your Own Mind* stumbles over Murphy's characteristic failing, the excessively complex plot. Four marriageable women, five suitors, a wit, a maleficent hypocrite, a vacillating protagonist, a sensitive orphan, and an overbearing guardian constitute just too much story to hold easily in mind or to enjoy. Murphy appears not to have been entirely in control; as in most of his earlier mainpieces he finds five acts a bit unwieldy, and tends to carry over from his afterpieces the reliance on situational comedy that was their forte.

Emery also praises the changes made by Murphy in the Larpent MS for the 1778 edition, but seems to have mistaken their nature. Most of the numerous alterations redirect histrionic scenes, orienting them toward a reader's pleasure. In the first scene of the MS Murphy communicates the vicissitudes of Sir John Millamour's temper through its effect on his household: servants hurry confusedly, shouting, colliding, counter-manding. Probably because this was considered too "low" for readers, Murphy substituted in the 1778 edition a conversation between Bygrove and Sir John that imparts the same information in expository, nonvisual fashion. The printed version generally replaces the humors of servants and any ridicule with verbal paragraphs in the novelistic mode, e.g., Miss Neville's sentimental outburst in II.i, Dashwould's word-portraits of London in III.i, and Sir John's didactic address to his son (IV.i). Murphy thus showed his usual care with printed editions, and his customary acumen as to audience.

In the play's prologue Murphy said his farewells to the stage after more than two decades as a dramatist. It was the passing of a theatrical generation as much as the end of his own career that moved him.

> Lost are the friends who lent their aid before;
> ROSCIUS retires, and BARRY is no more.
> . . . .
> For them our Author lov'd his tale to weave;
> He feels their loss; and now he takes his leave;
> Sees new performers in succession spring,
> And hopes new poets will expand their wing.

Of what there was to mourn Murphy's own contribution was not the least, yet it is difficult to escape the conclusion that his most artistic and satisfying creations were the afterpieces that he sometimes denigrated; that his longer comedies, however laudable the effort that went into them, were futile attempts to recapture a lost chord. In the farces and short comedies of manners satire—*The Apprentice, The Upholsterer, The*

Way to Keep Him, What We All Must Come To—where direct observation of his own society was called for and made, Murphy was most in his element.

OLIVER GOLDSMITH (1728–1774)

If Murphy sometimes attempted a singlehanded recapitulation of laughing comedy, his fellow Irishman Oliver Goldsmith sought to define it throughout his brief career as a playwright. By precept in the preface to *The Good-Natured Man,* the essay "On the Theatre" and the prologue to *She Stoops to Conquer,* and by example in his comedies, he tried to distinguish between the laughing and sentimental varieties. Though Goldsmith left unanswered some of our questions about these terms, probably in his own time their usage was sufficiently clear. The components of laughing comedy he variously described as "nature and humour," "humour and character," the "low," a "natural portrait of human folly and frailty," and—a distant last—"ridicule." In his sentimental limbo Goldsmith placed comedies that were "genteel," "elevated," "weeping" or "mawkish," "sententious," and preoccupied with "distress" ("a detail of calamities"). Whether the term *bastard* (or *tradesman's*) *tragedy* was meant to include the bourgeois prose tragicomedy of Lillo and others or was simply his epithet for *comédie larmoyante* is not entirely certain, but the basic distinction has been generally accepted by posterity, and Goldsmith has been admitted as the champion of laughing comedy.

For all his rhetoric in defense of the comic muse, however, Goldsmith proved unsteady in practice. Of his three plays *The Grumbler* is a sketchy low farce and *The Good-Natured Man* basically a sentimental comedy. Even *She Stoops to Conquer,* unquestionably a laughing comedy and one of the best of the century, shares some ground with the sentimentalists. Goldsmith cannot be explained simply as a reactor against sentimental comedy, then, for he is a station on the main line of the benevolization of humor from Shaftesbury to Dickens. Probably because he enjoyed a larger extratheatrical reputation and wrote less for the theater than any other dramatist discussed in these chapters, Goldsmith was less influenced by purely dramatic traditions than any of them. Judged on the grounds of sustained effort and quantitative output, his contribution to comedy of a poor afterpiece and a strong mainpiece would be meager. Were it not for that one comedy and his timely theorizings Goldsmith would find no place here, and it is a measure of the excellence of *She Stoops* that his omission is unthinkable.

By the time Goldsmith turned to the theater in his late thirties he was already widely known as a poet, essayist, and novelist; he had powerful literary friends and well-defined ideas of what was amiss in comic drama and what he wanted to do about it. Unless the thoughts prefaced to *The Good-Natured Man* (1768) are wholly after the fact, he intended to challenge the advocates of the "genteel" and strike a blow in favor of the comedy "of the last age," even if that led him to the "mean." He failed in this desire partly because his play was outshone by Hugh Kelly's *False Delicacy*, but mainly because the shadow had fallen between his conception and his creation. Whatever else it may be, *The Good-Natured Man* is not a straightforward laughing comedy. It still divides critics as do few other eighteenth-century plays; some call it laughing, some sentimental, some mixed.[9] The second or third views seem most tenable. Goldsmith's *olla podrida* provides something for every palate: benevolism, comic scenes, manners satire, humors, reform. John Forster, his early biographer, contributes the interesting detail that, when he began to write, Goldsmith had Farquhar, *The Jealous Wife* and *The Clandestine Marriage* in mind.[10] If this is true he fell considerably short of his models, and was evidently amenable to a compromise position on sentiment. But Goldsmith's mixture is such that sentimentality weakens the *vis comica*, as a brief review of the plot will show.

Young Honeywood's uncle Sir William returns incognito from a period of foreign travel to observe his nephew's behavior. Young Honeywood loves Miss Richland, who reciprocates, but he will not make overtures; he fears that she just "likes" him, and that he would make her miserable, so he resigns her to the blowhard politician Lofty. A second plot concerns the Croakers, their son Leontine, and Olivia. She is passed off by Leontine as his sister; actually they are in love and want to marry. Eventually, Young Honeywood's characteristic attempts at universal benevolence lead him to do them a disservice at their elopement. The same scene fortunately discredits Lofty, frees Leontine for Olivia, and reunites Young Honeywood with his uncle and with the long-suffering

Miss Richland, who had earlier bailed him out of debt. The young benevolist vows to refine and discipline his thoughtless good nature.

If the proposed redefinition of sentimental comedy along the lines of "total psychological effect" is allowed to work both ways, then *The Good-Natured Man* falls into the sentimental category. It is not just a question of sentimental devices such as the benevolent incognito relative, used by Foote and Sheridan in laughing comedy as well as by Cumberland in *The West Indian*, but of character and its handling. Young Honeywood, rather like Winworth in *False Delicacy*, has an obsessive refinement that complicates his own and others' lives and prevents him from seeing through even the most transparent feminine subterfuges. This was a very common theme in the period; versions of it had already appeared in Garrick's *The Guardian*, Whitehead's *The School for Lovers*, and Colman's *The Deuce Is in Him* before Kelly and Goldsmith used it, and would occur later in *The Rivals* and in Charles Stuart's *The Experiment* (1777, unpublished). Honeywood's problem, however, is neither delicacy nor suspicious insecurity but imprudent benevolence, a trait not of personality or manners but of character, and a difficult object for satire to undercut. "False delicacy" can be separated from "true delicacy" as the Augustans had distinguished true and false wit, but when Goldsmith attempts this division with the benevolent heart the effect is that of *Tom Jones* and *The West Indian:* the emphasis falls more on benevolence than on imprudence. The title itself belies the idea that Young Honeywood's character has been seriously compromised by his course; he is good-natured, not falsely good-natured. When he talks in the last scene of perceiving his errors and receives righteous rebukes, we feel uneasy at his contrition and the self-righteousness of his rebukers. He has not done wrong, merely too much indiscriminate right; he must curb the excesses of a good propensity. The play has other sentimental characteristics, to be sure—sententious dialogue, recognition and reform motifs, a drawn-out moralizing close—but the character of Young Honeywood remains the crux.

In his inexperience as a dramatist Goldsmith had stumbled on intractable material that could not be wrought to his purpose; realizing this, perhaps, he seems to have planned or even started a novel based on the play. But what would come off in prose fiction (Tom Jones, Yorick) did not necessarily work as laughing comedy. The actor Powell reportedly warned Goldsmith that "he could do nothing" with Young Honeywood; as a stage character he simply could not be treated as Goldsmith had tried to treat him. No more than Cumberland could he place such a character in a central position and hope to avoid sentimentality. Seeing him there before us during the entire play is fatal; his benevolent emanations permeate its atmosphere. *The School for Scandal* is nearly asphyxiated in a similar fashion, but whereas Sheridan finds ways to make us laugh at Charles Surface, and so distances him to some extent, Goldsmith permits us to empathize with his hero's distresses. Undistracted by satire or ridicule, we are alarmed when Young Honeywood's misplaced generosities begin tumbling about his head in act 5 and Leontine actually draws his sword on him: comic decorum, the "law of no consequences," is violated. And the scene that was already dark becomes sentimental and melodramatic when Honeywood, instead of, say, reaching for a witticism, responds with the aside: "Ha! 'contemptible to the world'! that reaches me."[11] Through him it reaches us, just at a moment when some wry retort (such as Sheridan would have given us) could lighten the moment by making us laugh. The larger difficulty here is that a "good heart" was beginning to function in the Shaftesburian system like grace in the Puritan: a sign of irrevocable salvation. Who are we to criticize one of the elect? Only Sterne's Smelfungus or Mundungus would undertake such a task. If Young Honeywood seems troublesome, that is a consequence of our own imperfections. To bring such a character into distress and retrieve him comically was beyond Goldsmith's powers at this time.

Although *The Good-Natured Man* was offered, and by some accepted, as the comic antidote to Kelly's sentimentalism, that polarity now seems misleading, if not downright meretricious. Both deal ambiguously with sentimental materials, contradicting themselves and confusing us; their plots have a generally antisentimental shape, yet some characters and speeches fall on the other side of the question. If anything, *False Delicacy* scores the heavier hits on sentiment, but its target is a relatively superficial point of manners. *The Good-Natured Man* attempts to operate on the heart of the matter, benevolence, and discovers that radical surgery does not mix with laughter or satire. Goldsmith's heavy touch on reforming a character who is, after all, only too good for this world, his turgid sermons, his use of prolonged distresses, above all the language at crucial points inevitably create a melodramatic atmosphere of which sympathy and sentimentality are the principal constituents. Of comedy there is only an occasional whiff. To a greater extent than Kelly's play, *The Good-Natured Man* contributes to the comic tradition negatively, by providing a failed experiment.[12]

Somewhat bruised by the public's reception of his play, Goldsmith salved his pride by printing it whole, including the bailiff scene that the Covent Garden audience had hissed off as "low," and had the satisfaction of a good sale. He did not return to the lists with a new comedy for five years, and then he took the precaution of mounting a preliminary bombardment. The anonymous essay "On the Theatre" that appeared in the *Westminster Magazine* for January 1773 was obviously a preparation for *She Stoops to Conquer;* it also shows how far Goldsmith's conception of comedy (for it is assumed to be his essay) had developed in the interim. The language in which he describes the "weeping sentimental comedy" fits *The Good-Natured Man* much more closely than do the Aristotelian terms employed to define traditional comedy. If all "distress" is really the province of tragedy, then Young Honeywood is tragic, and Goldsmith had misplaced him. Similarly, if the purpose of comedy is to "expose" the "vices" and "faults of mankind," to "ridicule foibles," then the aesthetics of *The Good-Natured Man* stand discredited. It is noteworthy that, in the same year, Goldsmith's friend Dr. Johnson narrowed his 1775 *Dictionary* definition of comedy—"a dramatick representation of the lighter faults of mankind"—by adding the words, "with an intention to make vice and folly ridiculous."

In *She Stoops to Conquer*, dedicated to Johnson, Goldsmith solved the problems that had plagued his earlier play both by keeping such neoclassic definitions firmly in mind, and by treating them liberally. "Folly" is plentiful but "vice" nonexistent, for example, and "ridicule" is sparingly applied. It is no more a "straight" laughing comedy that his previous attempt had been, for under its simple surface *She Stoops* is a rather complicated play, blending various strains. Yet its complexities are under control; the many currents, intellectual as well as dramatic, join and make sense, while comic emotion is held at a perfect poise between sentiment and ridicule. The great wonder is that Goldsmith could have learned so much in five years; he achieves the finest dramatic synthesis of eighteenth-century feeling and makes it look easy.

She Stoops to Conquer is a peace treaty between the various comic traditions. Diverse and hitherto contradictory elements are brought together, not simply to be maintained in balance or wary truce, as they were in *The Suspicious Husband,* but for fusion into an integral structure. Benevolence and satire on sentimental absurdities, farce, romance, and Restoration comedy mingle harmoniously. Largely because of Goldsmith's own critical theories, however, *She Stoops* is usually regarded as an indictment of *comédie larmoyante* that reasserts the characters and values of traditional laughing comedy. Since this interpretation takes us some distance into the play, it is a convenient place to start. Goldsmith either avoids or mocks sententiousness, "conscious virtue," and the prudential reform in situations deliberately contrived so that we might expect them. The first interview between Kate Hardcastle and Marlow in act 2 is conducive to sentimental conversation, for example; not only *The Conscious Lovers* but such recent sentimental comedies as *The School for Lovers* (1762), *The Double Mistake* (1765), and *The Sister* (1769), by Charlotte Lennox, had used such a meeting for an exchange of aphoristic sentiments. Instead, Goldsmith gives us a parody of the convention, inept and faltering on one side, ironic and amused on the other. During the vogue of sentimental comedy this exchange would have been especially pertinent, but it remains excellent theater. Similarly, Marlow's bold courting of Kate under the illusion that she is a barmaid resembles Cibber's device of having Loveless woo the disguised Amanda in *Love's Last Shift*—in that each man treats the woman distantly *in propria persona*, then is emboldened by a freer appearance to take liberties—but there is an important difference. Loveless lusts for Amanda as long as she is vizarded; only when she unmasks does he repent and vow fidelity. Marlow, however, develops honorable intentions *before* the full revelation of the barmaid's (or poor relation's) identity, simply because he perceives and loves her natural qualities. Cibber's false virtue and prurience are exposed by this telling revision, which substitutes for the specious coin of the sentimentalists ("they are lavish enough of their *tin* money upon the stage") true good nature. What he failed to achieve in his whole previous comedy Goldsmith thus brings off at one stroke here.

So far a reaction against sentimental comedy may seem an adequate rationale for the action, but the rest of the play cannot be explained in these terms. As soon as Marlow begins to fall in love with Kate, he drops into sentimental jargon: "conscious virtue," etc. We know that such speech was rigidly conventional between lovers, but it is a strange convention for Goldsmith not to break in this play. There are also occasional displays of domestic affection, such as Mr. Hardcastle's fondness for his wife (anathema in Restoration comedy but a desideratum of Steele and Cumberland) in the first scene, and the fellow-feeling between Hardcastle and Diggory in act 2. Then the character of Tony, unknown in sentimental comedy, is too important to be dismissed merely as an attempt to revive the Shakespearean humorist. And how are we to view the central action of the play, Miss Hardcastle's "stooping" to win Marlow? This ploy, if not its treatment, can be parallelled in early sentimental comedy. The answers to all these questions lie far afield in different directions.

That peculiarly eighteenth-century development, the "cult of feeling," is one answer. A love of "natural goodness," encouraged by deist and Shaftesburian philosophy and domesticated by Steele and Addison, had been emerging since about 1700.[13] As a broad aesthetic movement that eventually embraced Rousseau it remained distinguishable from its dramatic counterparts, the sentimentalizings of Cibber and the moralizings of Steele. The highest expression of this philosophy in a human being was benevolence of character; thus the benevolent or "good-natured man" became a popular ideal, highly valued both in life and art as the individual aspect of this humanizing, civilizing, and eminently British movement in thought and feeling. Soon this relatively recent development, the benevolent man, was attracted to and fused with the older humor character, no longer dangerous (as it had been for Swift) but lovable, because he followed the natural impulses that Shaftesbury and his followers deemed good.[14] Good nature, the basis of good humor and a trait greatly to be desired, could be expected to occur in eccentric, "humorous" guises. Sterne's Yorick in *A Sentimental Journey* is a good example of this fusion; Uncle Toby and Parson Adams are others.

There is no doubt that Goldsmith was carried along in this tide of taste, for Dr. Primrose and Young Honeywood are creations quite in accord with its premises, and if *She Stoops to Conquer* is approached with this idea of sentiment in mind rather than Cibber's a good deal falls into place. Natural, unaffected goodness, the benevolist's summum bonum, is the means by which farce, romance, sentiment, and Restoration materials are welded into a concordant whole. Tony is another "amiable humorist," and Goldsmith's approbation of him is evident from the extent to which he is allowed to influence the action. A "natural man," he has at bottom better manners and a shrewder wit than the London blades. He is at home in the late eighteenth century, not in Shakespeare; if he has a Falstaffian charm, it is that of the eighteenth century's Falstaff, not Shakespeare's. The Hardcastles' domestic warmth and the genial sympathy subsisting between several characters have also reminded some readers of Elizabethan dramatic romance, others of Farquhar, but nowhere in earlier comedy is there a parallel so close as *The Jealous Wife*, and we can imagine Murphy's Sir Bashful Constant (in the 1761 *Way to Keep Him*) finally achieving a peace of the affections much like Hardcastle's if he has the courage to leave London. The hostility of the urban beau monde to married love was not only a Restoration cliché but an abiding Georgian theme, and one of the comic problems Goldsmith avoided by setting his play in the country.

The "stooping" of Kate Hardcastle is somewhat more difficult, and, as the central action, deserves all the light we can shed. Her role-playing has aspects of the sentimental heroine's gesture (Amanda), the romantic heroine's device (Rosalind), and the reformer's exemplum (Lady Easy, Lady Lovemore). It is best understood, however, as a humanistic development from late Restoration comedy. Like many other eighteenth-century playwrights Goldsmith looked there for inspiration and ideas, but he reworked its characters and motives in accordance with his own values. In *The Way of the World* Congreve had separated the conventional rakish hero into a good rake (Mirabell) and a bad one (Fainall).[15] Similarly, Goldsmith gives each half of his principal romantic couple a pair of masks, or, to put it another way, each subsumes comic types familiar from Restoration drama. Kate is both the witty virtuous heroine (Millamant, Dorinda) and the clever attractive servant (Cherry). Corresponding to these, Marlow plays either the rake *manqué* (Pinchwife) or the unscrupulous rake (Horner, Archer, Fainall). To Mr. Hardcastle he shows yet another face: the *bienaisé* rake, the somewhat foppish man-about-town (a mixture of, say, Dorimant and Sparkish). Marlow, of course, is everywhere mistaken, showing the wrong face to each audience, basing his conduct on appearances and caste, in short, not being himself. Yet he is not contemned and rejected as he would have been a century earlier; Kate Hardcastle shows him his error by winning his love in the lowly character of a barmaid. Like a Dorinda who would be willing to disguise herself as Cherry for the sake of an Aimwell-Archer unable to communicate with a lady, she intimates that "worth conquers birth," that "nature will shine through nurture": venerable humanist saws greatly prized by Enlightenment social thought. Goldsmith thus completes the action that *The Beaux' Stratagem* cries out for. Archer is genuinely attracted to Cherry, and when Farquhar has to leave her dangling we are painfully aware that only class has interfered.

Of course Kate is not an innkeeper's daughter merely because she impersonates one. Neither Goldsmith nor the eighteenth century would go that far. The revolution is only dramatic, not social, but we are to assume that Marlow has profited from wooing the supposed barmaid and loving the "poor relation" who turns out to be his equal and future wife. When the final revelation comes there are no philosophical aphorisms, for Goldsmith wisely gives the moment over to humor. But radical change has already begun; Marlow's two characters are synthesizing into one as Kate Hardcastle, like the play, brings unity from diversity. "It must not be, madam. I have already trifled too long with my heart. My very pride begins to submit to my passion. The disparity of education and fortune, the anger of a parent, and the contempt of my equals, begin to lose their weight" (*Works*, 5:210), says the tormented Marlow, on the point of departure from the "poor relation." Admittedly this is no barmaid, though he still believes her a housekeeper; it is mainly a question of fortune now, and he still intends to go. But no, a moment later, "I am now determined to stay, madam, and I have too good an opinion of my father's discernment, when he sees you, to doubt his approbation. . . . I can have no happiness but what's in your power to grant me. Nor shall I ever feel repentance, but in not having seen your merits before" (*Works*, 5:211). If he has learned anything from this encounter (and he will have Kate constantly by him as a teacher), Marlow has seen that humble women deserve more of his respect, and great ones less of his diffidence, than he had thought. He has acquired a "new" standard of discrimination—character in lieu of rank—which is at least as old in English as the Wife of Bath's Tale. It is the genius of Kate to perceive and evoke a happy middle ground of his manner, partaking of, but moderating, both the ardor and the reserve of his previous extremes. The contrasts with Loveless and Amanda, Archer and Cherry, are too pointed to miss.

As in character, so in values does Goldsmith transform his seventeenth-century comic heritage. Manners and wit had ruled the world of Restoration comedy; those at the top used manners to mask themselves as they wittily manipulated others, while nonmanipulators—witless fops and fallen women—were at the bottom of the heap. In *She Stoops to Conquer,* however, natural goodness is the indispensable quality. Wit has been deposed by good humor, and manners have only the negative importance that their misuse, affectation, is a vice. Instead of providing a useful means of social distinction, they tend to disrupt social intercourse. Marlow is a naturally affable fellow who freezes up when confronted with a "woman of reputation." Only in his low-life character, freed of a set code of manners, can he relax and be himself. Kate Hardcastle's stooping to a barmaid's role dramatizes her conviction that love, sympathy, and the flow of natural spirits are superior to correct manners. Both lovers know the two sets of manners (social and natural), but communicate only on the natural level. The rustic Tony is even allowed to rebuke the sophisticate Hastings on a point of manners (v.ii), and though he is not a wit, he is a better manipulator than Marlow. The "niceness" of Tony's companions at the Three Pigeons in aping their betters ("O damn anything that's *low,* I cannot bear it") is one of a number of eighteenth-century dramatic statements that manners do not make the man; *High Life below Stairs* (1759) is another, and Murphy's *What We All Must Come To* shows the bourgeois affecting upper-class tastes in landscape gardening. Nature and benevolence, then, have replaced the artifices of Restoration comedy as both status symbols and touchstones of worth in *She Stoops to Conquer,* though superficial resemblances in theme and character remain.[16]

Sentimental comedy falls victim to the same reformation of values, and also, of course, to a sense of humor. Twice at least we are lulled into the sentimental idiom and both times Goldsmith crashes the cymbals. Marlow's "pretty smooth dialogue" with Kate mocks the emptiness and artificiality of those sententious exchanges between lovers popularized by Steele; they are seen as an unnatural distortion of self. Again, the sentimentalist's handling of the "stooping" plot would be either (in

Cibber's day) to let Marlow sleep with Kate *qua* barmaid and then provide an affecting revelation, or, in nicer times, to have him abstain until an affecting revelation by Mr. Hardcastle that the barmaid is his long-lost and well-dowered daughter. Goldsmith avoids both the prurience and harshness of the first and the prudential sentimentality of the second by treating the situation as humorous, and by making its psychological denouement depend on unselfish love, free of either lawless lust or considerations of fortune. He thus takes up the recurrent motif of true-false distinctions in emotion and thought; his satire upon the cheap, absurd, inhuman conduct of sentimental comedy is at the same time an assertion of its opposite. With Kate and Marlow natural goodness, "true delicacy" if you will, replaces (successfully this time) the false.

Farce and *farcical* were words often on the lips of Goldsmith's contemporaries when they criticized this play. The central mistake, the disguise, the horse-pond deceit were so described by friend and foe alike, and cries of "low" were heard about Tony and his associates. But the functions of these devices, apart from their considerable entertainment value, are at one with the largest purposes of the comedy. Tony's various antics (he causes the mistake and hence the disguise) underscore the eccentricity and benevolence of the humorist. The same freedom of mind and heart that gives vent to his lovable goodness unleashes his pranks, and the latter are excused by the former. Marlow's mistake, besides generating humor, begets Kate's disguise, which brings out Marlow's characteristic foible of basing manners on assumed rank. But in her disguise she is also able to find Marlow's more natural and appealing side, and teach him that innate qualities can overcome all the accidentals of rank, fortune, and appearances.[17] Thus farcical devices, like sentimental and romantic ones, are made to subserve the central idea of the comedy. Forster's remarks on the titling of the play point up Goldsmith's awareness of what was being subsumed and what must remain central:

> What now stands as the second title, *The Mistakes of a Night,* was originally the only one; but it was thought undignified for a comedy. *The Old House a New Inn* was suggested in place of it, but dismissed as awkward. Reynolds then . . . triumphantly named it *The Belle's Stratagem.* This name was still under discussion . . . when Goldsmith hit upon *She Stoops to Conquer.* (*Life of Goldsmith,* p. 627)

"The Mistakes of a . . ." was a title coming into vogue for farces, Spanish intrigues, and comedies of errors: e.g., *Mistakes of a Day* (1789), *Mistakes of a Minute* (1787), *Mistakes in Madrid* (1814). Connotatively, such a name aroused expectations of an episodic plot crammed with surprising incident and stage business. Friedman gives Goldsmith's original title as *The Novel; or, The Mistakes of a Night,* which would implicate the "Spanish novel" as well (*Works,* 5:88). *She Stoops to Conquer* certainly has a connection with this genre, but Goldsmith's rejection of the "undignified" title shows that he placed his emphasis elsewhere. The second name, with its strained glance at Elizabethan comedy, was wisely refused as "awkward." *The Belle's Stratagem* must have tempted Goldsmith; its reference to Farquhar is apt and it evokes the world of romance. But is Kate Hardcastle a "belle"? At this point the dawn broke. The play should be named for its crucial action, of course, yet "stratagem" sounds devious and would be needlessly vague. *She Stoops to Conquer* provides not only a terse summary of the action, but also nice ambiguities relevant to the theme (Is this really "stooping"? Whose is the conquest? What is conquered?) and a pleasing humanitarian paradox ("A man never stands so straight as when he stoops to help a child").

Both of Goldsmith's major comedies are cut from eighteenth-century fabric, and nowhere is this more obvious than in the way they repeat the comic characters, devices and concerns of the age. If we need "originals" apart from the entire comic tradition living on the London stages of the time, they were close at hand. Lofty of *The Good-Natured Man* resembles the character of Luke Limp in Foote's *Lame Lover,* and "Lofty" is the name of Foote's Patron. The imprudent philanthropy of Young Honeywood is simply a special case of the now-familiar "false delicacy syndrome"; Felton, a character in *The Politician* (unpublished farce, 1758), has the same problem: his generous temper stands in the way of a happy marriage and settlement. The relationship of Sir Charles and Young Honeywood is anticipated by Governor Cape and Young Cape in Foote's *The Author.* Marlow's *mal à la tête à tête* when confronting Kate is foreshadowed by Clerimont and Miss Harlow in Murphy's *The Old Maid.* Horsey squires like Tony were ubiquitous in prose fiction and dramatic comedy (Sir Harry Beagle in *The Jealous Wife*). The attack on sentiment was anticipated and probably assisted by Foote's *Piety in Pattens,* which opened only two weeks before *She Stoops* (*Works,* 5:90[n. 1]). Enough of

Goldsmith's ore came from eighteenth-century mines to make an alloy in which native and contemporary elements predominated. *She Stoops to Conquer* may have seemed "Shakespearean" because not since his time had a play so completely epitomized what an age had to say.

His one effort at afterpiece-writing, however, reveals Goldsmith as a poor *farceur*. *The Grumbler* (1773; published by Harvard Press, 1931), his last play, was a benefit piece for John Quick, the young comedian who, as Tony Lumpkin, had helped to put over *She Stoops*. A token gesture of gratitude, *The Grumbler* derives ultimately from *Le Grondeur* (1691) by de Brueys and La Palaprat, by way of Sir Charles Sedley's translation of 1702 and an anonymous, unpublished 1754 adaptation. Goldsmith's version has the thinnest plot, the flattest characters and the poorest dialogue of any of the four. By using only half of the original plot— omitting the grumbler's daughter and her entourage—he completes the story in one act (the 1754 production had two, Sedley's three, and the original five). The piece uses a Theophrastan– La Bruyèresque "character" (here, the self-tormenting misanthrope) as the *senex amans*. In Goldsmith's farce the grumbler covets his son's intended spouse (he also opposes his daughter's match in the original) because he finds the gruff manner she puts on to please him attractive. The problem is solved when she reverses this humor and gets a French dancing-master to bully him into resigning her to his son. The crudity of dialogue and character, the utter indifference to verisimilitude, the casualness of the saturnalia and the absolute lack of contemporaneity mark this as a "mere farce," to be distinguished from afterpiece comedies such as *The Mock Orators* or even *The Upholsterer*. It was, as its editor, Alice I. Perry Wood, says, a "hasty trifle" (p. xviii).

Goldsmith's stage career ended on this discordant note, for he died the next year. Given the success of *She Stoops*, and due time, he would certainly have written dramatic comedy again. His loss was a major blow to English comic theater, which sorely needed him just then. Though he made substantial contributions to the essay and the novel and wrote some passable verse, Goldsmith was not indispensable to those genres; equal or better talents were at work. The same cannot be said of the drama, where no one was more promising. *She Stoops to Conquer* has as much merit as any single comedy of the century, *The Good-Natured Man* was at least an interesting failure, and his essay "On the Theatre" is still the indispensable brief analysis of the sentimental challenge to the laughing tradition. His early death deprived that tradition of one of its mainstays at a critical moment.

RICHARD BRINSLEY SHERIDAN (1751–1816)

It is helpful to recall the context, both personal and dramatic, in which Sheridan began his career. His roots were in the literary-theatrical world of Dublin: Thomas Sheridan was an actor, elocutionist and writer of farces, while Frances Chamberlaine Sheridan composed several novels and plays, including sentimental comedies. When he settled in London in the spring of 1773, the season of *Piety in Pattens* and *She Stoops to Conquer,* Richard Sheridan was an ambitious and needy young man. On the strength of his wit and charm he had just married Elizabeth Linley, the blooming singer celebrated by Foote in *The Maid of Bath,* and was eager to provide for her. Moreover, with Goldsmith's death in 1774 the cause of laughing comedy was languishing: Foote and Garrick were tiring, Murphy was quiescent, and Colman was flirting with sentimental comedy. There was room for a new champion, and, to judge by the profits Foote and Goldsmith had realized from their attacks on sentiment, the defense of the older tradition needed not be unrewarding. Given these circumstances and his penchant for the chivalrous adventure, it is not surprising that Sheridan stepped forward with a play that he subsequently described as another assault on sentimental comedy in the name of laughter; nor, given his upbringing, that the play, when examined, proves to be less monolithic than his description would suggest.

When first produced at Covent Garden in January 1775 *The Rivals* failed; withdrawn and rewritten in ten days, however, it scored the success that made Sheridan's career. In his second prologue, written for the revised version "and spoken on the tenth night," Sheridan explicitly rejected "the Goddess of the woeful countenance — The Sentimental Muse." His speaker (Julia) points to an actress impersonating Comedy:

> —Look on her well—does she seem formed to teach?
> Should you *expect* to hear this lady—preach?
> Is grey experience suited to her youth?

Do solemn sentiments become that mouth?
Bid her be grave, those lips should rebel prove
To every theme that slanders mirth or love.[18]

"Mirth" and "love," then, are to be the twin pillars of Sheridan's comic credo, and the play largely redeems this pledge. Both halves of the plot are stories of romantic love (used previously in short laughing comedies) that end happily in marriage; both are adorned with a wealth of mirthful characters from traditional comedy: humorists such as Sir Lucius O'Trigger and braggadocio Bob Acres, clever servants (Fag and Lucy), a blocking father, and the illimitable Mrs. Malaprop. Sheridan's comic treatment of the duel would then have called to mind not only *Twelfth Night*, but also Garrick's *Miss in Her Teens*. Satire upon contemporary manners, especially the sentimental fashion, is ubiquitous. Ridicule is employed freely if lightly upon the excesses of Lydia and Faulkland and the cowardly blustering of Acres. The *double vie*, the *double-entendre*, the mistaken identity and other comic devices hoary with age are brought forth in fresh paint. By any standard *The Rivals* has a broad, solid basis in the laughing tradition.

While most readers have agreed with this verdict on the play as a whole, however, many have felt that the subplot of Faulkland and Julia is, despite Sheridan's professions, in the style of sentimental drama.[19] Any case for a significant "sentimental alloy" in *The Rivals* must indeed be drawn from this story, for references to sentimentalism in the main plot—Lydia's romantic vapors and the circulating libraries full of sentimental novels—are clearly satirical and slighting; and playgoers of 1775 would have noticed Lydia's resemblance to the heroine of Colman's *Polly Honeycombe* (revived in the spring of 1773), a "Dramatick Novel" spoofing the vogue of sentiment. It was unusual for a laughing comedy to have a sentimental subplot—the reverse was more common—but even in view of the second prologue Sheridan might have constructed his play thus, either as a sop to the devotees of sentiment or because the idea appealed to him. A review of the subplot may clarify the situation. Julia Melville is Lydia's cousin and the ward of Sir Anthony Absolute. Before her father's death she was contracted to marry one Faulkland, who now delays assuming his right, taxing her with his absurd jealousies and generally playing the role of the capricious lover. (This was thought to be Sheridan's self-portrait, just as other characters and circumstances of the play approximate his own romantic experiences as Elizabeth Linley's suitor at Bath.) Faulkland reaches the pinnacle of outrageous suspicion when, as a test, he tells the faithful Julia that he has duelled and must flee the country. She wants to marry him at once regardless, and he declares himself at last satisfied, but Julia is so offended by this unwarranted trick that she dismisses him "forever." In the end, of course, she is led by her affections to accept a penitent Faulkland.

Although many have found this subplot and its characters sentimental, the opposite view has also been advanced. Allardyce Nicoll sees in Faulkland "the satire of sentimental self-torture", and for George Nettleton he is a "humour character, in whom jealousy is carried to comic exaggeration," even though "some of his and of Julia's speeches seem rather an unconscious echo of sentimental diction than raillery at its extravagance."[20] The disagreement over Faulkland is understandable. He is a tortuous character for light comedy, almost three-dimensional with his annoying vacillations, and needs to be scrutinized in the light of the comic traditions of the period. His framework, the outline of his character, is that of the conventional "capricious man," a Georgian humorist. Colonel Tamper in Colman's *The Deuce Is in Him* is so similar in his desire to test an obviously devoted mistress that he ranks as one possible source; Beverly, in Murphy's *All in the Wrong*, is another.[21] Henrietta Pye's *Capricious Lady* (1771, unpublished) states the idiom in its baldest terms, building its afterpiece comedy around the whimsical changes of a central character. Mrs. Partlet, the "domestick tyrant" in *The Spirit of Contradiction* (1760) by John Rich (?), produces much the same effect by her compulsion to oppose the views of everyone she meets.

Faulkland's particular affliction, the source of his changeability, is represented by Sir Anthony Absolute as "the *delicacy* and *warmth* of his affection" for Julia (v.iii), which Captain Absolute finds "a subject more fit for ridicule than compassion" (iv.iii). Is he not another case of "false delicacy"? Like Sir John Doulant in Whitehead's *The School for Lovers,* Winworth in *False Delicacy,* and Goldsmith's Young Honeywood and Marlow, Faulkland possesses a self-torturing sensibility that seriously impedes the attainment of his destined saturnalia. If Faulkland may be seen as false delicacy or sensibility, Julia is "sense." Unlike the young ladies who play opposite the sentimentalists mentioned above, she in no way contributes to the miserable delay of comic fulfillment. She reacts to

Lydia's "romantic" ideas about penniless marriage with "Nay, this is caprice!" And when Lydia retorts that a lover of Faulkland should be inured to caprice, Julia admits, "I do not love even *his* faults" (I.ii). Julia is thus a critic of sentimental delicacy, and her treatment is as sympathetic as that of any character in the play. The story and characters of Julia and Faulkland, then, have an inherent tendency to satirize or undercut the hypersentimentalist.[22]

The management of this story is another matter: something in Sheridan's handling of the subplot has sent intelligent readers off in widely different directions. The lovers' language seems to be the core of the problem; often moral and sententious, it does sound more like an echo than a satire of sentimental diction. We have seen, however, that sententious conversation between the romantic leads was a widely observed convention that held in laughing as well as sentimental comedy, and as soon as we begin to discuss specific language here we encounter a textual problem. Sheridan, an inveterate polisher of his dialogue, left multiple versions of both his major comedies. In the case of *The Rivals*, the original version is lost; we have the Larpent MS, which seems to approximate the revised acting text, and several editions issued during Sheridan's lifetime. The first of these combines parts of the lost original with recent revisions, and the third moves back toward the then-current acting version.[23] Ordinarily we can live with such discrepancies in prose comedy, but here the issue is complicated by the debate over the sentimentality of the subplot, which centers on the flowery idiom of Faulkland and Julia. The problem is twofold: which text should we be working with, and how should we interpret the changes made by Sheridan from one to the other? The first is easily answered, given the existence of the second: we should take into account both the stage and printed versions, i.e., at least the Larpent MS and the first edition. Cecil Price takes the latter as his copy-text, but students of the theater will also wish to learn what transpired onstage.

In making the comparison we discover approximately what chapter two led us to expect. The first edition cultivates a reading audience by toning down Sir Lucius and Sir Anthony, moralizing the language generally, and adding more ornamental sentiments by Faulkland and Julia (Purdy, pp. xxvi-xxxi). The elaboration of the Julia-Faulkland interviews has been used as evidence of an emergent sentimental strain

217

in Sheridan; in reality, Purdy argues, he liked the sententiousness of these scenes, and the critics simply encouraged him (pp. xlii-xliii). This argument assumes both that the changes do sentimentalize the subplot and that Sheridan made them voluntarily. Purdy, however, adduces no reason why we should think that Sheridan was fond of sentiments except that some of the press said that they favored them, and then he wrote more. But given the circumstances it is equally probable that he was clutching at straws. We know how anxious Sheridan was to succeed, and how perilous the situation was after the play's initial failure. He was more than vulnerable to pressure: he was eager to please the public (Auburn, *Comedies*, p. 32). We also know that the critics expressed approbation of Faulkland and Julia in at least three London newspapers during the period of revision (18–27 January), though they liked little else in the play (Purdy, pp. xv, xlii–xliii). As for the omnipotent opening-night audience, one of its members reported that "Faulkland and Julia . . . were the characters which were most favorably received; whilst Sir Anthony, Acres and Lydia, those faithful and diversified pictures of life, were barely tolerated; and Mrs. Malaprop . . . was singled out for peculiar vengeance."[24] That Sheridan heard and heeded this audience is beyond reasonable doubt: a review of the first revised performance in *The London Chronicle* for 30 January (Beinecke Collection, Yale) remarks of an excision from a speech by Lydia, "The hiss *that occasioned this cut* was that of party or ignorance, not of judgment" (my italics). Sheridan's heavier emphasis on Faulkland and Julia in the second version thus becomes quite understandable, and probably his hasty revision, which could only encompass matters of dialogue, not produce a complete alteration, accounts for our confusion and disagreement. Faulkland, in particular, *does* appear to oscillate between capricious humorist and sentimentalist, depending on which scene or speech or text is under the lens.

The changes Sheridan made in the subplot certainly produce a change in effect, whether or not they represent an actual shift in intention. We can only guess what Sheridan intended, what he thought his public wished to have heightened; we can at least analyze how the alterations affect the play. Purdy and others think they sentimentalize it, and, if Arthur Sherbo's analysis may be credited, simple prolongation of the distresses of the virtuous is a major part of the sentimental effect. On the other hand,

Sheridan's revisions may have been designed simply to give the audience more of Faulkland and Julia without further sentimentalizing them. Some of the revisions emphasize Faulkland's jealous humor, such as the addition to his speech in III. ii (ending "may I lose her forever") of the lines "and be linked instead to some antique virago, whose gnawing passions, and long-hoarded spleen, shall make me curse my folly half the day, and all the night!" (*Works*, 1:108, ll. 35–37) The Larpent MS is more conducive to the idea of satire on Faulkland, and is hence less sentimental, chiefly because it treats him more tersely, and "brevity," according to Sherbo, "is inimical to sentimentalism" (p. 36). It is worth noting that the famous antisentimental prologue to the revised version was composed shortly after these alterations. If Sheridan intended to appease the sentimentalists or give rein to his own pathetic tendencies the second time around, this was a strange way of going about it.

The "compromise with sentiment" has been one ruling passion of Sheridan criticism; the other is "the spirit of Congreve," or Wycherley, or Vanbrugh. Sheridan, it is often said, "looks back to the Restoration." Sometimes these statements refer to his penchant for the five-act comedy of manners, while at other times they mean that nothing so good had been done in this vein since so-and-so, but either way they undervalue Sheridan's considerable debts to the comic idiom of his own time. No one who has examined *The Rivals* and its immediate dramatic milieu closely has failed to find many connections, and the extent to which Sheridan was influenced by Georgian afterpiece comedy is especially striking. The genesis of *The Rivals* may have been his mother's unfinished farce *The Journey to Bath* and/or another, rather mysterious "little farce."[25] The main plot resembles Garrick's *Miss in Her Teens,* and there are parallels between the subplot, Colman's *The Deuce Is in Him* and Murphy's *All in the Wrong.* Several of the characters were virtually stock figures at the time. Faulkland was a well-established type, and Lydia Languish, like Polly Honeycombe, was a takeoff on the heroines of sentimental comedies such as *The School for Lovers* and *The Platonic Wife.* Mrs. Malaprop had a long genealogy and numerous family still living: Penelope Trifle in *The Knights,* Heel-Tap in *The Mayor of Garret* and Mrs. Clack in *The Trip to Calais,* all by Foote; Lady Autumn in Mrs. Lennox's *The Sister*; Termagant in Murphy's *The Upholsterer*; Brush in Joseph Reed's *The Register Office,* and so on. For that matter, *The Journey to Bath* has a malapropist as well. The sentimental materials used and abused so liberally are of mid-eighteenth-century vintage, and the full-scale comedy of manners was still a living form. Little or nothing in *The Rivals* necessitates an expedition into the seventeenth century; most of it echoes or transforms contemporary drama which he could have seen on the London stage by 1775.

Between *The Rivals* and *The School for Scandal* Sheridan was not inactive, but the kind and quality of his work are insubstantial. *St. Patrick's Day; or, The Scheming Lieutenant* (1775) is a sketchy two-act farce drawn from Farquhar's *The Recruiting Officer*. Like Goldsmith's *The Grumbler*, it is a "thank-you" piece, written for the benefit of an actor who had helped to put across the playwright's big comedy. One senses Sheridan yawning through its mediocrities. *The Duenna* (1775), on the contrary, shows Sheridan the opportunist, wide awake to the rage for comic opera and committed to no principle save theatrical success. His plot is a well-worn piece of Spanish intrigue that he treats with the superficiality it deserves; the libretto is gay, bubbling, and empty (cp. Auburn, *Comedies*, pp. 79–80). With music by his father-in-law Thomas Linley it succeeded hugely, enabling the entrepreneurial young Sheridan to buy out Garrick's share of the Drury Lane patent the following season (1776). Garrick then wrote the prologue for Sheridan's next play, *A Trip to Scarborough* (1777), altered from Vanbrugh's *The Relapse*. The prologue prepares us for the predictable "moralization"; the ravishment of Berenthia is replaced by Loveless' (latest) reform, and Townley does not assault Amanda. Sheridan's chief improvement is to cut and smooth Vanbrugh's messy fifth act by setting it entirely at Sir Tunbelly Clumsy's in Scarborough, and by simplifying the recognition and reconciliations. Sheridan expended a lot of energy between his two original comedies without trying to reach beyond his grasp.

The School for Scandal (1777) was worth waiting for, however; it is still often called "the last great English comedy" or "the most finished product of the English comedy of manners," and was certainly the last significant comedy of Sheridan and his age. *The School for Scandal* has also endured its share of detractors, and a critical tradition has grown up about it like the briar hedge around Sleeping Beauty. Breaching this tradition is the most difficult part of the quest; the beauty within is relatively accessible, partly because Sheridan was as consistent as his critics. Like *The Rivals*, *The School for Scandal* is professedly and basically a laughing comedy but has sentimental elements that are something of an interpretative problem, and though often seen as a throwback to the Restoration comedy of manners, in character and device it has close affinities with its own age. These two antinomies are near relations.

The main line of interpretation was founded by John Pinkerton in 1785. Pinkerton wrote that *The School for Scandal* reestablished the style of Congreve, though Sheridan's characters were weak and kept "blundering upon sentiments."[26] The limited usage of *sentiments* here is worth noting—"Everything like a sentiment is sure to meet with applause in our theatre; which the actors well express by calling sentiments *claptraps*"—because Charles Lamb, who formulated the classic phrasing in broader and more damning terms, may have meant the same thing as Pinkerton: "This comedy grew out of Congreve and Wycherley, but gathered some allays of the sentimental comedy which followed theirs."[27] At about the same time *The School for Scandal* was described by William Hazlitt as "a genteel comedy," a term that usually connoted "sentimental" or at least "moral."[28] For the largest and most influential group of modern critics, clearly derived from this tradition, the play is a wedding of Congreve's brilliant dialogue with the plot line of *L'École des femmes* by way of *The Country Wife*, the whole constrained by the "sentimental decorum" of the day.[29] One finds other writers on both sides of this centrist position, but most agree that Restoration and sentimental influences are mingled in Sheridan's masterpiece.

Other resemblances closer to home have been pointed out, however, of which the most interesting is to *Know Your Own Mind*. Murphy's play was produced only a few weeks before *The School for Scandal*, but had been finished, according to the author, in 1768, and may have circulated in manuscript. There are reasonably close parallels between Murphy's Malvil, with his "musty sentences," and Joseph Surface; between Dashwould and the Scandalous College; between Miss Neville and Maria; and between the two sets of opposed brothers (though that idea goes back to Terence's *Adelphi*). Almost every character and situation of the play has analogues in the comedies of the preceding quarter century. The story of the Teazles is certainly reminiscent of Molière and Wycherley, but it also approximates the "Bashful Constant" plot of *The Way to Keep Him* (1761). The point is not that Sheridan was following Murphy instead of Molière, but that a laughing tradition in comedy linked all three and continually passed along such devices from each to each and onwards, so that the very idea of an "original" is a bit naive.[30] Eighteenth-century parallels, however, abound. The main idea of the Sir Oliver Surface plot—the benevolent incognito relative—also occurs in Foote's *The Author* (1757), as well as in *The Good-Natured Man* and *The West Indian*. The characters and circumstances of Charles and Sir Oliver parallel those of George and Sir William Wealthy in Foote's *The Minor* (1760). Even the famous screen scene may be partially modelled on the screen trick in act 5 of Isaac Bickerstaffe's *The Hypocrite* (1767).[31] Many influences, from Plautus and Terence to Foote and Murphy, may be discerned in Sheridan's comedy; those of the Restoration are simply the latest that are well known to most of his modern critics.

As for the Congrevian wit that some find in *The School,* Sheridan's play does have better sustained dialogue than any other comedy of its time except *She Stoops,* but whether the impulse was Restoration brilliancy is another question. As often as not, humor of situation, not verbal wit, is the charm of the conversation:

> CHARLES: Yes he [Sir Oliver] breaks apace I'm told—and so much altered lately that his nearest relations don't know him—
> SIR OLIVER: No! ha! ha! ha! so much altered lately that his relations don't know him! ha ha ha! that's droll egad—ha ha ha! (III.iii)

Unquestionably Sheridan can be witty too, but wit in general occupies a different place and has another nature than in Congreve's work. At its ordinary level Sheridan's style has a balanced periodic ease that is closer to the relaxed smoothness of Goldsmith, "sipping at the honey-pot of his mind," than to the more violent energy and paradoxical turns of Congreve or Vanbrugh. Again it is difficult to discuss Sheridan's language specifically because of numerous disparate versions and the absence of an authorized edition in his lifetime, but every version has the ring of Georgian literary conversation. And it is not true that Sheridan's servants, like Congreve's, trade banter as witty as their masters'. Trip shocks Sir Oliver by his aristocratic dissipation, not by his wit (III. ii), and while this motif does occur in the Restoration (*The Man of Mode*), it is more highly developed in the eighteenth century (*High Life below Stairs*).

The School for Scandal, then, is a child of the eighteenth-century comic tradition, not a throwback merely because it also resembles its grand-parents. As a Georgian mainpiece, however, it was expected to be moral, and the character of Maria (especially in II. ii), the reforming of Charles, the "moral tag" and, negatively, the avoidance of licentiousness, fulfil that expectation. For some it is also sentimentalized, but this proposition is more controversial, the question being whether "sentimental de-corum" is crudely juxtaposed with comedy of manners, or whether something more integral emerges. In support of the play's integrity, it should be pointed out that the Restoration form is made the vehicle of Sheridan's ideas on two characteristically Georgian concerns, wit and good nature; and that the sentimental materials, far from being an "alloy" or a "varnish," are central to the comedy—though it is not a sentimental comedy. This seeming paradox requires some explanation.

A "true versus false" motif, familiar from the "false delicacy" plays, is even more pervasive in *The School for Scandal* than in most comedies.[32] The forms it assumes here are benevolence—in the story of the Surfaces—and wit: the school for scandal and its effects on others, especially the Teazles. Though this analysis might seem to promote the separateness of the two plots, in fact the two themes are inextricably linked.[33] Their close kinship and interdependence is indeed the central assertion of the play about them. As Sir Peter remarks to Lady Sneerwell and her circle, "Madam, true wit is more nearly allied to good-nature than your ladyship is aware of" (II.ii). His observation accords with general eighteenth-century thought on the topic. The distinction and separation of true from false wit had been a concern not only of Pope and his circle and of moral essayists such as Addison and Steele, but of philosophers and estheticians and popularizing pamphleteers such as Corbyn Morris.[34] This semantic distinction, a post-Restoration de-velopment, was basic to the Georgian redefinition of humor and humorists. The trouble with Sir Benjamin Backbite's "neat rivulet of text" meandering "through a meadow of margin" (I.i) is that it consists of "satires and lampoons on particular people." Too often, the "wit" is a hypocrite and seducer such as Joseph Surface, smoothly assuring Lady Teazle that "when a husband entertains a groundless suspicion of his wife, . . . it becomes you to be frail in compliment to his discernment" (IV. iii). Obviously Sheridan is having it both ways here, enjoying what he criticizes and inviting us to do likewise, yet the structure of the plot and of our sympathies works against these characters and brands their wit as false as their natures are base. "True wit," then, as Sir Peter says, must be found in "good natures": Charles and Sir Oliver, chiefly. This distinction is largely lost on us because we follow Morris in calling them "humorous" rather than "witty," but it generates what moral purpose the play has. It is not a school where one goes to learn scandal, but one in which scandal may learn to know itself.

With benevolence as with wit, true and false are confronted in Charles and Joseph Surface, who form the crux of critical disagreement over the play. The problem can be formulated as follows. Certainly *The School* is loaded with a charge of satire aimed against sententiousness and sentimental heroes (Joseph), yet no play that retains benevolent Charles Surface as its hero, virtuous Maria as his mate and genial Sir Oliver as their benefactor can be said to wage all-out war on sentiment. Thus, runs the argument, Sheridan had a sentimental side, or he was still at the beck of the sentimentalists in the audience.

The problem evaporates, however, as soon as we look closely at what kind of sentiment we are dealing with in each case. Joseph is par excellence the conventional "man of sentiment," as Kate Hardcastle teasingly called Marlow, the grave, moral young man of the sentimental comedies; his descent is from Steele's Bevil, Jr., via Sir John Doulant in Whitehead's *School for Lovers,* Sir William Belville in Elizabeth Griffith's *The Platonic Wife,* and Winworth in *False Delicacy.* Sir Peter's remark about Joseph (II. iii) could be applied to each of them: " 'Tis edification to hear him converse; he professes the noblest sentiments. But lately an odd thing had been happening to this figure as it uttered a sentiment. *Profess* was beginning to sound ironic. Either his good intentions and moral purity were creating problems of their own, or the sentences were coming out all wrong (*Piety in Pattens*), or else he was losing his glib tongue when he needed it most. Obviously the family was in trouble by 1777; both Joseph and Murphy's Malvil are hypocrites who use sentimental gravity as a cloak for villainy. As in Rodgers' "White Christmas," their "soft plush / Of sentiment . . . embosoms all / The sharp and pointed shapes of venom, . . . / And into obese folds subtracts from sight / All truculent acts"—their own. Sheridan, that is to say, was making the distinction basic to our modern distrust of sentimentality. Joseph is one of Foote's puppets, a sentimental machine to be turned on or off as the occasion requires:

> JOSEPH: Poor Charles! I'm sure I wish it were in my power to be of any essential service to him; for the man who does not share in the distresses of a brother, even though merited by his own misconduct, deserves—
> LADY SNEERWELL: O Lud! you are going to be moral, and forget you are among friends.
> JOSEPH: Egad, that's true!—I'll keep that sentiment till I see Sir Peter. (I.i)

His reputed benevolence is all pretense and gesture (v.i). Cecil Price surmises that the character could have been suggested by Chesterfield's letters to his son (*Works,* 1:305–6), though Fielding also provided several models.

Charles, on the other hand, has nothing falsely delicate about him, and his genealogy is quite distinct from his brother's. He is "exceeding frank" (III.iii), and prosecutes his benevolence with such animal vigor that it gets him out of trouble as well as into it. Sheridan does not permit us to worry on this head: it is not that kind of comedy. The temperature is kept low and the tension slack. At the outset Sir Oliver assures Rowley that "if Charles has done nothing false or mean, I shall compound for his extravagance," and thus there is no real danger in Charles's admission that "Justice is an old lame hobbling beldame, and I can't get her to keep pace with Generosity for the soul of me" (IV. i). The portrait of Charles is a celebration of the good heart and the good impulse; he has the robust virtues of Tom Jones and Belcour without the indecorous refinement of Bevil, Jr. Unquestionably the character participates in the Georgian benevolization of humor, and could easily have turned the play into a sentimental comedy, but Sheridan deliberately avoids that destination by skirting opportunities for pathetic distress, heavy moralizing, or any serious attempt at reforming Charles. That in him which appeals to our hearts is not treated sentimentally. In the picture-auction scene, for example, Charles's loyalty to "poor Noll" and his unwitting flattery of his uncle tickle Sir Oliver's vanity so comically that the maudlin and senti-mental possibilities are upstaged; his subsequent charity to old Stanley is hastened over with a flippant allegory. Sheridan's light touch was never more needed, more evident, or more admirable than here. Charles is presented favorably to an age nourished on Shaftesbury and waking to

Rousseau and humanitarianism, but he is not what was meant by a sentimental character. Sheridan, like Congreve and Goldsmith, had subdivided a dramatic type. The blundering sentimentalist, such as Winworth or Faulkland, is here split into two characters: the calculating utterer of sentiments (Joseph), and the imprudent benevolist (Charles). The intent of the play may have been to kill sentimental comedy, but its achievement was to separate its human gold from its dross.

At twenty-six, Sheridan had written two comedies that could stand comparison with any in the century, and had seen them produced successfully. He was the bright young hope for laughter which, in one way or another, had lost Goldsmith, Foote, Garrick, and Murphy in the preceding three years. Incredibly, Sheridan never wrote another comedy. Such a run of ill luck defies probability; if the laughing tradition was comatose after 1777, this withering away of individual talent was a principal malefactor. The next play we can confidently ascribe to Sheridan is *The Critic* (1779). He may possibly have worked on a "dramatic entertainment" called *The Camp* (1778), although Tate Wilkinson insists (in *The Wandering Patentee*) that Sheridan never wrote a line of it (but cf. Auburn, *Comedies*, p.149). If he did not there is no great loss to his canon, for *The Camp* is an ambiguous piece of fluff, a satiric farce with aspects of comic opera. On the other hand, the incisive wit, some mild but well-aimed social satire and a few good topical touches (the theatrical scene-painter, the great ladies following the military camp) argue a dramatist of some talent. *The Camp* is unambitious and merely histrionic, but not worthless.

The Critic is not a comedy, but stands within the laughing tradition. It has no plot, only incidents. The first act is dramatic satire somewhat in Foote's manner, while the latter portion is a theatrical burleque, a descendant of *The Knight of the Burning Pestle*, *The Rehearsal* and *Tom Thumb*, to name only its best-known forebears. At the time Sheridan's debts to Fielding's *Pasquin* (1736), Garrick's *A Peep behind the Curtain* and Colman's *New Brooms!* were also recognized (*Works*, 2:473) The play provides abundant satire of sentimental conventions. In 1.i, Dangle, Mrs. Dangle, and Sneer discuss Sir Fretful Plagiary's new tragedy and drama in general. Mrs. Dangle, supported by Sneer, upholds "genteel" comedy and deplores the return of the "ridiculous," while Mr. Dangle waxes hot against "nicety" and hypocritical moralization. (Sneer contemptuously agrees with him, too.) Subsequently we are introduced to Sir Fretful

himself—a cruel but recognizable portrait of Richard Cumberland—
and taken to a rehearsal of Puff's play. This amusing, sometimes brilliant,
takeoff on the more absurd and bombastic conventions of English
tragedy also contains a few passing hits at sentimental comedy and some
satiric commentary on social modes. *The Critic* has been called Sheridan's
Dunciad (*Works*, 2:472), and the analogy is biographically apt in suggest-
ing that Sheridan was standing aside from the theater and letting off a
farewell blast. He did in effect depart the next year by standing for
Parliament, though he managed to write some new scenes for a revival of
the pantomime *Harlequin Fortunatus* and authored a pantomime of his
own, *Robinson Crusoe*, produced in 1781. (There is an old tradition that
he once acted Harlequin, but it is unsubstantiated.) Soon Sheridan was
involved in the spectacular Hastings trial and his dramatic output dwin-
dled to nothing; his contributions to Drury Lane were purchases of
lavish scenery and the enlargement of 1794. Five years later he concluded his playwrighting career with *Pizarro,* an adaptation of von
Kotzebue's melodrama *Die Spanier in Peru,* although his association with
Drury Lane lasted until it burned in 1809. The fire left him with little
except the glass of port in his hand, but this prop, and a friend's cue, gave
him an exit line in the old style as he watched the ruinous conflagration:
"Cannot a man take a glass of wine by his own fireside?"

Sheridan's major comedies have been described as "deltas" of received
comic modes, and this metaphor can be helpful if taken to refer to all of
his drama and to the confluence of an entire network of tributaries, not
just sentiment and Restoration manners. His parentage and his precoc-
ity together may explain his extensive use of inherited eighteenth-
century comedy throughout his career; in all of his plays Sheridan was
either altering or recombining earlier works. His dramatic corpus is in
the last analysis a motley assortment: two fine comedies, an altered
comedy, a comic opera, a farce, a burlesque, an adapted melodrama, one
pantomime and part of another, perhaps a "dramatic entertainment."
More than Murphy or Goldsmith or Foote he wrote expediently, to
please the taste of the town. His willingness to pursue a profitable
illegitimacy where it led was as characteristic of Sheridan as were his
satires on sentimentalism; after all, he was not so much an artist or a man
of the theater as an ambitious and talented careerist. Sheridan always
needed money, and the stage must pay.

The germ of his casual recipience of nontraditional comedy can be detected at the outset of his career, in the second prologue for *The Rivals*, where in rejecting the "sentimental Muse," he asks,

> Can our light scenes add strength to holy laws?
> Such puny patronage but hurts the cause:
> Fair Virtue scorns our feeble aid to ask;
> And moral Truth disdains the trickster's mask.
>
> (*Works* 1:75, ll.7–10)

Perhaps it does, although the trickster's mask is not the comic mask, and the phrase does not do justice even to Sheridan's own comedies. But there is no point in arguing with Sheridan: what is important is to realize that this amoral conception of comedy brings us full circle from John Dennis's attack upon sentimental comedy as immoral back in 1722. In *A Defence of Sir Fopling Flutter* Dennis had reasserted the implicit morality of traditional comedy, as had most major theorists since Aristotle and Horace; but the sentimentalists, for whom morality took the less subtle forms of didacticism and exemplary characters, had kept insisting from about the turn of the century that sentimental comedy had a monopoly upon morality, that laughing and low comedies, because they exhibited vice, were vicious. This idea fitted into the eighteenth century's generally reformist attitude toward the excesses of Restoration manners, and eventually the point was carried. As early as 1702 Dennis had complained (in his *Large Account of the Taste in Poetry*) that few qualified judges of comedy remained in the audience; by 1775, it seems, not even a comic playwright could or would make the distinction that Dennis had considered fundamental. Sheridan talks about comedy the way Joseph Reed had defined farce in 1761: "With pleasantry alone . . . to laugh a thoughtful hour away" (prologue to *The Register Office*, Larpent MS 196). In order to oppose the "school of morality" it was apparently thought necessary to forswear morality. But comedy, once it has been thus stripped, has leave to become mere farce, entertainment—all those things, in fact, that Sheridan wrote. The usurpation of morality was the unkindest cut perpetrated by sentimental comedy, a fatal wound left in the body of its "victorious" opponent: "Not so deep as a well, nor so wide as a church-door; but 'tis enough, 'twill serve."

Epilogue

Epilogue

Eighteenth-century comedy eventually came to recognize two different and opposed faces of sentiment: the maudlin or hypocritical cant of sentimentality on the one hand, constructive benevolence and genuine sensibility on the other. It would be exaggerating to say a debate raged, and excessive to argue that progress was everywhere evident. But there was a dialectic, and the development from *Love's Last Shift* and *The Conscious Lovers* to *She Stoops to Conquer* and *The School for Scandal* is encouraging. Some false starts necessitated new beginnings; some sense of the civilizing influence and utilitarian value of good nature was emergent. In such characters as Marlow, Faulkland, Malvil, and Joseph Surface certain prototypes of sentimental man were rejected as false without being allowed to discredit the ideals against which they were measured and found wanting. The history of comedy from Cibber to Sheridan forms a continuation of the Augustan attempt to build the City of Good Sense, which included a Neighborhood of Good Feeling. Yet the artifact was fragile, as its short life testifies; for only a decade or two was it viable. In working out a compromise between laughter and sentiment, the dramatists acquired unstable and potentially dangerous allies. Heart, Sympathy, and Admiration were useful while they could be controlled, but without a master's hand they tended to set up independent bases of power and turn on their host. Comedy, in a word, cannot survive too large an admixture of fellow-feeling, though in moderate amounts it gives the finest wine. This is why our story breaks off on the eve of the "humanitarian period" in drama, an age better for society than for comedy. The debate we have been tracing passed into other forms—*Sense and Sensibility* is an obvious example—while stage comedy took up winter quarters.

231

Why the eighteenth century was such an awkward period for comedy is a troublesome question that does not finally admit of a single answer. At best the complex of factors might be reduced to two: one a feature of intellectual and one of social history. Northrop Frye's discussion of the age of sensibility is a good introduction to the first; he views the Garrick era as one devoted to Longinian psychology and interested in literature-as-process, rather than to an Aristotelian aesthetic concerned with literature-as-product: "Where there is a strong sense of literature as aesthetic product, there is also a sense of its detachment from the spectator. . . . Where there is a sense of literature as process, pity and fear become states of mind without objects, moods which are common to the work of art and to the reader, and which bind them together psychologically instead of separating them aesthetically."[1] This generalization is based chiefly on nondramatic literature, and once again we must be wary of transferring its full force to the stage; but drama is influenced by what its audience is doing and thinking outside the theater (hence the intellectual factor shades easily into the social) and Frye's terms are useful for their adaptability to dramatic comedy. To the extent that he is right about this general bent of eighteenth-century spectators and that Henri Bergson was right about comedy, they were a poor audience, and the laws by which they judged it were alien to its traditions. In Bergson's classic treatment comic laughter is unfeeling, impartial, detached: in short, aesthetic and Aristotelian. Some eighteenth-century theorists, however, argued that you may laugh with rather than at a comic figure, a response that undermines comic detachment. According to Frye's theory, the natural dramatic expression of an age of sensibility is sentimental drama, but the Georgian drama's patrons seem to have found other novelties—farce, vaudeville, and spectacle—more congenial in the long run. Actually the two alternatives to traditional comedy soon found each other out, and mated to produce hybrids. As sentimental comedy became stylized and drifted towards melodrama (*The Brothers, The Maid of Kent*) its "farcical" features gradually became apparent, and the theater of Vincent Crummles and Gilbert & Sullivan was the eventual result. These nontraditional types harried legitimate comedy on both flanks, and by the time of Garrick's retirement had captured almost three-fifths of the comic repertoire.

The "sociological" factor stems from another aspect of the relationship between the producers and the consumers of drama. Most of our information points to a serious gap between the audiences—heterogeneous, unpredictable, cranky—and the professional dramatic community, which was relatively unified and more traditional in its outlook on comedy. Broadly speaking, the latter drew up a ragged front against the vulgarians in the former. Both the gap and the front had precedents (and are not unknown today), but they were nonetheless crucial in the development of Georgian comedy. During and after the Restoration circumstances combined to drive an especially thick wedge between theater and society. As the patronage of the drama passed from royalty or nobility to the audience, that audience metamorphosed from aristocratic to bourgeois. In trying to please the less educated, more commercial tastes that were coming to dominate the theater, playwrights lost the respect of intellectuals and *literati,* moving to a middle ground between artists and philistines, firmly identified with neither. The introduction of actresses altered the internal society of the theater and attracted rakes from outside; the stage remained a "demi-rep," on the fringes of polite society. The memoirs of eighteenth-century actors, actresses, and managers emphasize their tenuous social footing, while their direct addresses to the audiences and dramatists' representations of the spectators in plays point up the numerous tensions that existed.

How these conditions may have affected drama is suggested by G. K. Chesterton's essay "On the Comic Spirit."[2] He believed that comedy depends on certain distinctions being made and held by the dramatist and his audience; some shared assumptions and values are necessary in order for the comic and satiric to flourish. "There must be something serious that is respected," writes Chesterton, "even in order that it may be satirized." Obviously as the eighteenth-century dichotomy between playwright and public increased, such common ground became harder to find: hence the wranglings, the grudging compromises, the wild swings in taste. "You cannot unmask a mask, when it is admittedly as hollow as a mask," says Chesterton. "You cannot turn a thing upside down, if there is no theory about when it is right way up." Here is the central and persistent problem of comic artists (or artisans) trying to laugh with *nouveaux arrivés* and socialites and tired businessmen seeking light entertainment as an escape from the complexities of society. Probably the general shrinking of eighteenth-century comedy's forms and

233

concerns was due in part to this diminution of common grounds for laughter. There was, literally, not as much that all could agree to laugh at, except the timeless, classless, mindless jokes of farce.

Locked in this social context, breathing this intellectual atmosphere, dramatic comedy lived an increasingly attenuated existence in the latter half of the eighteenth century. An impoverishment and a dwindling of the comic spirit were felt and commented upon at the time. George Colman defined the subject of comic artists in his day as "the comic stubble of the moral scene."[3] Foote's phrase in the same context and at about the same time was "a bankrupt age."

> Equally sunk, our credit and our wit,
> Nor is the sage more solvent that the cit.
> . . . .
> For wit's keen satire, and this laughing stage,
> What theme so fruitful as a Bankrupt Age?
> (Prologue to *The Bankrupt*, 1773)

There was a general conviction that the great and abiding comedies of the past (which of course were still being seen, brilliantly acted) had harvested the great and abiding subjects, leaving to moderns only "the comic stubble." It was already an old theme in English drama; as early as 1677 Dryden wrote nostalgically of the Elizabethan summer as he huddled by the embers of *All for Love*. The idea implicit in such comments was more fully articulated by William Hazlitt half a century after Foote: "Comedy naturally wears itself out—destroys the very food on which it lives; and by constantly and successfully exposing the follies and weaknesses of mankind to ridicule, in the end leaves itself nothing worth laughing at."[4] This diagnosis—that society had ceased to provide comedy with fuel—is predicated on a more optimistic view of the social efficacy of comedy than most of us are likely to accept, and eighteenth-century dramatists did not really believe it either, at least not in this extreme form. The sarcasm with which they assured their audiences that humanity was now too virtuous to be laughed at and their ingenuity in uncovering fresh follies belie the notion that the trouble was merely a lack of material. The sickness lay within the genre itself, which tended more and more to reflect the image of the "comic stubble" that it took as its subject. Lesser forms sufficed to treat lesser material, as dramatic comedy withdrew in scope and aspiration. Original full-length comedies showed signs of padding, alterations of old plays habitually shortened them by as much as one act (e.g. Sheridan's *Trip to Scarborough;* cf. *The Relapse*), and seemingly fatigued authors turned to writing afterpieces in weary relief:

> This foolish poet's no where, take my word.
> He's jaded at two heats, as I'm alive,
> 'Tis well it's out of rule to start for five.[5]

As the farces, short comedies, dramatic satires, pantomimes and burlettas multiplied, mainpiece comedies shrank proportionately in the repertoire. Foote (who had called farce a reduction of Attic comedy) rose to the challenge of gleaning the stubble with ingenuity and even a kind of doomsday vision: in an age bereft of both intellectual and financial credit, what apter target can a theatrical satirist find than this same bankruptcy? To look farther is evasive and unnecessary; the very littleness of the contemporary creative spirit in drama, which leads him to write in dwarfish forms, also affords him materials. And the comic stubble ought to be satirized in miniatures, as accurate reflections of the malaise. It is thus appropriate that much of the comic tradition that lingered on did so in terse forms. In them it endured, as befits comedy, until the next spring. Reduction was necessary to survival.

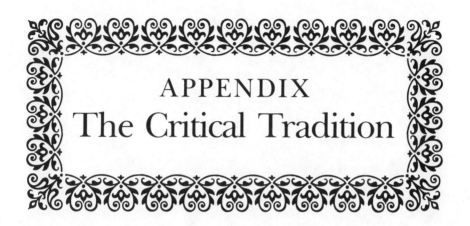

APPENDIX
The Critical Tradition

Appendix
The Critical Tradition

From one point of view this book is an inquiry into the vagaries and possible sources of error of historical criticism in the humanities, a forbidding but important subject. Everyone who works with events or ideas more than a few years old also reckons with opinions and interpretations of them; they shed various lights on the events and ideas, and assessments of such opinions therefore turn one back towards evaluation of the original works or occurrences. The "reality" of history to us is our image of it, and in debating what to make of the past and what others have made of it, we affect our modes of interpreting the present and the future. A researcher therefore perceives a divided duty, to the primary material on the one hand, and to the commentators on the other, and hence develops an ambivalence toward his predecessors. For there is no denying that once a critical tradition has built up a certain momentum it tends to perpetuate itself; inertia will carry it forward a considerable distance past the point where the impulse (i.e., evidence) ceases. The later critic is in part the servant of this tradition—he must deal with it whether he will or no, if only to reject it—and the original material is its prisoner as well as its protegé. The tradition forms around a work or an author or a period from the inside out, like a cocoon around a larva; it encloses protectively, but also renders the emergence of the next stage more difficult. In order to understand the whole process, the historian has to go back to the pupal stage, when the earliest statements were being spun out.

Many of the critics and criticisms adduced below have been mentioned previously, but as those references are scattered it will be convenient to group them as follows.

239

The relatively small body of contemporary criticism that discussed general trends rather than particular plays is interesting now chiefly for what it says (and does not say) about sentimental comedy. To the Georgians this interest would doubtless appear a distortion, since for them sentimentalism did not seem the all-pervasive issue of the period; it is not even mentioned in the anonymous *Essay upon the Present State of the Theatre in France, England and Italy* (1760), which concerns itself with such issues as spectacle, reading versions, stage business, and pantomimes. By 1775, however, it was very much on William Cook's mind as he expounded *The Elements of Dramatic Criticism*. He distinguishes traditional from sentimental comedy, associating the latter with the novel and attacking it as "a driveling species of morality" (p. 142). Like Goldsmith in his well-known essay "On the Theatre" published two years earlier, Cook is reluctant to accept it as a kind of comedy at all, and does so only because of current taste and practice. He traces the genre back to Steele, though the chronology from the 1760 *Essay* to Goldsmith to Cook suggests that such a continuum was not universally perceived. In 1785 sentiment was already being spoken of in the past tense. "Robert Heron" (alias John Pinkerton) claimed in that year that "sentimental comedy bore a very short sway in England" ("On Comedy," in *Letters of Literature*, p. 46). This writer began the tradition of relating Sheridan to Congreve, devoted considerable space to farce and satire, and deplored the rapid decline of the stage since 1780 (pp. 202–3), a lament echoed in Murphy's anecdotal *Life of Garrick* (1801). Charles Dibdin corroborates Pinkerton's chronology of sentiment, dating the span of the vogue from *False Delicacy* to *She Stoops to Conquer* (in *A Complete History of the Stage*, 1795, 5: 277, 282–84). He also wonders if sentimentalism might not be another cultural bow to France (5:6), distinguishes "genteel" from "sentimental" comedy (5:8) and notes the prevailing taste for spectacle (5: 43, 125–29). Major eighteenth-century commentary ends on this note, quite unlike the tradition that developed as the plays receded into the past.

Little important criticism of Georgian drama was published in the following century, a period of more or less malign neglect, but the few general appraisals that did appear included some classics and established the main lines of early modern studies. William Hazlitt's voluminous theatrical writings include general remarks on comedy, some of them discussed in my epilogue. He speaks nostalgically of Sheridan and Foote, lamenting that they were no longer well acted or well received, and denigrates Steele's "homilies in dialogue" while accepting the moral mission of the stage. Today Hazlitt seems an odd though important and entertaining drama critic, with his love of puppet shows and his dislike of small theaters that destroyed the scenic illusions he cherished. Charles Lamb is more dignified. His classic piece "On the Artifical Comedy" in *The Essays of Elia* (1821) echoes Hazlitt's judgment that comedy of manners was no longer understood or appreciated by moralistic audiences, and adds the influential opinion that *The School for Scandal* "a mixture of Congreve with sentimental incompatibilities."

Sir Walter Scott's "Essay on the Drama" (1819) is inadequate in several respects, for example when it asserts that "genteel comedy" was "borrowed from the French," but Scott's remark that Sheridan unites Congreve with Farquhar seems to refine on Pinkerton and may have passed that tradition on to Lamb. Frederick G. Tomlins's *Brief View of the English Drama* (1840), Percy Fitzgerald's notoriously unreliable *New History of the English Stage* (2 vols., 1882), and Dutton Cook's *On the Stage* (1883) deserve only passing mention.

By 1889 most Georgian comedies were rather old books to be read than plays to be seen, and the literary rejection of sentimentality had begun. Whether for these reasons, or because of the need to simplify a general survey, Sir Edmund Gosse's one chapter on "Drama after the Restoration" in his prestigious *History of Eighteenth-Century Literature 1660–1780* ends with Farquhar. Sheridan appears briefly and unexpectedly (looking back to the Restoration) under "Poets of the Decadence." Gosse dismisses mid-century comic drama (Fielding to Goldsmith) with the mention of two comedies and two farces, and remarks that the decade of the 1770s witnessed the return of conventional comedy after an interval of *drame larmoyante* (pp. 317–18, 338). At this point most of the main planks of the platform of twentieth-century criticism were in place.

Modern historians have published voluminously on eighteenth-century comedy. With most of the comedies no longer being produced, and many of them not even readily accessible in print, however, clichés and oversimplifications were perhaps inevitable. George Nettleton, for example, who wrote the chapter on eighteenth-century drama and the stage for *The Cambridge History of English Literature*, vol. 10 (1913), as well as the standard *English Drama 1642–1780* (1914), characterized two adjacent periods thus: "Whether comedy laughs with the sins of the Restoration, or weeps with the sentimentality of the eighteenth century, it bears the form and pressure of the age" (*English Drama*, p. 12). As he progresses, Nettleton modifies this position considerably. Halfway through the book he has already remitted over fifty years of the sentence: "The moral reform of English drama was won at the expense of almost half a century during which comedy bowed her head in the presence of Sentimentality" (p. 165). Before the end Nettleton seems to have come half circle: "At times the poverty of the comic spirit before Goldsmith and Sheridan has been exaggerated into too positive an insistence upon its extinction.... The comic spirit was not dead.... It is idle to maintain that [Goldsmith] was the first to turn comedy back from tears to laughter" (p. 262). Whether Nettleton is referring to Gosse or to his own earlier pages is not clear, but it makes a little difference, since the original characterization stands.

Generally critics of Nettleton's generation, especially in America, shared his views without indulging in "weeping age" rhetoric to the same extent. H. V. Routh in his chapter on Georgian drama in volume eleven of the *Cambridge History* (1914) sees genteel comedy prevailing in the 1760s, Sheridan and Goldsmith "reverting" to "classical comedy" (p. 266), and sentimental drama winning the day in the 1770s (p. 272). His pages on Cumberland as the proto-Wordsworth of drama are still worth reading (pp. 263–65). Ernest Bernbaum's valuable *Drama of Sensibility* (1915) falls into the trap of many special studies: it finds what it is looking for everywhere. Sentimental comedy is described as "dominant and prolific" (p. 222) between 1750 and 1767, while from 1768 to 1772 it "overwhelmed" traditional comedy "by sheer weight of numbers" (p. 224), and the period 1773–80 saw its "final triumph" (p. 247).

In 1923, however, William Archer announced that "sentimentalism" had become merely "a vague term of abuse" and that the decline of eighteenth-century drama was not due to sentiment (*The Old Drama and the New,* p. 203), but to "clinging to an outworn formula" (p. 222). Joseph Wood Krutch's *Comedy and Conscience after the Restoration* (1924) follows Nettleton and Bernbaum in finding that "by 1725 . . . sentimentalism had become the prevailing spirit" of comedy (p. 221), with *The Conscious Lovers* marking the "final victory of the new type" (p. 225). In the next year Stanley T. Williams described the tears of Loveless in *Love's Last Shift* as "typical . . . of the normal mood of the theatre" for three quarters of a century ("The English Sentimental Drama from Steele to Cumberland," *Sewanee Review,* 33 [1925]:407).

During the twenties a transatlantic dialogue developed on the subject, with most American critics upholding the sentimental tradition while British scholars tended to play it down. Allardyce Nicoll's *British Drama* (1925) attempts to subdivide all sentimental drama into three types: false, true, and humanitarian. "It must not be supposed," he wrote, "that sentimentalism completely dominated the age" (4th ed. rev., p. 289). Sheridan and Goldsmith "had been preceded by many dramatists who kept to the older paths" (p. 290). The same author's six-volume *History of English Drama* 1660– 1900 (1927) repeats these contentions and adds a warning that "those writers on our dramatic literature who class all the comedies between 1750 and 1800 as 'sentimental' (always excepting the work of Sheridan and Goldsmith) are building a hasty theory on an incomplete foundation of fact. Indeed, when we look at the typical dramatic fare of the period, we may be inclined to wonder whether, after all, it was not sentimentalism which was the fashion insecurely planted on the theatre" (3rd ed. rev., 1952, p. 171). Ashley Thorndike, whose *English Comedy* was published in New York in 1929, was struck by the "dearth of comedy" at midcentury; it is wrong, he wrote, to assume "that there was something in between" Fielding and Goldsmith. "As a matter of fact there were almost no new comedies" from 1735 to 1760 (p. 377). He balanced his chapters on the period 1760– 1800: one on "the revival of comedy," one on "sentimentality triumphant." Completing this group, F. W. Bateson generally supports Archer; in *English Comic Drama 1700–1750* (1929) he argues that sentimentalism does not explain eighteenth-century comedy, for "the tone of the age was not predominantly sentimental" (p. 11), and sentimental comedies were an "aberration" (p. 13). Bateson maintains that it was the novel and essay that carried the extreme sentimentalism.

The postwar generation of scholars kept the tradition intact. L. J. Potts wrote that "while [sentimental comedy] was in possession of the stage, Fielding, Sterne, and Smollett kept true comedy alive in the novel; and in the 1760's Goldsmith and Sheridan recaptured the stage for comedy" (*Comedy*, 1948? p. 144), thus reasserting the line of Nettleton and Bernbaum. In 1950 Louis I. Bredvold's *The Literature of the Restoration and Eighteenth Century 1660–1798* (volume 3 of *A History of English Literature*, ed. Hardin Craig) took the position that the "middle years" of the century saw the "triumph of sensibility" in drama: "Ultimate victory was already certain to the new forces. The laughing comedies of Goldsmith and Sheridan could not rival the popularity of the drama of sensibility" (rpt. Collier Books, 1962, p. 161). This kind of statement could not, of course, be debated until the full repertoire became available. F. S. Boas summarizes his views in the preface to his *Introudction to Eighteenth Century Drama 1700–1780* (1953): "The immoral wit of Restoration comedy, battered by the powerful attack of Jeremy Collier, yields place, though not fully, to the sentimentalism of Steele and his followers. This, in its turn, becoming stereotyped, meets with the satire which reaches its peak in *The School for Scandal*" (p. vii). Another preface of the same year, that of James J. Lynch's *Box, Pit and Gallery,* characterizes eighteenth-century comedies as either "sugary or solemn" (p. vii), for they generally followed "the fashion of Steele and Cibber" (p. 3). Lynch found sentiment the dominant mode (p. 288), too "deeply embedded" (p. 190) for Goldsmith's efforts to overcome, and a part of the pre-Romantic preparation for Wordsworth and Shelley (p. 305).

In the next few years American scholarship began to explore the contrary evidence. Harry Pedicord's *The Theatrical Public in the Time of Garrick* (1954) examines the repertoire closely and obtains surprising results. Garrick's audience, Pedicord concludes, favored sentimental plays only if they also had amusement value, and "the proportion of plays of this type was exceedingly low in comparison with the bulk of the playhouse fare" (p. 154). Then Arthur Sherbo reexamined sentimental comedy itself, finding evidence that it was mostly closet drama aimed at a reading public and commenting that it reflected "adversely on the seriousness and depth of the sentimental attitude in the century" (*English Sentimental Drama*, 1957, p. 145). Testing his consensus definition of sentimental comedy, he questioned the accepted sentimentality of several plays and the "sentimental advance" of 1750–1800, during which he found nonsentimental comedies at least holding their own (pp. 159–60). The view that sentiment triumphed in this period, Sherbo concludes, is unfounded (p. 163); sentiment was present but not dominant. Capping these efforts, *The London Stage 1660–1800* began to appear in 1960. As successive parts were published in 1961 (1729–1747) and 1962 (1747–1776) its revolutionary potential and likely impact on criticism became clear. It showed, for example, how few comic performances in the mid–eighteenth century were actually of sentimental plays. A good deal of earlier scholarship was thus partially invalidated, as having proceeded on false assumptions, and it seemed likely that the course of future studies would be deflected.

The older tradition possessed considerable momentum, however. Louis Kronenberger in *The Thread of Laughter* (1962) visualizes a "darkness" or "swamp" of sentimental comedy in the eighteenth century (p. 151), so that by Goldsmith's time comedy was "drowned" in sentiment (p. 185) and left the stage for the novel. Leonard R. N. Ashley's *Colley Cibber* (1965) mentions that "as the century went on, the vogue of sentiment increased" (p. 38); "This view ruled the drama absolutely until Goldsmith" (p. 39). Often enough, the tradition has been perpetuated in just such passing references. So Allan Rodway's "Goldsmith and Sheridan: Satirists of Sentiment" contains the remark that sentimental comedy was "dominant" in Goldsmith's day (*Renaissance and Modern Essays Presented to Vivian de Sola Pinto*, ed. G. R. Hibbard, 1966, pp. 66). Much less casual is A. N. Kaul: "The history of English comic drama," he writes, declines from Shakespeare to the Restoration, "and then it further deteriorates into the monotonous vapidity of sentimental drama" (*The Action of English Comedy* 1970, p. 131). Kaul asserts that by 1775 the Muse of Comedy was "virtually defunct" on the stage, the Sentimental Muse having "long usurped the theater as her own exclusive realm" (p. 134). In the annals of the friends of the sentimental tradition it would be difficult to find a critic more extreme in his dedication, though Kaul is by no means alone in his convictions.

But a reaction has been gathering, of which the best single example is

Robert D. Hume's essay "Goldsmith and Sheridan and the Supposed Revolution of 'Laughing' against 'Sentimental' Comedy" (*Studies in Change and Revolution: Aspects of English Intellectual History 1640–1800*, 1972). Building on information in *The London Stage* and leads in earlier scholarship, Hume rejects most major tenets of the accumulated critical tradition as "nonsense" (p. 248), sharpens the relevant distinctions and definitions (pp. 243–44), and inspects closely a number of comedies and their production records from 1760 onward. "The perspective given by the concept of a struggle to reassert laughing against sentimental comedy is quite misleading," he begins (p. 237), and concludes that "Goldsmith and Sheridan inherited a thriving comic tradition" (p. 271). Hume denies that sentimental comedy ever "achieved so much as a temporary dominance" between 1760 and 1773 (p. 257), and supports that denial with a careful examination of the comedies of that period; his views are generally endorsed by John Loftis in *Sheridan and the Drama of Georgian England* (1976 pp. 4–15). The best general booklength study in recent years, Cecil Price's *Theatre in the Age of Garrick* (1973), gives a more middle-of-the-road appraisal of the question. Price finds tears and sensibility in such comedies as *False Delicacy* and *The West Indian*, but also humor, satire, and criticism of sentiment; and he wonders if it was the "fun" or the sentiment that attracted crowds (pp. 161–64). According to Price's calculations, only three important laughing comedies appeared in the three decades before *She Stoops to Conquer* (p. 164), yet the best stage entertainment of the time was comedy and satire (p. 174). The stage was moral in outlook, Price concludes, and audiences delighted in didactic sentiment (p. 197), but he speculates that it was tragedy, not comedy, whose place in the repertoire was usurped by sentimental comedy (p. 174). *Theatre in the Age of Garrick* is admirable in its balance and its degree of independence from the critical tradition we have been tracing.

Since I have myself sketched a view of eighteenth-century comedy sharply differing with much of this tradition, I may fairly be asked to account for the disagreement. First, access to the full repertory and the acting texts of the plays, which *The London Stage* and the Larpent Collection make available, shows us what really happened on the stages of Georgian London. I take issue with some of my predecessors on their literary approach to the theater of this period; too often, it seems to me, they have accepted as representative and "major" a few plays that were successful in print, and been content to trust the published versions. The extent to which the acted theater might have diverged from the booksellers' theater has not usually been considered, nor has sufficient importance been attached to the short comedy and farce, probably because they interest readers less than spectators. Early critics were unlucky in two important respects. Trusting to the printed drama (the Larpent Collection was not catalogued until 1939), some were misled by the popularity of sentimental literature; and deprived until 1962 of complete and reliable information about production, they sometimes guessed wrong about the standard theatrical fare. The error was understandable, and in any one case it was small, but it was fairly constant, and multiplied by three hundred–odd comedies in the period it acquired significant dimensions.

The second cause of variance is closely related to the first. Lacking adequate knowledge of specifically theatrical transactions, some critics were tempted to transfer what they knew of poetry, the novel, and the essay into the realms of drama. Doubtless it seemed unlikely that dramatic taste stood aside from the pre-Romantic mainstream, yet to an extent this appears to have been the case. Stuart Tave's useful book *The Amiable Humorist* (1960) traces the transition from satiric to benevolent laughter during the eighteenth century, but one must be wary about applying his statements to the theater without some allowance for its oblique development. For some of the less cautious, their general non-dramatic literary learning has proved a *faux ami*. A similar problem in transference is that *our* interest and pleasure in discussing the phenomenon of sentiment have sometimes been projected onto the audiences who witnessed it: there is evidence to indicate that they tired of it soon enough, usually rejecting its extreme manifestations outright. Some of the "major" sentimental comedies of today's anthologies showed little staying power in eighteenth-century playhouses. *The Conscious Lovers* was less popular than *The Suspicious Husband* in the long run; *False Delicacy* was a veritable flash in the pan. The dozen or so comedies that circumstances have made most famous in our textbooks do not necessarily give an accurate picture of the standard theatrical fare, in this or any other age. It is not a question of worshipping box-office success, but of taking a second look at what constitutes an "influential" or otherwise "significant" comedy, as well as asking how representative these plays were.

Where I differ from earlier historians, then, it is partly because of primary material that has come to light in the last few decades, partly because I believe that their treatment of the material they did have sometimes involved unrepresentative part-sampling and unwarranted generalization upon insufficient evidence. At the same time I must record my admiration of other critics such as Archer and Nicoll who, navigating under the same conditions, avoided these shoals and directed their successors along what now seems the right course.

Notes

Notes

PROLOGUE

1. For a survey of relevant criticism see the appendix, "The Critical Tradition."

2. By, for example, John Dennis, in "Remarks on a Play Call'd, *The Conscious Lovers*" (1723), and Oliver Goldsmith, in "An Essay on the Theatre; or, A Comparison Between Laughing and Sentimental Comedy" (*Westminster Magazine* for Dec. 1772 to Jan. 1773). See Richard Cumberland's "Dedication" to his *The Choleric Man*, 3d ed. (London, 1775) for the sentimentalists' response: that Terence and other ancients had provided classical precedents for sentimental comedy.

3. "There has never been a time since Garrick's day when so many representative English comedies could be seen in a single season. The public constantly had plenty of first-rate comedy." Ashley Thorndike, *English Comedy* (New York: Macmillan Co., 1929), p. 379. Many of the older comedies, however, were altered to adapt them to Georgian taste.

4. *The World Upside-Down: Comedy from Jonson to Fielding* (Oxford: Blackwell, 1970), p. 23.

5. Leonard R. N. Ashley, *Colley Cibber* (New York: Twayne, 1965), p. 72.

6. *An Apology for the Life of Colley Cibber, Comedian*, (1740) ed. B. R. S. Fone (Ann Arbor: Univ. of Michigan Press, 1968), p. 147.

7. See Kenny, ed., *The Plays of Richard Steele* (Oxford: Clarendon Press, 1971), p. 191; and Dobrée, *English Literature in the Early Eighteenth Century* (Oxford: Clarendon Press, 1959), p. 235.

8. Kenny, ed., *Plays of Steele*, p. xiii. She calls it "his most light-hearted and comic play" (p. 191).

9. Henry Fielding, *Joseph Andrews* (London, 1742), book 3, chapter 11.

10. John Wilson Bowyer, *The Celebrated Mrs. Centlivre* (Durham, N.C.: Duke Univ. Press, 1952), p. v.

11. *The London Stage, 1660–1800* (5 pts. in 11 vols.), pt. 4, *1747–1776*, ed. George Winchester Stone, Jr., 3 vols. (Carbondale, Ill.: Southern Illinois Univ. Press, 1962), 1:clxv.

12. See also chapter four and Cibber, *Apology*, pp. 153–62; Watson Nicholson,

The Struggle for a Free Stage in London (New York: Houghton Mifflin, 1906), chaps. 3 and 4; Frank Fowell and Frank Palmer, *Censorship in England* (London: Palmer, 1913), pp. 130–54; P. J. Crean, "The Stage Licensing Act of 1737," *Modern Philology* 35 (1938):239–55; and John C. Loftis, *The Politics of Drama in Augustan England* (Oxford: Clarendon Press, 1963), pp. 129–52.

13. The Larpent Collection, housed at the Henry E. Huntington Library and Art Gallery, San Marino, California. See Dougald MacMillan, *Catalogue of the Larpent Plays in the Huntington Library* (San Marino: Huntington Library, 1939).

14. For recent contributions to this discussion, see Jean B. Kern, *Dramatic Satire in the Age of Walpole 1720–1750* (Ames, Iowa: Iowa State Univ. Press, 1976), pp. 51, 54–55, 96; John Loftis, in *The Revels History of Drama in English* (8 vols.), vol. 5, *1660–1750* (London: Methuen, 1976): 27, 31–32, 70, 72–73; and A. H. Scouten, in *The Revels History*, 5:287.

15. *Letters of Literature* (London, 1785), pp. 202–3.

16. *The Life of David Garrick*, 2 vols. (London, 1801), 1:118; 2:159.

1: THE NOISE AND TUMULT

1. For a fuller treatment of the subject matter of this chapter, see Alwin Thaler, *Shakespere to Sheridan* (Cambridge, Mass.: Harvard Univ. Press, 1922), esp. pp. 117–47; James J. Lynch, *Box, Pit and Gallery* (Berkeley and Los Angeles: Univ. of California Press, 1953), esp. p. 294; V. C. Clinton-Baddeley, *All Right on the Night* (London: Putnam, 1954); Harry W. Pedicord, *The Theatrical Public in the Time of Garrick* (New York: King's Crown Press, 1954); *The London Stage*, esp. the introductions to pt. 3, *1729–1747*, ed. Arthur H. Scouten, 2 vols. (1961), and pt. 4, *1747–1776*; Leo Hughes, *The Drama's Patrons* (Austin, Texas: Univ. of Texas Press, 1971); Cecil Price, *Theatre in the Age of Garrick* (Oxford: Blackwell, 1973), esp. pp. 123 and 196; and Kern, *Dramatic Satire*, esp. pp. 56 and 99.

2. For a different view of the failure of Jacob's play, see *The London Stage*, pt. 3, 2:699. Kelly makes his claim in an "Address to the Public" prefaced to the first edition of his play (London, 1770). Price discusses this incident (*Theatre*, p. 124), and all of the major authorities cite similar occurrences.

3. *The London Stage*, pt. 4, 1:142. The play, anonymously altered from Beaumont and Fletcher, was not published.

4. Clinton-Baddeley, *All Right*, pp. 46–47. While corroborating this general picture Hughes thinks it somewhat exaggerated. But he admits that "far too often the audience . . . came prepared to damn" (*Drama's Patrons*, p. 37). Cf. also Michael Booth in *The Revels History of Drama in English*, vol. 6, *1750–1880* (London: Methuen, 1975), p. 21.

5. Benjamin Victor, *History of the Theatres of London and Dublin*, 3 vols. (London, 1771), 3:66. The mainpiece was *No One's Enemy But His Own*.

6. Clinton-Baddeley, *All Right,* p. 167. Robertson Davies writes in *The Revels History* that "the success or failure of a particular playwright was often a matter of luck, and our period [1750–1880] abounds in examples of what seem to be caprice and injustice affecting the fortunes of a play. This is especially true in comedy" (6:149).

7. Lynch, *Box, Pit, and Gallery,* p. 139; Murphy, *Life of Garrick,* 2:97. Jean Kern notes that James Miller's *Art and Nature* was shouted down by Templars incensed at his previous play, *The Coffee House (Dramatic Satire,* p. 56).

8. *A Discourse Upon Comedy* (1702), in *The Works of George Farquhar,* ed. Charles Stonehill, 2 vols. (London: Nonesuch, 1930), 2:338; Cibber, *Apology,* pp. 99–100; and Virgil Stallbaumer, "Thomas Holcroft: A Satirist in the Stream of Sentimentalism," *E L H* 3 (1936):42.

9. Printed in my *Eighteenth-Century Drama: Afterpieces* (London: Oxford, 1970).

10. *A Will and No Will* was edited by Jean Kern for the Augustan Reprint Society (nos. 127–28, 1967), and also appears in my *Afterpieces,* where it is briefly compared to Regnard's and King's plays (pp. 37–38).

11. William W. Appleton describes Macklin's legal victory over some hecklers in 1775 as one that benefited the entire profession. *Charles Macklin, An Actor's Life* (Cambridge, Mass.: Harvard Univ. Press, 1960), p. 196.

12. Simon Trefman, *Sam. Foote, Comedian* (New York: New York Univ. Press, 1971), p. 200, says that after 1768 Foote published only his unsuccessful plays so that he could make some profit from them, but this was unusual, if not unique.

13. "A new edition" (London, 1788), p. 28, p. 6.

14. Quoted by Dobrée, *English Literature,* p. 225.

15. Thaler, *Shakespere to Sheridan,* p. 7, dated this development from "the decades just preceding . . . 1642." Cibber, *Apology,* p. 54, attributed it to interplayhouse rivalry after the Restoration. See also Hughes, *Drama's Patrons,* pp. 97–119, 185–86; Price, *Theatre,* chap. four; and Stone, in *The London Stage,* pt. 4, 1:cxix–xx.

16. First edition (London, 1767), p. 67 (I.ii).

17. Larpent MS 401. The authorship is uncertain.

18. *Prose on Several Occasions,* 3 vols. (London, 1787), 1:208–9.

19. Lynch: the characteristics of the audiences "are necessarily reflected in the repertory" (*Box, Pit, and Gallery,* p. 206). Hughes: "the audience assumed an important role in determining the content of eighteenth-century plays" (*Drama's Patrons,* p. 7).

20. Stone, in *The London Stage,* pt. 4, 1:clxix.

21. See Pedicord, *Theatrical Public,* chap. one; cf. Stone, in *The London Stage,* pt. 4, 1:xxx–xxxi; and Hughes, *Drama's Patrons,* pp. 182, 185.

22. William Archer, *The Old Drama and the New* (London: Heinemann, 1923), p. 228. Appleton describes special exercises developed by Charles Macklin "to

cope with the visual and aural problems of the increasingly large theatres" (*Macklin*, p. 158). The worst of this development took place after 1780, but the forces that brought it about were operative in Garrick's time.

23. Thaler comments that in the eighteenth century "playhouse finance began to be high finance indeed," and managers fought a running battle with bankruptcy (*Shakespere to Sheridan*, pp. 213–14); see also p. 244.

24. *European Magazine* 4 (Sept. 1783):168.

2: STAGE VS. CLOSET

1. Based on MacMillan's *Catalogue of Larpent Plays*. His information on publication is quite reliable, and the few missing plays (conjecturally, 28 in the first 790 items: see MacMillan, p. vii) do not seriously damage the statistics.

2. *English Drama 1642–1780* (New York: Macmillan Co., 1914), p. 224.

3. *English Comedy*, p. 372. Dobrée's verdict that "comedy as such was temporarily dead" (*English Literature*, p. 240) is clarified by his remark "the comic spirit fled to farce" (p. 229). See also Leo Hughes, *A Century of English Farce* (Princeton, N.J.: Princeton Univ. Press, 1956), pp. 282–83.

4. *English Comedy*, p. 415. See also Allardyce Nicoll, *British Drama*, 5th ed. rev. (London: Harrap & Co., 1962), p. 189; and W. J. Lawrence, *Old Theatre Days and Ways* (London: Harrap & Co., 1935), chap. 19. Some recent writers have gone further: "After Gay and Fielding the major vehicle for so-called 'laughing comedy' . . . was . . . the afterpiece" (Robert Findlay, "The Comic Plays of Charles Macklin," *Educational Theatre Journal* 20 [1968]:400). Philip K. Jason, "Meteors of an Hour," Ph.D. dissertation, Univ. of Maryland, 1971, holds that by the late eighteenth century afterpieces were more important than mainpieces. And see *The London Stage*, pt. 4, 1: cxlv, clxi.

5. *English Comedy*, p. 464, quoting Mrs. Inchbald in the last phrase.

6. Prologue to *The Man of Reason*, thought to be Kelly's.

7. Hughes, *English Farce*, p. 153. His whole chapter "The Actors" is germane.

8. *English Sentimental Drama* (East Lansing, Mich.: Michigan State Univ. Press, 1957), p. 152.

9. See Sherbo, *Sentimental Drama*, p. 75; Allardyce Nicoll, *A History of English Drama 1660–1900*, 6 vols., 4 ed. rev. (Cambridge: Cambridge Univ. Press, 1952; rpt. 1961), 3:71–73; and Eugene R. Page, *George Colman the Elder* (New York: Columbia Univ. Press, 1935), p. 133.

10. Nicoll, *History*, 3:156.

11. *The Works of Hugh Kelly* (London, 1778), p. 86.

12. First edition (London, 1762), p. 7 (I. i). The play was "formed on a plan of M. de Fontenelle's, never intended for the stage," says the Advertisement.

13. Prologue to *Polly Honeycombe*.

14. *The Dramatic Works of George Colman*, 4 vols. (London, 1777), 4:118 (I.i).

15. Prefatory note to *The Discovery* in vol. 21 (London, 1791).

16. See Nicoll, *History,* 3:72 and chapter on melodrama; and Lynch, *Box, Pit, and Gallery,* pp. 287–88.

17. Price, *Theatre,* pp. 49, 153–54.

18. Murphy, *Life of Garrick,* 2:52.

19. Richard Purdy, ed., *The Rivals* (Oxford: Clarendon Press, 1935), p. xlvi.

20. See John P. Emery, ed., *The Way to Keep Him and Five Other Plays by Arthur Murphy* (New York: New York Univ. Press, 1956), p. 245; and MacMillan, *Catalogue of Larpent Plays,* p. 43.

21. *An Essay upon the Present State of the Theatre* (London, 1760), p. 126.

22. *Life of Garrick,* 1:103. In fact the piece became quite popular, with about sixty-five performances in its first thirty seasons (1745–76).

23. Purdy, ed., *The Rivals,* pp. xxvi ff. and xlvi ff.

24. *The Good-Natured Man* constitutes a notable exception, in that the bailiff scene had been hissed off the stage and was thereafter omitted, but Goldsmith had a particular point to make, so he reinstated it in the printed version.

25. For example, cf. act 1 of William Kenrick's *Widowed Wife* in Larpent MS 275 and in the first edition (1767).

26. Ernest Bernbaum, *The Drama of Sensibility* (Boston and London: Ginn, 1915), p. 248; and Thorndike, *English Comedy,* p. 449.

27. Larpent MS 362: "laughable." The change produces a closer echo of Horace.

28. This was untrue. See Claude E. Jones, "Dramatic Criticism in the *Critical Review,* 1756–1785," *Modern Language Quarterly* 20 (1959); 18–26, 133–44.

3: THE MUSE OF THE WOEFUL COUNTENANCE

1. B. Ifor Evans paraphrases Meredith's position thus in *A Short History of English Literature* (Penguin Books, 1940; rpt. 1962), p. 70. Tennyson and Arnold among poets, Hardy and Dreiser of the novelists, afford other examples. As for turn-of-the-century criticism, Sir Leslie Stephen called sentimentalism a kind of "mildew" on eighteenth-century literature.

2. Samuel Chew describes the Imagists as "opposed to exuberance, sentiment, and cloudily romantic lushness" in *A Literary History of England,* ed. A. C. Baugh (New York: Appleton-Century-Crofts, 1948), p. 1580. Similar views are expressed by David Daiches in his introductions to the modern period in *The Norton Anthology of English Literature,* 4th ed. (New York: Norton, 1979).

3. E.g., Paul Parnell, "The Sentimental Mask," *P M L A* 78 (Dec. 1963): 529–35. Possibly this wave has crested, however. John Traugott argues that sentimentalism is not the death of comedy, but an opportunity for the inventive, in "The Rake's Progress from Court to Comedy," *Studies in English Literature* 6 (1966): 406; and Michael M. Cohen (countering Parnell) has maintained that

the most serious flaw in *The Conscious Lovers* is not that it uses the sentimental code but that it violates it. See "Reclamation, Revulsion, and Steele's *The Conscious Lovers*," *Restoration and Eighteenth-Century Theatre Research* 14, no. 1 (May 1975): 23–30.

4. See Stuart Tave, *The Amiable Humorist* (Chicago: Univ. of Chicago Press, 1960), p. ix.

5. *Steele at Drury Lane* (Berkeley and Los Angeles: Univ. of California Press, 1952), pp. 196–97; *Comedy and Society from Congreve to Fielding* (Stanford: Standford Univ. Press, 1959), p. 127.

6. Joseph J. Keenan, "The Poetic of High Georgian Comedy: a study of the comic theory and practice of Murphy, Colman and Cumberland," abstract, Ph.D. dissertation, Univ. of Wisconsin, 1969. See also Robert J. Detisch, "High Georgian Comedy: English Stage Comedy from 1760 to 1777," Ph.D. dissertation, Univ. of Wisconsin, 1967.

7. *The Theory of Comedy* (Bloomington: Indiana Univ. Press, 1968), pp. 61, 63.

8. See, for example, Robert D. Hume, "Goldsmith and Sheridan and the Supposed Revolution of 'Laughing' against 'Sentimental' Comedy," *Studies in Change and Revolution, Aspects of English Intellectual History 1640–1800* (n.p.: Scolar Press, 1972), p. 244.

9. F. W. Bateson, *English Comic Drama 1700–1750* (Oxford: Clarendon Press, 1929), pp. 8–11.

10. Two interesting examples of that period are Robert Baddeley's *The Swindlers* (1774) and George Colman's *The Suicide* (1778), both unpublished but extant in the Larpent Collection. The *Critic* quotations may be found in *The Dramatic Works of Richard Brinsley Sheridan*, ed. Cecil Price, 2 vols. (Oxford: Clarendon Press, 1973), 2:501–2.

11. Stanley T. Williams put it well: "In single speeches these flexible folk throw off the habits of a lifetime" ("The English Sentimental Drama from Steele to Cumberland," *Sewanee Review* 33 [1925]:408).

12. Price, *Theatre*, p. 164. Cf. Arthur Friedman, "Aspects of Sentimentalism in Eighteenth-Century Literature," in *The Augustan Milieu*, ed. Henry K. Miller and others (Oxford: Clarendon Press, 1970), p. 249, who classes it with *Tom Jones* and *The School for Scandal* as works "productive of laughter."

13. *Dramatic Character in the English Romantic Age* (Princeton: Princeton Univ. Press, 1970), p. 112.

14. For a different view see Mark Schorer, "Hugh Kelly: his place in the Sentimental School," *Philological Quarterly* 12 (1933):392.

15. Colman, *Dramatic Works*, 4:130. On the French influence, see especially Willard A. Kinne, *Revivals and Importations of French Comedies in England 1749–1800* (New York: Columbia Univ. Press, 1939).

16. *A Complete History of the Stage*, 5 vols. (London, 1800), 5:277, 283–84.

17. *The Devil Upon Two Sticks* (London, 1794), p. 57 (act 3).

18. Murphy, *Life of Garrick*, 2:52; and Thomas Davies, *Memoirs of the Life of David Garrick*, 2 vols. (London, 1780), 2:140–41.

19. Preface to *The Town Before You*, 2nd ed. (London, 1795), pp. x–xi. That the rhetoric here and in *The Contract* has a self-serving aspect is evident.

20. Pp. 163–66. Robert Hume has since virtually demolished Bernbaum's analysis in "Goldsmith and Sheridan."

4: HARLEQUIN'S INVASION

1. A descendant of the Italian commedia dell'arte, pantomime had been prominent on the seventeenth-century French stage, especially in Molière's adaptations; like sentiment, pantomime was often thought of as French in England, where it had been naturalized from about 1715.

2. "The Victorian theatre witnessed the complete subordination of comedy to spectacle, signs of which were apparent in the last years of Georgian theatre" (George Rowell, *The Victorian Theatre* [Oxford: Clarendon Press, 1956]), p. 64. See also Booth in *The Revels History*, 6:30–31; Clinton-Baddeley, *All Right*, p. 105 and chap. six; and Charles Dickens, *Nicholas Nickleby*, chaps. 22–25 and 29–30.

3. Thaler discusses the growing demand for melodrama, spectacle, and music from the late Caroline period onward in *Shakespere to Sheridan*, pp. 7 ff.

4. Colman, *Dramatic Works*, 4:334–35 (scene 2).

5. Clinton-Baddeley, *All Right*, p. 162. Nicholson paints a similar picture in *Free Stage*, pp. 281 ff. See also Rowell, *Victorian Theatre*, chap. one; Joseph Donohue, "Burletta and the Early Nineteenth-Century English Theatre," *Ninteenth-Century Theatre Research* 1 (1973):29–51; P. T. Dircks, "The Eighteenth-Century Burletta: Problems of Research," *Restoration and Eighteenth-Century Theatre Research* 10, no. 2 (Nov. 1971:44–52; and Edward T. Byrnes, "The English Burletta, 1750–1800," Ph.D. dissertation, New York University, 1967.

6. Philip James de Loutherbourg, scenic director at Drury Lane 1771–81 and the leading creative spirit of spectacularism. See Price, *Theatre*, esp. pp. 80–82. The quotation appears in Price, ed., *Works of Sheridan*, 2:729.

7. See among others Price, *Theatre*, chap. four; Clinton-Baddeley, *All Right*, p. 205; Pedicord, *Theatrical Public*, pp. 27 ff.; and Dibdin, *Complete History*, 5:43, 125–29.

8. An interest in exotica was a minor feature of the rise of irregular drama and the history of Georgian taste. Plays such as Bickerstaffe's *The Sultan* (1775), Edward Thompson's *St. Helena* (1776, unpub.) and George Stevens's *French Flogged* (1760), set in America, as well as numerous burlettas and pantomimes, catered to an interest in the faraway and picturesque. See Mitchell Wells, "Spectacular Scenic Effects of the Eighteenth-Century Pantomime," *Philological Quarterly* 17 (1938):67–81.

9. See Price, *Theatre*, pp. 71–76; Lynch, *Box, Pit, and Gallery*, pp. 232 ff.; and Hughes, *Drama's Patrons*, pp. 97 ff.

10. See Colley Cibber's interesting account of "how our childish pantomimes first came to take so gross a possession of the stage" in chap. 15 of his *Apology;* and Nicholson, *Free Stage*, p. 52.

11. Larpent MS 96, ed. Jean Kern for the Augustan Reprint Society, no. 116 (1965), pp. 6, 18.

12. *Collected Works of Oliver Goldsmith*, ed. Arthur Friedman, 5 vols. (Oxford: Clarendon Press, 1966), 4:96.

13. Northrop Frye notes that "moral comedy" often leads to melodrama: *Anatomy of Criticism* (Princeton: Princeton Univ. Press, 1957), p. 167. He is referring to comedy that makes moral judgments, not to "moralization" as distinguished from "sentimentalization," but his description of melodramatic themes (p. 47) could easily be applied to most Georgian sentimental comedies.

14. See Dircks, "Burletta," pp. 44–45; and Pedicord, *Theatrical Public*, p. 27.

15. Stone quotes Garrick, for example, to the effect that any improvement of the drama must begin with the audience's reforming its "errors and prejudices"— then managers and actors will follow or starve. *The London Stage*, pt. 4, 1:cxcii.

16. For standard views of Rich as a seducer of public taste, see Loftis, *Politics of Drama*, p. 152; and Hughes, *Drama's Patrons*, pp. 101–2. Paul Sawyer attempts a mild defence of his career in "John Rich's Contributions to the Eighteenth-Century London Stage," in *The Eighteenth-Century English Stage*, eds. Kenneth Richards and Peter Thomson (London: Methuen, 1972).

17. *The Critics in the Audience of the London Theatres from Buckingham to Sheridan* (Albuquerque: Univ. of New Mexico Publications in Language and Literature, no. 12, 1953), p. 36.

5: LAUGHING COMEDY

1. Friedman, ed., *Works of Goldsmith*, 3:212.

2. Cf. Hume, "Goldsmith and Sheridan," p. 240.

3. Louis Kronenberger, *The Thread of Laughter: Chapters on English Stage Comedy from Jonson to Maugham* (New York: Knopf, 1962), p. 185.

4. *The London Stage*, pt. 4, 1:clxiii–clxv.

5. *In Praise of Comedy* (London: Allen and Unwin, 1939), p. 60.

6. "To say that there was not a strong vein of laughing comedy flourishing throughout the period 1760–80 is ridiculous" (Hume, "Goldsmith and Sheridan," p. 256).

7. Newell Sawyer, *The Comedy of Manners from Sheridan to Maugham* (Philadelphia: Univ. of Pennsylvania Press, 1931), p. 1.

8. See his *Large Account of the Taste in Poetry*. In support of Sawyer's definition, see especially Nicoll, *History*, 1:12–13; Norman Holland, *The First Modern Com-*

edies: The Significance of Etherege, Wycherley, and Congreve (Cambridge, Mass.: Harvard Univ. Press, 1959), pp. 9–12; and Kenneth Muir, *The Comedy of Manners* (London: Hutchinson, 1970), p. 11.

9. On the difficult question of class in the theaters, see Pedicord, *Theatrical Public*, pp. 43, 154; Stone, in *The London Stage*, pt. 4, 1:cxci; James Sutherland, *English Literature of the Late Seventeenth Century* (Oxford: Clarendon Press, 1969), p. 152; Hughes, *Drama's Patrons*, p. 178; Price, *Theatre*, p. 93; and Booth, in *The Revels History*, 6: 3–7, 28.

10. See Dennis's "A Defence of Sir Fopling Flutter" (1722) and "Remarks on a Play, Called, *The Conscious Lovers*" (1723); and Goldsmith's "On the Theatre."

11. Dedication to *The Choleric Man,* 3d ed. (London, 1775).

12. *An Essay Towards Fixing the True Standards of Wit, Humour, Raillery, Satire and Ridicule* (London, 1744), p. 32. Hurd also takes a balanced position in "On the Provinces of Dramatic Poetry," *The Works of Richard Hurd,* 8 vols. (London, 1811), 2:58–72.

13. *Gray's Inn Journal* 96 (17 Aug. 1754):279 (interpolation from p. 276).

14. *Anatomy of Criticism,* p. 163. The standard reference work for borrowings and influences in this period is Nicoll's *History,* vols. 2 and 3.

15. Murphy, *Life of Garrick,* 1:118.

16. *An Examen of the New Comedy, call'd "The Suspicious Husband"* (London, 1747).

17. First edition (London, 1747), p. 28 (II.iv).

18. First edition (London, 1768), p. 4 (I.i).

19. Donohue views the play as finally ambiguous (*Dramatic Character,* pp. 117–18). Its humor is emphasized by Price, *Theatre,* pp. 162–64, and by C. J. Rawson, "Some Remarks on Eighteenth-Century Delicacy, with a note on Hugh Kelly's *False Delicacy," Journal of English and Germanic Philology* 61 (1962):1–13.

20. Quoted by W. Moelwyn Merchant, *Comedy* (London: Methuen, 1972), p. 80.

6: THE COMBRUSH OF THE COMIC MUSE

1. See Hughes, *English Farce;* Lawrence, *Old Theatre Days,* chap. 19; and Leslie Hotson, *The Commonwealth and Restoration Stage* (Cambridge, Mass.: Harvard Univ. Press, 1928), esp. pp. 16–17. A useful early source, *The Wits, or Sport Upon Sport* (1672), by Francis Kirkman, is quoted by Hotson and other authorities. Philip Jason's dissertation "Meteors of an Hour" includes a history of the afterpiece.

2. Lynch, *Box, Pit, and Gallery,* p. 238; and Stone, in *The London Stage,* pt. 4, 1:xxv. Lawrence (*Old Theatre Days*) also makes the point, and as noted above Jason ("Meteors") argues that late in the century afterpieces were more important than mainpieces.

3. See the works by Donohue, Dircks, and Byrnes cited in chap. four, note five; and Booth, in *The Revels History*, 6:42.

4. According to Stone, about 40 percent of the afterpieces performed between 1747 and 1776 were farces; roughly 30 percent were pantomimes (*The London Stage*, pt. 4, 1:clxvi–vii).

5. Isaac Bickerstaffe wrote a quite different play with the same title in 1768.

6. *The Divine Average: A View of Comedy* (Cleveland and London: Case Western Reserve Univ. Press, 1971), p. vii. See also Eric Bentley, *The Life of the Drama* (New York: Atheneum, 1965), pp. 222–54. An early contributor to the reassessment of farce was Gustave Lanson, who argued that "l'origine de la comédie de Molière, de toute cette comédie, jusqu'en ses plus hautes manifestations qui sont la comédie de moeurs et la comédie de caractère, doit être cherchée dans la farce" ("Molière et la farce," *Revue de Paris* 8, no. 3 [May–June 1901]:132.

7. Stone, in *The London Stage*, pt. 4, 1:cxlv.

8. Amateurs joined "spouting clubs" or the Robin Hood Society; professionals such as Thomas Sheridan and James "Orator" Henley gave public lectures and demonstrations. In 1754 Charles Macklin offered a series of lecture-debates called "The British Inquisition," apparently referred to in the play. This fad was also satirized by Murphy in *The Apprentice* (1756) and by Foote in *The Orators* (1762) and *The Commissary* (1765).

9. *The London Stage*, pt. 4, 1:clxvii. Stone classifies it as a "farce," but, internal evidence aside, most printed editions call it "a dramatick satire."

7: WE THAT LIVE TO PLEASE

1. "Plays of Macklin," pp. 401–2.

2. *Four Comedies by Charles Macklin* (London: Sidgwick & Jackson; Hamden, Conn.: Archon Books, 1968), p. 23. But see Jean Kern's edition of *Covent Garden Theatre* (ARS no. 116, 1965), p. i.

3. Thorndike's opinion that the play's conclusion is sentimental (*English Comedy*, p. 421) seems to confuse a convention of plot (the test) with tone. The situation is handled humorously.

4. Bartley says this version was never printed (*Comedies by Macklin*, p. 26), but MacMillan's *Catalogue of the Larpent Plays* mentions a 1795 printing, while a note in with the Larpent MS says the first edition was 1783. Someone has evidently confused the two versions.

5. Respectively Larpent MSS 311, 500, and 558. For an account of the entire episode see Dougald MacMillan's "The Censorship in the Case of Macklin's *Man of the World*" in the *Huntington Library Bulletin* for Oct. 1936.

6. *David Garrick, Director* (Pittsburgh: Univ. of Pittsburgh Press, 1961), p. 16.

7. *The Letters of David Garrick*, ed. David Little and George Kahrl, 3 vols. (Cambridge, Mass.: Harvard Univ. Press, 1963), 1:xlix.

8. Charles B. Woods, "The 'Miss Lucy' Plays of Fielding and Garrick," *Philological Quarterly* 41 (1962):296.

9. Robertson Davies notes: "As a playwright Garrick shows no growth; he writes as well in his earliest pieces as he does at the end of his career" (*The Revels History*, 6:152).

10. See Lillian Gottesman, "Garrick's *Lilliput*," *Restoration and Eighteenth-Century Theatre Research* 11, no. 2 (Nov. 1972):34–37.

11. *An Essay upon the Present State of the Theatre*, p. 151. Elizabeth Stein calls the play "a little comedy of manners" in *David Garrick, Dramatist* (New York: M L A, 1938), p. 42.

12. Gerald M. Berkowitz lists this as an adaptation rather than an original play in "David Garrick: An Annotated Bibliography," *Restoration and Eighteenth-Century Theatre Research* 11, no. 1 (May 1972):3.

13. Nicoll's attributions of the play to Colman in *A History of Late Eighteenth-Century Drama* and *British Drama* (both 1925) were modified to allow "collaboration" with Garrick in the revised editions (respectively 1952 and 1962). See also Joseph M. Beatty, "Garrick, Colman, and *The Clandestine Marriage*," *M L N* 36 (Mar. 1921):129–41; and Page, *Colman the Elder*, pp. 111–23. Stein stated the case for Garrick's dominance in *Garrick*, chap. six, esp. pp. 229 and 245. See also Frederick L. Bergmann, "David Garrick and *The Clandestine Marriage*," *P M L A* 67 (Mar. 1952):156. Ann T. Straulman divides the authorship about equally in "George Colman and David Garrick, *The Clandestine Marriage*: A Critical Edition," Ph.D. dissertation, Univ. of Wisconsin, 1968. An important early source is George Colman the Younger's edition of *Posthumous Letters* addressed to his father (1820), which contains relevant documents.

14. For a fuller treatment see Martha England, *Garrick's Jubilee* (Columbus, Ohio: Ohio State Univ. Press, 1964); Christian Deelman, *The Great Shakespeare Jubilee* (London: Michael Joseph, 1964); and Levi Fox, *A Splendid Occasion* (Oxford: Dugdale Society, 1973).

15. Cf. Robertson Davies, who comments that the play "may be said to embody Garrick's managerial policy to perfection" (*The Revels History*, 6:173). E. Wind maintained that both Harlequin and Shakespeare in this piece would have been understood as Garrick. "Harlequin between Tragedy and Comedy," *Journal of the Warburg and Courtauld Institutes* 6 (1943):224–25.

16. Those interested in the anecdotal side of Foote may consult William Cooke's edition of the *Table-Talk and Bon Mots*, 2 vols. (London: Myers & Rogers, 1902); any indexed Boswell's *Life of Johnson;* Percy Fitzgerald's *Samuel Foote: A Biography* (London: Chatto & Windus, 1910); and Trefman's *Foote*, which is also an adequate guide to other early sources.

17. J. Aikin and A. L. Aikin, "On the Province of Comedy," in *Miscellaneous Pieces* (London, 1775), pp. 16, 18.

18. See pp. v–vi of the dedication to *Taste* in vol. 1 of *Foote's Life and Dramatic Works*, 2 vols. (London, 1809).

19. *A Letter from Mr. Foote, to the Reverand* [sic] *Author of "The Remarks, Critical and Christian, On the Minor"* (London, 1760).

20. See Grzegorz Sinko, *Samuel Foote, The Satirist of Rising Capitalism* (Warsaw: Dom. Ksiazki, 1950), p. 51; and Giacomo Oreglia, *The Commedia dell' Arte*, trans. Lovett F. Edwards, intro. Evert Sprinchorn (New York: Hill & Wang, 1968), p. 19.

21. Mary M. Belden, *The Dramatic Work of Samuel Foote*, Yale Studies in English 80 (New Haven: Yale Univ. Press, 1929), p. 65. See pp. 61 ff. for an account of how *Diversions* mutated into *Taste*.

22. Martha W. England thinks that Blake saw *Tea* at the the Haymarket and that it influenced *An Island in the Moon*. See "Apprenticeship at the Haymarket?" in *Blake's Visionary Forms Dramatic*, eds. David B. Erdman and John E. Grant (Princeton: Princeton Univ. Press, 1970). *The Auction* satirizes, among others, Henry Fielding, who had staged puppet shows to compete with *Tea* (Trefman, *Foote*, p. 31). *The Virtuoso* is the title of Larpent MS 93, produced as *Taste* in 1752.

23. I have recounted the published version (1770); the ending of the Larpent MS, probably closer to the acting text, is even quicker, more equivocal and less satisfactory.

24. See "Samuel Foote's *Primitive Puppet-Shew* Featuring *Piety in Pattens: A Critical Edition*," eds. Samuel N. Bogorad and Robert Gale Noyes, *Theatre Survey* 14, no. 1a (Fall 1973). Both the Huntington and Folger MSS are printed.

25. Bogorad and Noyes, "Foote's *Puppet-Shew*," p. 34, citing the Larpent MS. The editors point out (p. 6) a parallel speech in *The Maid of the Mill* they think Foote was parodying.

26. Belden notes the influence of *The Capuchin* on Sheridan's *Duenna*, and of *The Trip to Calais* on Murphy's *Know Your Own Mind* (*Work of Foote*, p. 190).

27. See *Le Rire* (1900), section 2. In *Comedy*, ed. Wylie Sypher (New York: Doubleday Anchor, 1956), pp. 127, 130.

28. See the essay from *The Gentleman*, no. 6 (Dec. 1775) in *Prose*, 1:208–10.

29. *Colman*, p. 85.

30. Page believes that the translation of Terence caused Colman to change direction towards the sentimental (*Colman*, pp. 106–7); I think that Pulteney's death was the more important event, and that Colman's later mainpieces moved away from sentiment.

31. Percy Fitzgerald, *The Life of Mrs. Catherine Clive* (London: A. Reader, 1888), p. 68.

32. Keenan's "Poetic of High Georgian Comedy" argues that Colman in fact achieved the *drame*.

33. *The Suicide* has been edited, along with *The Separate Maintenance*, by Ross Grossman. See "Two Unpublished Comedies by George Colman the Elder," Ph.D. dissertation, Claremont Graduate School, 1976.

8: TRUE-BORN IRISHMEN

1. See Thorndike, *English Comedy*, p. 422; and Nicoll, *History,* 3:162.

2. *Elements of Dramatic Criticism* (London: Kearsley), p. 171.

3. *Gray's Inn Journal* 96 (17 Aug. 1754):276–80.

4. See *New Essays by Arthur Murphy*, ed. Arthur Sherbo (East Lansing, Mich.: Michigan State Univ. Press, 1963), p. 12 (n. 60), 71, 91 (n. 203).

5. This is the copy-text used in my *Afterpieces* volume, where it is compared to the versions of 1757 and 1758.

6. Edited by John Pike Emery in *The Way to Keep Him and Five Other Plays by Arthur Murphy* (1956). The three-act version is included in my anthology.

7. Tuvia Bloch argues that Beverly in this play was one of "The Antecedents of Sheridan's Faulkland," in *Philological Quarterly* 49 (1970):266–68.

8. According to the prologue it had "lain hid" (from fear of critics) for nine years before its performance. Emery concludes that Murphy began it in 1760 and was almost finished by 1764 except for some rewriting (*Way to Keep Him*, p. 333).

9. A modern selection: in the first category, see W. T. Gallaway, Jr., "The Sentimentalism of Goldsmith," *P M L A* 48 (1933):1167–81; R.B. Heilman, "The Sentimentalism of Goldsmith's *Good-Natured Man,*" in *Studies for William A. Read,* ed. Nathaniel M. Caffee and Thomas A. Kirby (Baton Rouge: Louisiana State Univ. Press, 1940), pp. 237–53; Clara M. Kirk, *Oliver Goldsmith* (New York: Twayne, 1967), p. 125; Robert H. Hopkins, *The True Genius of Oliver Goldsmith* (Baltimore: Johns Hopkins Press, 1969), p. vii; and Samuel L. Macey, "Sheridan: The Last of the Great Theatrical Satirists," *Restoration and Eighteenth-Century Theatre Research* 9 (Nov. 1970):36. Macauley's biography of Goldsmith in the *Encyclopaedia Britannica* (1860) also takes this view. The second group includes Bernbaum, *Drama of Sensibility,* pp. 227–28; and Allan Rodway, "Goldsmith and Sheridan: Satirists of Sentiment," in *Renaissance and Modern Essays Presented to Vivian de Sola Pinto,* ed. G. R. Hibbard (London: Routledge & Kegan Paul, 1966), pp. 65–72. Among those who consider the play either a subtle or a confused mixture, see especially Donohue, *Dramatic Character,* p. 118; Friedman, "Aspects of Sentimentalism," p. 250; Hume, "Goldsmith and Sheridan," p. 266; and Ricardo Quintana, "Oliver Goldsmith: Ironist to the Georgians," in *Eighteenth-Century Studies in Honor of Donald F. Hyde,* ed. W. H. Bond (New York: Grolier Club, 1970), pp. 301, 309–10.

10. *The Life and Adventures of Goldsmith,* 2nd ed. (London, 1848), p. 392.

11. Friedman, ed., *Works of Goldsmith*, 5:73. Hereafter cited in the text as *Works*. Friedman, among others, observes that Young Honeywood resembles the Man in Black and Sir William Thornhill in Goldsmith's nondramatic prose; the type was of course well known in other eighteenth-century literature (*Tom Jones*) and in Georgian life (Goldsmith himself).

12. Cf. Robertson Davies in *The Revels History,* 6:163–64.

13. See Ernest Tuveson, "The Importance of Shaftesbury," *E L H* 20 (1953):267–99; E. N. Hooker, "Humour in the Age of Pope," *Huntington Library Quarterly* 11 (1948):361–85; and R. S. Crane, "Suggestions toward a Genealogy of the 'Man of Feeling,' " *E L H* 1 (1934):205–30, reprinted in his *The Idea of the Humanities and Other Essays,* 2 vols. (Chicago: Univ. of Chicago Press, 1967), 1:188–213.

14. See Tave, *The Amiable Humorist.*

15. Traugott, "Rake's Progress," p. 404.

16. One could argue that the rake's native wit and control of manners constitute his "nature," in this case an antisocial one. Eighteenth-century comedy, influenced by the deist view of human nature, recognized a few such characters, making them villains (Joseph Surface). Goldsmith, however, admits no such cad to this comedy, and the optimism implied by this omission is a passive kind of sentimentalism.

17. An old lesson, of course: e.g., the Wife of Bath's Tale, *Fulgens and Lucrece, The Arcadia, The Shoemaker's Holiday,* and *The Duchess of Malfi.* Among Georgian comedies it also figures in Dodsley's *The King and the Miller of Mansfield* and its sequels, and Francis Waldron's *The Maid of Kent* (1773).

18. Price ed., *Works of Sheridan,* 1:74. Hereafter cited in the text as *Works.*

19. They include Bernbaum, *Drama of Sensibility,* p. 252; Thorndike, *English Comedy,* p. 431; Macey, "Sheridan," p. 37; and Kronenberger, *Thread of Laughter,* p. 62. Bloch thinks that the vacillations of Faulkland "are ultimately condoned because they result from his extreme sensibility" ("Antecedents," p. 268). For Mark S. Auburn, Julia and Faulkland "clearly partake of sentimentality," yet are "potentially comic" ("The Pleasures of Sheridan's *The Rivals,*" *Modern Philology* 72 [1975]:264–65). See also his *Sheridan's Comedies* (Lincoln and London: Univ. of Nebraska Press, 1977), pp. 55–58 and ch. 2 generally. Cited as Auburn, *Comedies.*

20. Nicoll, *History,* 3:160; Nettleton, *English Drama,* p. 296. See also Auburn, "Pleasures," p. 265; and John Loftis, *Sheridan and the Drama of Georgian England* (Oxford: Blackwell, 1976), pp. 52–53.

21. Miriam Gabriel and Paul Mueschke, "Two Contemporary Sources of Sheridan's *The Rivals,*" *P M L A* 43 (1928):237–50; see also Bernbaum, *Drama of Sensibility,* p. 252; and Bloch, "Antecedents," p. 266.

22. This was brilliantly realized in William Glover's production for the Ashland Shakespeare Festival in 1977.

23. See Purdy, ed., *The Rivals,* pp. xlvi ff. Though superseded by Price, Purdy's comparison of texts and parallel-columns format are still useful.

24. John Bernard, *Retrospections of the Stage,* 2 vols. (London: Colburn & Bentley, 1830), 1:144.

25. See Thomas Moore, *Memoirs of the Life of Richard Brinsley Sheridan,* 5th ed., 2 vols. (London, 1826), 1:123; Purdy, ed., *The Rivals,* pp. xxxix–xli; Price, *Works*

of Sheridan, 1:37–39; and Loftis, *Sheridan*, p. 45 (n. 6). *The Journey to Bath* is included in W. Fraser Rae's edition of *Sheridan's Plays Now Printed As He Wrote Them* (1902).

26. Pinkerton, *Letters of Literature*, p. 48.

27. "On the Artificial Comedy," in *The Essays of Elia* (1821), Everyman's Library (London, 1906), pp. 168–69.

28. *"The School for Scandal"* (1815), in *The Complete Works of William Hazlitt*, ed. Percival P. Howe, 21 vols. (London and Toronto: Dent, 1930), 5:250. Hereafter cited as *Complete Works*.

29. See Nettleton, *English Drama*, pp. 305–6; Thorndike, *English Comedy*, p. 433; Nicoll, *History*, 3:161; and Andrew Schiller, *"The School for Scandal*: The Restoration Unrestored," *P M L A* 71 (1956):694–704.

30. Cf. Arthur C. Sprague, "In Defence of a Masterpiece: *The School for Scandal* Re-Examined," in *English Studies Today*, 3rd series, ed. G. I. Duthie (Edinburgh: Edinburgh Univ. Press, 1962), p. 128.

31. Peter A. Tasch, *The Dramatic Cobbler: The Life and Works of Isaac Bickerstaff* (Lewisburg, Pa.: Bucknell Univ. Press, 1971), p. 172.

32. Cf. Macey, "Sheridan," pp. 38–40.

33. On the idea that there were originally two plays, see Schiller, *"School for Scandal,"* p. 699, and Price, *Works of Sheridan*, 1:293. My point is that the two plots are thematically connected, however they originated.

34. *An Essay towards Fixing the True Standards of Wit, Humour, Raillery, Satire and Ridicule* (London, 1744) argues that humour (i. e., Sheridan's true wit) is "more pleasurable" than wit (Sheridan's false wit), being more natural (p. 24).

EPILOGUE

1. "Towards Defining an Age of Sensibility," *E L H* 23 (June 1956):149.

2. In *Generally Speaking* (1929; rpt. Freeport, N.Y.: Books for Libraries Press, 1968).

3. Prologue to Charlotte Lennox's *Old City Manners* (1775, an alteration of *Eastward Hoe!*). It is Hogarth who is spoken of as having gleaned "the comic stubble," but dramatists are exhorted to adopt this "aim."

4. "On the Comic Writers of the Last Century," *Lectures on the Comic Writers* (1819), in *Complete Works*, 6:149.

5. Epilogue to Richard Cumberland's *The Note of Hand* (1774).

Index

Index